# WHY CITIES CHANGE

# Why Cities Change

URBAN DEVELOPMENT AND
ECONOMIC CHANGE IN SYDNEY

Edited by Richard V. Cardew,
John V. Langdale and David C. Rich

GEOGRAPHICAL SOCIETY OF NEW SOUTH WALES
GEORGE ALLEN & UNWIN Sydney London Boston

First published in 1982 by
George Allen & Unwin Australia Pty Ltd
8 Napier Street, North Sydney, NSW 2060 Australia

George Allen & Unwin (Publishers) Ltd
Park Lane, Hemel Hempstead, Herts HP2 4TE England
Allen & Unwin Inc.,
9 Winchester Terrace, Winchester, Mass 01890 USA

National Library of Australia
Cataloguing-in-Publication entry:

Why cities change.

   Bibliography.
   Includes index.
   ISBN 0 86861 252 9.
   ISBN 0 86861 260 X (pbk.).

   1. Urban economics.   2. Sydney (N.S.W.) — Economic
   conditions.   I. Cardew, R. V. (Richard V.).
   II. Langdale, John V.   III. Rich, David C.
   (David Charles).

330.9

Set in 10/11 pt Baskerville by Graphicraft Typesetters

Printed by the Singapore National Printers (Pte) Ltd.

# Contents

# Tables

# Figures

# Abbreviations

| | |
|---|---|
| AAP | Australian Associated Press |
| ABS | Australian Bureau of Statistics |
| ACTU | Australian Council of Trade Unions |
| AFR | Australian Financial Review |
| AGPS | Australian Government Publishing Service |
| AIUS | Australian Institute of Urban Studies |
| ALP | Australian Labor Party |
| ANU | Australian National University |
| ASIC | Australian Standard Industrial Classification |
| BIE | Bureau of Industry Economics |
| CBD | Central business district |
| CCC | Cumberland County Council |
| DMR | Department of Main Roads, New South Wales |
| DURD | Department of Urban and Regional Development |
| FCL | Full container load |
| GM-H | General Motors-Holden |
| IAC | Industries Assistance Commission |
| ISD | International subscriber dialling |
| km | Kilometre |
| L | Litre |
| LCL | Less-than-container load |
| LGA | Local government area |
| MDB | Macarthur Development Board |
| Ml | Megalitre |
| MSB | Maritime Services Board of New South Wales |
| MWSDB | Metropolitan Water Sewerage and Drainage Board (Sydney) |
| MWSSDB | Metropolitan Water Supply, Sewerage and Drainage Board (Perth) |
| NRMA | National Roads and Motorists Association |
| NSW | New South Wales |
| OPEC | Organisation of Petroleum Exporting Countries |
| PEC | New South Wales Planning and Environment Commission |

| SATS | Sydney Area Transportation Study |
| SMH | Sydney Morning Herald |
| SPA | State Planning Authority of New South Wales |
| SPCC | State Pollution Control Commission (of New South Wales) |
| TEU | 20 foot equivalent container units |

# Contributors

**Ian Alexander** is Lecturer in Urban and Regional Planning, Western Australian Institute of Technology.

**Graeme J. Aplin** is Lecturer in Geography, School of Earth Sciences, Macquarie University.

**John A. Black** is Head of the Department of Transport Engineering, School of Civil Engineering, University of New South Wales.

**Ian H. Burnley** is Senior Lecturer in Geography, University of New South Wales.

**Richard V. Cardew** is Senior Lecturer in Urban Studies, Centre for Environmental and Urban Studies, Macquarie University.

**Peter Crabb** is Senior Lecturer in Geography, School of Earth Sciences, Macquarie University.

**Maurice T. Daly** is Professor of Geography, University of Sydney.

**Bill Faulkner** is Principal Research Officer, Special Studies Branch, Bureau of Transport Economics; he was formerly Lecturer in Geography, University of Wollongong.

**John V. Langdale** is Senior Lecturer in Geography, School of Earth Sciences, Macquarie University.

**Ellis Nugent** is employed in the Commonwealth Department of Trade and Resources, Sydney.

**Michael Poulsen** is Lecturer in Geography, School of Earth Sciences, Macquarie University.

**David C. Rich** is Senior Lecturer in Geography, School of Earth Sciences, Macquarie University.

**Peter J. Rimmer** is Senior Fellow, Department of Human Geography, Research School of Pacific Studies, Australian National University.

**Peter L. Simons** is Senior Lecturer in Geography, University of New South Wales.

**Susanne R. Walker** is Lecturer in Geography, University of New South Wales.

# Preface

This book has been written for the Geographical Society of New South Wales as part of its role in disseminating geographical knowledge to the profession and wider community. We felt that there was a need to bring together recent research on Sydney's economic geography and had two goals in editing the book. The first one was to present up to date material outlining Sydney's changing pattern of development. The second and more important was to interpret this recent development in terms of the processes of economic change. The book thus emphasises the mechanisms underlying contemporary urban change: Sydney is the empirical focus, but because many of the processes of change are common to Australian cities and indeed most metropolitan areas in the western world, the book has much wider relevance.

With its focus on the processes of change the book reflects recent trends in much geographical writing. Its particular contribution is to bring together research on urban development with that on macro-economic change, including finance, property development, industrial recession and reorganisation of the distribution sector. In so doing, we hope to improve understanding of recent urban change and increase awareness of the nature and causes of the problems facing urban planners.

In assembling material for the book, we have deliberately chosen to restrict our focus to the economic aspects of urban change (even so there are some obvious gaps in our coverage). Clearly, urban development has an important social dimension and there is undoubtedly scope for a companion volume exploring this.

Many people have assisted in the preparation of the book. Ian Alexander acknowledges the assistance of Coralie McCormack with data analysis and Lucie Caricnan with field work. Peter L. Simons is grateful to A. D. Winter and T. Beed for supplying data, the University of New South Wales for financial support and D. Spicer for research assistance. Peter Crabb thanks A. Small, Public Relations Officer of the Metropolitan Water Sewerage and Drainage Board. Peter J. Rimmer and John A. Black thank the Study Director of the Urban Transport

Study Group, Frank Jordan (State Transport Study Group, Ministry of Transport), Ross Blunden (Emeritus Professor, School of Civil Engineering, University of New South Wales), the Traffic Accident Research Unit of the Department of Motor Transport, and the Maritime Services Board of New South Wales. H. W. Faulkner acknowledges the assistance of Helen Match who typed his original manuscript and Tai Ta who provided data.

As editors we are indebted to Rod Bashford for the cartography. He prepared the majority of maps and the task of representing the material to meet the publishing format was no small challenge. Our special thanks must go to Gwen Keena who typed several versions of most chapters and in the final days worked long hours to enable us to submit the manuscript on time.

# 1 Themes in urban development and economic change

DAVID C. RICH, RICHARD V. CARDEW AND JOHN V. LANGDALE

## 1.1 Introduction

Sydney is a unique city. The harbour, Opera House, CBD skyline and Harbour Bridge create strong impressions among visitors and locals alike. These landmarks in the central area dominate most people's image of the city, yet Sydney has sprawled in a vast, complex intermingling of activities linked together by a mesh of transport and communications networks. Understanding these aspects of Sydney's development requires consideration not only of purely local characteristics such as the distinctive physical environment but also of wider international, national and regional economic forces.

The last decade has been a period of dramatic economic change around the world. The long postwar boom turned into deep recession. Successive energy price rises sent a series of shocks through the international economy. Recession hit Australia and accelerated changes in its economic structure and world role. In Sydney the impact ranged from increased unemployment to a reevaluation of the role of motor vehicles in urban sprawl. These and many other features of Sydney's recent development are essentially products of global and domestic economic change, rather than local conditions.

This book explores Sydney's development, especially over the last decade or so, concentrating on the interrelationships between that development and contemporary economic change. Though the 13 remaining chapters probe diverse topics, they are closely connected by four themes. First is the evolving physical structure of the metropolitan region, including expansion of the built up area, rapid but varying dispersal of activities into the suburbs, redevelopment of inner areas, most notably the CBD, and the growing importance of suburban centres. Second is the nature of contemporary economic change, associated especially with the expansion and changing role of the financial sector, rapid organisational change in most fields of business, and widespread and pervasive technological change. The interplay between Sydney's physical restructuring and these economic mechanisms thus

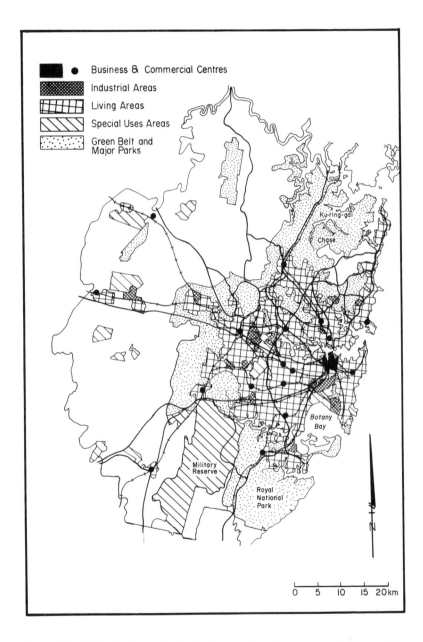

**Figure 1.1    Major land uses in the Sydney metropolitan area as designated by the Planning Scheme for the County of Cumberland, 1948**

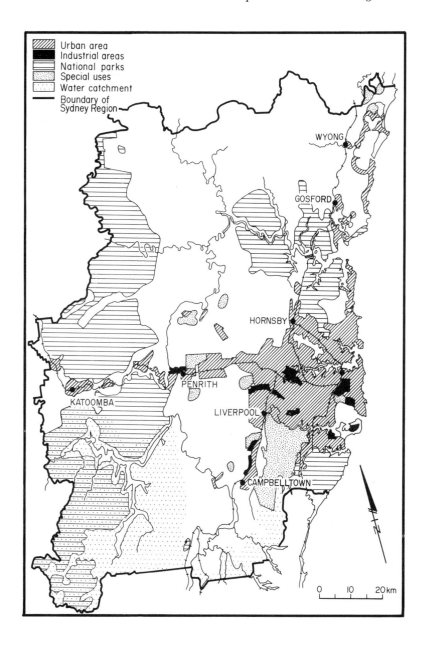

**Figure 1.2    Major land uses in the Sydney Statistical Division, 1981**

forms the primary focus of the book. But urban change has enormous implications for the inhabitants of the city, so that the community impact of change forms the third theme. The fourth is the role of government both in stimulating metropolitan change through conscious and unconscious urban policy and in reacting to and attempting to control it. This chapter develops each of these four themes. It identifies the main features of the patterns and processes of change, thus providing a broad introduction to the more detailed chapters that follow.

## 1.2   Sydney's postwar development

Like most major cities, Sydney has expanded massively since the Second World War. Numbers of people and jobs have almost doubled. The built up area has expanded from approximately 400 square kilometres in 1945 to nearly 1,200 square kilometres in 1981. The metropolitan region has also been much enlarged. The planning region defined by the CCC (1948) was confined to the Cumberland Plain (Figure 1.1), but since 1976 the metropolitan area has included for planning and statistical purposes fringe LGAs which incorporate Sydney's discontinuous dormitory suburbs (Figure 1.2). The current boundary is to some extent arbitrary and this is reflected in the varying interpretations used in succeeding chapters. To the south, the northern part of Wollongong LGA accommodates increasing numbers of commuters to Sydney but is excluded from the metropolitan area. Conversely, to the west and north, for example in Gosford and Wyong LGAs, some settlements are included even though they remain fairly independent of Sydney. Similarly, although the metropolitan area is large by world standards and includes extensive agricultural districts, national parks and even wilderness areas, it incorporates only a portion of the water catchment used to service the metropolitan population (Crabb ch 11).

Population growth has also been substantial. In 1947 the CCC planning region accommodated 1.70 million people, while the Sydney metropolitan area housed an estimated 3.23 million in 1980. Until the 1970s it attracted larger absolute population increases than any Australian city except Melbourne and the rate of growth was well above the national average, though lower than in most other capitals (Neutze 1977:49). Expansion slowed in the late 1960s, and between 1971 and 1976 Sydney's population growth rate fell to only one third of the Australian average of 1.8 per cent per annum. The bulk of postwar growth has been due to natural increase (excess of births over deaths) and immigration from overseas. Migration from elsewhere in Australia contributed little to growth and, indeed, since the mid 1960s has generally been a negative influence (Rowland 1979:79). The reduced volume and rate of growth in the 1970s has been a product not only of increased net migration to the rest of Australia but also of lower immigration rates and reduced natural increase (Burnley 1980; Choi and Burnley 1974), though there were signs by the end of the decade that downward trends in the latter two components had been reversed.

Most of Sydney's population increase has been accommodated at or near the metropolitan fringe (Neutze 1977:73-7; Spearritt 1978:255). The zone of most rapid population increase thus moved progressively from areas such as Bankstown and Parramatta in the 1950s to more distant LGAs such as Liverpool, Warringah and Sutherland in the 1960s and 1970s, while Hornsby, Penrith and Baulkham Hills became important areas of development in the 1970s. In contrast, the inner city has lost population since the 1940s. Even so, the population of some inner LGAs has stabilised (e.g. Drummoyne) or increased slightly (e.g. Marrickville) because of infilling of vacant lots, redevelopment with flats and other medium to high density accommodation, rejuvenation and gentrification, or housing demand from overseas migrants.

Despite moves towards the geographical consolidation of metropolitan development, peripheral expansion remains the dominant feature of Sydney's growth. Like other Australian cities, the overall density of development is still low by world standards (Logan *et al.* 1981:89). These characteristics reflect the relative lateness of urban development, community preference for detached housing, availability of land at the fringe, along with weak public controls on and strong lobbies for peripheral expansion (Logan *et al.* 1981; Sandercock 1975b). As a consequence of metropolitan sprawl, there have been many problems such as equitable and efficient provision of public transport and other community facilities, provision of infrastructure, lengthy journeys to work (Aplin ch 13) and latterly difficulties in finding sufficient land for expansion.

Paralleling Sydney's demographic expansion has been its economic growth. Employment (within the 1966 metropolitan boundaries) increased from 0.75 million in 1947 to 1.25 million in 1971. There was a further small increase (within the enlarged 1976 boundaries) between 1971 and 1976 (Table 1.1).

There have also been changes in the mix of industries. Manufacturing peaked in relative importance in 1954 and declined thereafter. Conversely, public administration, and financial, business and community services have all increased in relative and absolute importance. Examination of the occupations performed by individuals rather than the industry employing them reveals a similar picture. There was a growth of professional, technical and clerical occupations and relative or absolute decline of manual production and sales work (Neutze 1977:102; Table 1.2) These trends represent important changes in Sydney's economy and its economic role. They reflect in part the rise of

**Table 1.1   Employment change in the Sydney metropolitan area[a], 1971-1976**

| Industry | Employment | | Change | | % of total | |
|---|---|---|---|---|---|---|
| | 1971 | 1976 | Absolute | % | 1971 | 1976 |
| Agriculture, forestry and fishing | 11,922 | 11,192 | −730 | −6.12 | 0.9 | 0.8 |
| Mining | 5,587 | 4,718 | −869 | −15.55 | 0.4 | 0.4 |
| Manufacturing | 359,822 | 310,641 | −49,181 | −13.67 | 27.9 | 23.2 |
| Electricity, gas and water | 23,666 | 27,071 | 3,405 | 14.39 | 1.8 | 2.0 |
| Construction | 91,611 | 75,565 | −16,046 | −17.52 | 7.1 | 5.7 |
| Wholesale and retail | 251,687 | 258,428 | 6,741 | 2.68 | 19.5 | 19.3 |
| Transport and storage | 72,075 | 75,532 | 3,457 | 4.80 | 5.6 | 5.7 |
| Communication | 27,080 | 30,096 | 3,016 | 11.14 | 2.1 | 2.3 |
| Finance and business services | 121,460 | 129,660 | 8,200 | 6.75 | 9.4 | 9.7 |
| Public administration and defence | 70,011 | 79,877 | 9,866 | 14.09 | 5.4 | 6.0 |
| Community services | 131,883 | 172,932 | 41,049 | 31.13 | 10.2 | 12.9 |
| Entertainment | 69,165 | 67,707 | −1,458 | −2.11 | 5.3 | 5.1 |
| Other | 57,521 | 92,700 | 35,179 | 61.16 | 4.4 | 6.9 |
| *Total* | 1,293,490 | 1,336,118 | 42,628 | 3.30 | 100.0 | 100.0 |

*Note:* [a] The metropolitan area is the Sydney Statistical Division, as extended in 1976
*Source:* 1971 and 1976 Population Censuses

**Table 1.2  Occupational change among employed persons in the Sydney metropolitan area[a], 1971-1976**

| Occupation | No. persons | | Change | | % of total | |
|---|---|---|---|---|---|---|
| | 1971 | 1976 | Absolute | % | 1971 | 1976 |
| Professional, technical | 142,168 | 169,189 | 27,021 | 19.01 | 10.99 | 12.66 |
| Administrative, executive | 95,728 | 101,990 | 6,262 | 6.54 | 7.40 | 7.63 |
| Clerical workers | 253,852 | 270,099 | 16,247 | 6.40 | 19.63 | 20.22 |
| Sales workers | 102,901 | 104,725 | 1,824 | 1.77 | 7.96 | 7.84 |
| Farmers, fishermen etc. | 17,011 | 16,822 | −189 | −1.11 | 1.32 | 1.26 |
| Miners, quarrymen | 1,723 | 1,642 | −81 | −4.70 | 0.13 | 0.12 |
| Transport, communication | 79,686 | 69,859 | −827 | −1.17 | 5.46 | 5.23 |
| Production process workers, labourers | 438,789 | 409,097 | −29,692 | −6.77 | 33.92 | 30.62 |
| Service, sport, recreation | 94,450 | 103,915 | 9,465 | 10.02 | 7.30 | 7.78 |
| Armed forces | 16,413 | 13,453 | −2,960 | −18.03 | 1.27 | 1.01 |
| Other | 59,769 | 75,327 | 15,558 | 26.03 | 4.62 | 5.64 |
| *Total* | 1,293,490 | 1,336,118 | 42,628 | 3.30 | 100.00 | 100.00 |

*Note:* [a]The metropolitan area is the Sydney Statistical Division, as extended in 1976
*Source:* 1971 and 1976 Population Censuses

the 'post industrial' society with provision of personal and business services expanding more rapidly than production of goods, concentration of these higher order services in metropolitan areas, the historically more rapid rise of labour productivity in production than in service activities, and the industrial recession of the mid 1970s (Langdale ch 4; Rich ch 5).

There has been dramatic dispersal of economic activity in the period, although it came later than the dispersal of homes. The City of Sydney LGA provided 55 per cent of all jobs in 1945, but only 34 per cent in 1971; employment in the City rose from 345,000 in 1945, peaked at 422,000 in 1961 and fell to 406,000 in 1971 (Table 1.3). Subsequent chapters examine more recent developments. The largest employment increases have been in the middle and outer suburbs, the latter for example more than trebling their share of employment. Nevertheless, jobs are still rather less dispersed than people: for example, outer LGAs contained 19 per cent of jobs but 40 per cent of residents in 1971 (Neutze 1977:103).

The suburbs thus have an increasingly important economic role. No longer are they almost entirely residential dormitories. They contain a growing proportion of all economic activity, especially manufacturing (Cardew and Rich ch 6), retailing (Simons ch 8; Poulsen ch 9) and to a lesser extent wholesaling (Nugent *et al.* ch 7). Office activities are also becoming increasingly dispersed (Alexander ch 3), and although many head offices and high level service functions remain concentrated in the CBD, there is an emerging trend for these to move to the suburbs.

**Table 1.3    Distribution of employment in Sydney, 1945-1971**

| Area | '000 jobs | | | % of total | | |
|---|---|---|---|---|---|---|
| | 1945 | 1961 | 1971 | 1945 | 1961 | 1971 |
| CBD | | 244 | 228 | | 26 | 19 |
| | 345 | | | 55 | | |
| Rest of City[a] | | 178 | 178 | | 19 | 15 |
| Inner ring[b] | 119 | 171 | 213 | 19 | 18 | 18 |
| Middle ring[c] | 123 | 251 | 359 | 20 | 26 | 30 |
| Outer ring[d] | 38 | 110 | 227 | 6 | 12 | 19 |
| *Total* | 626 | 953 | 1,205 | 100 | 100 | 100 |

*Notes:* [a] The boundaries of the City of Sydney used are those existing between 1949 and 1968
[b] Mosman, North Sydney, Leichhardt, Drummoyne, Ashfield, Marrickvile, Botany, Woollahra, Waverley, Randwick
[c] Manly, Willoughby, Lane Cove, Hunters Hill, Ryde, Parramatta, Auburn, Concord, Strathfield, Burwood, Bankstown, Canterbury, Rockdale, Kogarah, Hurstville
[d] Warringah, Ku-ring-gai, Hornsby, Baulkham Hills, Blacktown, Windsor, Penrith, Holroyd, Fairfield, Liverpool, Camden, Campbelltown, Sutherland
*Source:* Neutze 1977:104

There have thus been major changes in the geographical structure of the metropolitan area. In the 1940s Sydney was still a single centred city with most activity focused on the CBD and surrounding area, and the inner city formed the main concentrations of employment, retailing and entertainment. Today, most activity is much more dispersed and there has been some trend towards a multicentred form: suburban centres have become increasingly prominent. Chatswood and Parramatta are two prime examples. Both have significant functions as office, retailing and transport interchange centres and have been the focus of recent medium to high density residential construction.

Nevertheless, because many activities are so widely dispersed, no one centre yet challenges the CBD. It remains the most important single node and has a more significant role than in most comparable US cities. It is still by far the largest centre of office activities (Alexander ch 3). Suburban shopping facilities are so widely spread that no one centre attracts the retail sales of the CBD (Simons ch 8). Even though fringe expansion is taking Sydney's centre of gravity progressively further west, the transport system remains essentially radial and focused on the inner city. Similarly, the inner area contains the major sea and air terminals: expansion of Port Botany has brought a realignment of traffic patterns (Rimmer and Black ch 12) without fundamentally changing Sydney's transport orientation.

There have, though, been important changes in the CBD and surrounding areas. The mix of economic activities has changed markedly, with rapid declines of employment in manufacturing, wholesaling and retailing and a growing specialisation in office based industries, notably finance and property, public administration, and community and business services (Neutze 1977:101). This specialisation remains strong, but the number of office jobs in the CBD has begun to fall (Alexander ch 3). Accompanying economic restructuring was the physical transformation brought by the massive office developments of the 1960s and early 1970s (Daly ch 2) and by several major transport developments. There has been extensive demolition of housing in some areas, but in others government sponsored schemes (in Glebe, Woolloomooloo and The Rocks) and private rehabilitation (e.g. in Balmain and Paddington) have brought rejuvenation of the physical fabric and often a changing social mix. In the industrial field, redevelopment has generally been preferred to rehabilitation, although some old warehouses have been converted to other uses, including offices and housing. Government institutions have played a role along with the private sector with takeover of large areas by hospitals, education and other activities.

The Sydney metropolitan area has thus undergone a transformation in the last three decades or so. These changes have brought many problems. For example, many journeys to work remain long (Manning 1978), while employment dispersal has meant a growth of intersuburban commuting, requiring greater use of private cars because of the inadequacies of the essentially radial transport system (Black 1977). For many, jobs are either non-existent or require difficult and costly journeys, because the labour market is segmented geographically and by occupation, skill and sex (Stilwell 1980). Development has brought many conflicts of interest between individuals and organisations, while the planning profession has encountered many difficulties in determining how best to control development pressures. There have been many problems in adequately servicing both the existing built up area and the expanding fringe. Such issues are explored in chapters 9 to 14.

Despite a distinctive character resulting from its attractive physical environment, many features of Sydney's recent development are, in general terms at least, similar to those observable in other major cities in Australia and overseas (see Carter 1981; Northam 1979; and Scargill 1979). Equally, though local characteristics and mechanisms — such as the topography, land use zoning and development control, or the preferred mode of housing — have influenced the nature of Sydney's development, they are in a sense no more than supplementary to a whole range of largely external influences, especially of an economic nature. It is to these influences that attention now turns.

## 1.3   Urban development and economic change

The nature of urban development is profoundly affected by international, national and local economic conditions. Studies of the impact of economic forces on urban development have conventionally used bid rent and movement functions to interpret land use and movement patterns (see Alonso 1964; Muth 1969; Richardson 1977). However, it is much more important to consider the wider economic forces which influence the volume and nature of economic activity in the city, the number, type and location of buildings required, and the volume and cost of capital available for construction. All of these need to be considered before the bid rent mechanisms allocate land uses to particular areas.

Sydney plays an important part in and is in turn much influenced by the Australian economy. At the same time, Australia is closely connected with the international economy and Sydney plays an important gateway role in linking the two. Consequently, this book explores Sydney's development in the context of its evolving economic function and as a product of the interaction of global and national change with local economic, political and social factors.

Six related developments with important implications for Australia have characterised international economic change over the last two decades (Fagan *et al.* 1981). First is the growing internationalisation of industrial production, to add to the long established pattern of international trade, portfolio investment and other financial flows (Hymer 1975; Perrons 1981). Second is the growing economic domination of transnational corporations, mostly based in USA, Western Europe and Japan (Barnet and Muller 1974; Hood and Young 1979). The third feature is the rapid industrialisation of certain third world countries and their increasing emphasis on high technology and/or capital intensive activities such as steel and electronics (Australia. BIE 1978; Fröbel *et al.* 1980). Next, technological change is having a vital impact on many aspects of the world economy and of individual countries (Freeman 1974). Fifth, rising energy prices are having serious effects on industrial economies built on imports of cheap oil, especially Japan and Western Europe, and leading to a rationalisation of energy intensive production in those countries (Fagan *et al.* 1981). The final development is the very rapid growth of international banking and rise of large scale international monetary transfers (Daly 1980).

Australia's international economic position has long been somewhat ambiguous (Taylor and Thrift 1981c). The country is prosperous and industrialised, but it relies heavily on primary production and is dependent on imports of capital and technology to sustain growth. These characteristics persist, but there have been changes in Australia's role in the world economy and a reorientation of its international contacts. Australia's trade with Japan, Asia and the Middle East has grown rapidly while that with Western Europe and USA has stagnated. Exports of agricultural commodities and associated processed goods have declined in significance, while minerals and part processed materials have become more important (Fagan *et al.* 1981:30-1). Likewise, reorientation of manufacturing away from import competing and durable goods production towards minerals processing, energy intensive production and related activities (Rich ch 5) is a product of Australia's evolving role in a changing world economy.

Three major components of Australian and international economic change have important consequences for Sydney's development. These are, first, the role of domestic and international capital flows and the activities of the finance sector; second, the changing nature of business and government organisations together with their evolving economic roles and locational requirements; and third, the impact of technological change. These issues form themes which underlie most of the subsequent chapters, but it is appropriate to consider each in a little more detail at this stage.

*Finance and urban development*

Changes in the financial system are vital features of Australia's recent economic development and Sydney's emerging economic role. Consideration of the finance sector is critical to an understanding of urban development and its links with economic change. Its role has been emphasised insufficiently, although a few writers have begun to explore it (Kilmartin and Thorns 1978; Vandermark and Harrison 1972). Several chapters in this book (Daly ch 2; Cardew and Rich ch 6; Cardew and Simons ch 8) investigate the relationships between financial flows and commercial or industrial development. Two features of the finance sector are particularly important in this context. One is the evolving nature of the international monetary system and Australia's position in it. The other is the increasing sophistication of the Australian financial system, the emergence of new institutions and the more rapid mobilisation of domestic capital. Both international and domestic capital have sought outlets offering good rates of return and/or secure investment; minerals and energy projects and urban property development have been favourite outlets in Australia (Daly ch 2).

The last two decades have seen a burgeoning of the international money supply (stimulated by demands of expanding transnational corporations, deficit financing and regulatory practices of US governments, and surplus funds accruing to OPEC countries) and the emergence of new institutions, such as international banks and the Eurodollar market, to handle it (Daly 1980). Consequently, very large volumes of funds now circulate internationally in search of portfolio investment, property development, commercial and institutional borrowers, and speculative outlets of one sort of another. Australia has been dependent on inflows of investment capital throughout European settlement (Butlin 1964, 1970; Cochrane 1980), but vastly increased funds have been made available by such global developments (Daly ch 2).

The increasingly complex world financial system involves diverse linkages between many countries and institutions. It is centred on London and New York, with Tokyo, Paris, Hong Kong and Singapore also important. In addition, many lesser ranking cities are closely linked to these major centres in a highly interdependent financial system. Sydney has developed as Australia's financial centre with an important role in the Pacific Basin as a whole (Daly ch 2). Sydney and Melbourne have long been important gateways for overseas funds into Australia, but since the mid 1960s new financial institutions have emerged, particularly in Sydney, to channel foreign capital into the country and, to a lesser extent, local capital into offshore development.

Accompanying global developments has been a diversification and growing sophistication of the Australian financial system. Building societies, finance companies and credit unions have expanded much more quickly than conventional banks (Reserve Bank of Australia 1979), thus tapping the higher disposable incomes brought by economic growth. The short term money market has grown rapidly because of the need of businesses to maximise their use of funds in an inflationary and increasingly competitive environment. Despite restrictions on the establishment of conventional overseas banks in Australia, there has been a rapid growth of branches and subsidiaries of foreign financial institutions, notably merchant banks, tying the country ever more closely into the world monetary system (Daly ch 2).

Changes in the financial system have had major consequences for the physical development of the metropolitan area. One of the most important is that they have channelled overseas and local capital into property development. The most spectacular evidence for this is in the surge of office construction which transformed Sydney's CBD in the 1960s and early 1970s (Daly ch 2), but there have been impacts on other aspects of urban form. Diversification of investment portfolios has provided ample capital for development of warehouses, factories, hotels and shopping centres as well as offices. Though the balance between sectors has varied considerably from time to time, a high rate of construction has been maintained despite the recession.

Many developments have been created simply as investment packages, bringing the rapid spread of leasehold tenure to all major property sectors except residential. This means that firms can occupy premises that are larger or otherwise more suited to modern modes of operation, and at the same time release capital from fixed assets in property to increase working capital for plant and machinery; those slowest to make the change have found their competitive positions undermined and have been vulnerable to takeover. Leasehold tenure has also facilitated higher mobility of most businesses and so encouraged the rapid dispersal of economic activity across the metropolitan area.

Speculation in land at the fringe by institutions and property developers, and construction of housing estates for sale have been important components of rapid peripheral expansion (Daly ch 2). Similarly on the demand side, the finance sector has long been important in providing funds for housing purchase. Along with government promotion of owner occupation, especially through control of mortgage interest rates, this has profoundly affected the nature and extent of urban development. Possible deregulation of the finance sector following the Campbell Inquiry will affect the availability and cost of finance for housing and may have a commensurate impact on future trends in urban form.

Domestic and foreign loan capital have historically been important in funding infrastructure and government services in urban areas. Interest rates on such borrowings are regulated by the federal government in return for guarantees of loan security. The federal government has recently attempted to limit overseas borrowings as part of its monetary policies. In the 1980s funding for infrastructure is likely to be limited because of the capital demands associated with resource developments (section 1.5). General economic developments and the distribution of financial flows may thus have both positive and negative impacts on the pattern of urban development.

## Organisational change

Paralleling and closely related to developments in the financial sector have been major changes in the organisation of business. Most important has been the increasing domination of the economy by a few large firms. Large businesses are not a new phenomenon in the Australian economy (Connell 1977), but the concentration of ownership has increased markedly in recent times and is now high by world standards (Byrt 1981; Logan et al. 1981:49). For example, although there were over 32,000 manufacturing enterprises in the mid 1970s, a mere 200 of them contributed half the total value added and employment (Australia. Committee to Advise on Policies for Manufacturing Industry 1975). The level of concentration appears to be highest in those activities most strategic to the future direction of the economy (Fagan et al. 1981:34). Increases in concentration have been closely associated with the emergence of transnational corporations and growing foreign investment in Australia. By the mid 1970s roughly half of mining output and one third of manufactured goods were produced by foreign owned companies (Australia. BIE 1981a).

Large firms are important products of economic change but they also initiate and control further change. They play a major role in directing worldwide and Australian economic trends and thus have a considerable impact on the nature of urban development. They wield considerable influence on government and profoundly affect the activities of smaller firms. Penetration of Australia by foreign firms transfers some control of the economy to overseas interests and increases its vulnerability to secular and cyclical shifts in international economic conditions. Large firms determine much of the demand for capital flows into and within Australia and, in the case of transnational corporations, form the medium through which much of the transfer of funds takes place.

An important feature of the increasing dominance of large firms is the growing spatial concentration of control in international and national economies. In Australia control has become progressively more concentrated in Sydney and Melbourne (Taylor and Thrift 1980, 1981a). These cities accommodate the great majority of the headquarters of Australian firms and Australian head offices of transnational corporations. They are linked with and dependent on the international control centres (mainly in the USA, Western Europe and Japan) and thus form part of an interlocking worldwide set of economic decision making centres. There is some evidence that Sydney has overtaken Melbourne as Australia's preeminent control centre except in mining (Rich ch 5). Along with its emerging role as Australia's major financial centre, this developing position is one of the most important features of Sydney's recent economic development.

Large firms have many impacts on urban structure. One of the most obvious relates to decisions about investment in production and distribution facilities. Large new projects help mould the pattern and speed of urban growth, while closure or changed use of existing facilities may have equally significant adverse effects. Both directly and through the effects on linked firms, there is an impact on the volume and spatial pattern of economic activity and employment, which in turn influence demand for housing, transport and urban infrastructure.

Concentration of head offices in Sydney has stimulated growth of business service firms (accounting, legal, financial and advertising), institutions facilitating the operation of markets (stock and futures exchanges), and federal and state government agencies regulating firms' activities. The greater the concentration of head offices in a city, the more specialised the set of associated organisations (Cohen 1977, 1979). Traditionally, these organisations have clustered in the CBD to communicate easily with each other; more recently there has been some decentralisation of offices to the suburbs (Alexander ch 3).

The impact of organisational change on urban development is clearly seen in the distribution sector (Nugent *et al.* ch 7; Cardew and Simons ch 8; Poulsen ch 9). The increasing dominance of large retailers in Sydney (Beed 1964; Bell 1981), their strategies to attract more trade, and investments by property developers have profoundly affected the pattern of shopping facilities, especially the rapid suburban expansion; small retailers still have an important place but they are in many respects pawns in the power plays of larger competitors. Likewise, the emergence of direct trading, whereby retailers buy goods from manufacturers rather than a wholesaler acting as intermediary, has been a dramatic organisational change in the industry: it has affected both the number of independent wholesalers and the role of survivors as well as being one factor influencing their rapid disperal.

## Technological change

Technological change is a major feature of economic development. Most technological change has occurred in response to the desire of producers and consumers for lower costs and better products and is a major feature of the competitive strategies of firms. It is characterised by reduced requirements for one or more factors of production (land, labour and capital) for each unit of output (Australia. Report of the Committee of Inquiry into Technological Change 1980; Australia. BIE 1981c).

Technological change has a widespread impact. For example, the growing dominance of transnational corporations and other large firms is both a product of and a stimulus to new production and distribution techniques and improvements in transport and communications. In particular, advances in computer communications systems, together with falling transmission costs, are vital to the effective coordination of national and international networks of offices and plants of large firms, and so underpin projects such as General Motors' world car concept. But technological change increasingly affects the methods of even the smallest firm and has many other effects on all aspects of the economy. A much publicised impact is the declining labour requirement of many industries and the deskilling of some semi skilled and clerical staff (Encel and Walpole 1980; Windschuttle 1979).

There is thus an intimate relationship between technological and economic change (Puu and Wibe 1980; Stubbs 1980). Technological change likewise has many effects on the urban environment, but the details of these are poorly understood, partly because of the difficulty of tracing the indirect impacts of technological change through the economy. It is clear, though, that technological change has been a factor encouraging the relocation of factories and warehouses out of cramped inner city sites to the middle and outer suburbs (Cardew and Rich ch 6; Nugent *et al.* ch 7). These changes combined with the national economic recession have created severe unemployment problems amongst migrants in inner city areas and school leavers in the western suburbs (Burnley and Walker ch 10).

Technological change has had an important impact on the distribution of goods and services in urban areas, although these changes must be seen in the light of overall changes in the nature of wholesaling and retailing (Nugent *et al.* ch 7; Cardew and Simons ch 8). A major component of technological change has been the introduction of information (electronic, computer and telecommunications) technologies in wholesaling and retailing. These changes combined with modern goods handling techniques, computerised stock control procedures and point of sale terminals have important implications for intraurban transportation and communications linkages (Langdale ch 4) and levels of employment in these industries.

Retailing and wholesaling have been traditionally labour intensive industries. However, technological change is likely to reduce labour requirements over the next ten years. Furthermore, the occupational mix of the workforce is expected to change significantly: the relative importance of semi skilled and unskilled white collar (clerical and sales) staff is expected to decline substantially, while increases will occur in skilled white collar (employers and computer staff) and, to a lesser extent, in blue collar groups (Australia. BIE 1981c:220-222).

Adoption of information technologies in the office sector has aroused fears of a massive reduction in the number of office workers as well as a deskilling of many of those left in the workforce (Alexander ch 3). While employment has been reduced in particular industries (printing, banking and insurance), the effect on overall employment in the economy is not clear as yet. Very few studies have attempted to examine the indirect impacts of the adoption of new technologies.

Technological change has been particularly important in altering the nature of Sydney's internal and external linkages. The automobile has dramatically changed the structure of the city (Neutze 1977). Other changes in transport technology have influenced commercial goods movements. For example, introduction of containers is related to the desire of firms to reduce shipping and handling costs (Rimmer and Black ch 12). This innovation has had repercussions on the nature of international and national modes of transport as well as on urban land uses and intraurban linkages.

As Sydney moves into an information economy, its internal and external communications linkages are undergoing significant change (Langdale ch 4). Improvements in telecommunications are integrating Sydney's industries more closely into the international and national economic system. At an intraurban level, adoption of these technologies is not only increasing the level of interdependency within the city, but reducing the relative importance of physically moving goods and people.

## 1.4   The community impact of urban change

Even though the primary concerns in this book are the links between economic change, physical restructuring of the city and the planning system, urban change does, of course, have major impacts on individuals and organisations in the city. The community impact of urban change is, then, an important theme, being the explicit focus of two chapters (Burnley and Walker ch 10; Rimmer and Black ch 12) and a strong subsidiary element in others (notably Aplin ch 13; Faulkner ch 14). Nevertheless, the intention is to illustrate some of the wide range of impacts rather than provide a comprehensive account.

Economic change, physical restructuring and government action all affect city dwellers in a great variety of ways. A key argument of much recent writing (e.g. Sandercock 1975b; Stilwell 1980; Troy 1981) is that this impact is an uneven one. In other words, urban change benefits some, may leave others unaffected, while still others suffer penalties of one sort or another. Rarely does any urban change bring universal benefits to all members of the community.

Some examples will help develop the point. One is provided by the changed state of the labour market. Reduced levels of economic activity and accelerating substitution of capital for labour have meant a declining rate of employment growth since about 1974 (Burnley and

Walker ch 10; Stilwell 1980). These factors combined with large numbers of entrants to the labour market have led to rising unemployment and underemployment, the latter through enforced part time working and a widespread tendency for individuals to occupy jobs below their level of skill (Callus and Quinlan 1979). But the impact has been uneven, falling most severely on those least competitive in the labour market — school leavers and other inexperienced workers, the unskilled and semi skilled, and recent immigrants. In contrast, there remains a shortage of workers in many skilled occupations, while most of those still in employment continue to gain higher incomes and improved working conditions. The unevenness of the impact of change is also clearly illustrated by the much increased absolute disparities in unemployment rates and the average duration of unemployment across the Sydney metropolitan area during the 1970s (Burnley and Walker ch 10; Stilwell 1980). The close relationship between unemployment and other social problems (Windschuttle 1979) intensifies the disadvantage of particular groups and locations, most notably inner LGAs and the outer west.

Variations in the incidence of unemployment are associated with the demographic, occupational and ethnic characteristics of the local population (Burnley and Walker ch 10). But they also reflect the physical restructuring of the city. Concentrations of high unemployment are associated with the more rapid suburbanisation of housing than of employment, and with inadequate ranges of job types in either the inner city or the outer suburbs. Especially in the remoter western and south western fringe, high unemployment is related to isolation from principal sources of employment, with the costs in time and travelling expense often so great that those out of work have little choice but to remain unemployed (Stilwell 1980).

Urban development has other direct and uneven community impacts. Most location decisions affect the distribution of income or welfare between individuals and organisations within the city, because changed urban form affects the cost of accessibility or proximity of any household to the city's facilities — employment, education, entertainment, shops, hospitals. Real income, if defined as total command over resources, including access to such public goods, is affected by location decisions, whether made by government or the private sector. Clear illustrations are provided by redevelopment of the CBD and inner suburbs (see Kendig 1979). Construction of new transport links or new offices has frequently involved demolition of substantial areas of low to medium priced housing. Such schemes undoubtedly benefited some — suburban commuters to the CBD or property developers and financial institutions — but, equally clearly, brought significant losses to others. Many of the dispossessed have been rehoused (often in physically superior property, it must be said) in outer western or south western suburbs. Aside from the physical disruption suffered, there are often substantial social impacts from such moves, including destroyed community social networks, unemployment and welfare problems, or at least significant economic costs (for example, through longer journeys to work and to urban facilities). Effectively, there has been a redistribution of real income away from such people (Sandercock 1975b). The worst excesses of such redevelopment schemes have been ameliorated in recent times because the economic downturn brought a reduced pace of development, while there have been greater government attempts to minimise the adverse effects (for example, by ensuring construction of more working class housing in the inner city). Nevertheless, virtually any redevelopment benefits some and disadvantages others.

Given the unevenness of the impact of urban change, it is not surprising that conflict arises between groups and individuals (Cox *et al.* 1974). Sometimes the conflict is implicit, reflecting merely a conflict of interests, though even this may represent real losses to some — those rehoused in the outer west or south west (Faulkner ch 14), or those suffering from heavy truck traffic (Rimmer and Black ch 12), for example. In other cases, physical conflicts arise, exemplified by police evictions of those occupying housing in Woolloomooloo threatened with demolition to make way for offices. In fact, urban development can be seen as a continuing sequence of conflict and its attempted resolution (Rimmer and Black ch 12).

Urban change thus affects everyone, but in different ways. Often, those least able to defend themselves and with fewest resources are the ones who suffer. Sometimes, inequities result directly from economic change; in other cases, physical restructuring is the immediate agent, though itself the product of economic stimuli. In either case, government is likely to play some role, as promoter of change or as regulator or as an agency to mitigate the most severe or inequitable consequences; in many cases, government attempts to perform all three roles.

## 1.5   Government and urban development

Government has a major impact on the nature of urban development; later chapters (notably chs 9, 11, 12, 13 and 14) explore various aspects of this. Two distinct roles can be identified. On the one hand, government is an initiator of urban change. On the other, it is a reactor to or controller of changes stimulated by external or internal mechanisms, attempting to regulate urban development in the interests of efficiency, community equity or its own political survival. These are extreme viewpoints and most government actions lie somewhere along the spectrum between the two. Rarely is government an entirely independent agent. Generally its decisions are taken in reaction to other events and are constrained by other factors, but in turn they provoke further shifts.

Government actions impinging on urban development are many and varied, in part reflecting the substantial number of bodies involved. All three levels of government take part and virtually all their manifestations, including government departments, semi-independent agencies (e.g. MWSDB) and advisory bodies (e.g. IAC), have direct or indirect impacts. There is thus a very complex web of government influence. For example, Linge (1971) identified more than 60 federal and state government departments and instrumentalities directly influencing development decisions in the City of Sydney LGA. Undoubtedly more would be found a decade later. Add similar situations for each of the more than 40 LGAs in the Sydney metropolitan area, plus the various functions within local government itself, and the number of linkages between public bodies becomes considerable. The pattern becomes even more complex when it is recognised that besides these formal linkages, informal decision making processes play a significant part in governmental actions (Linge 1971; Troy 1981). It is thus not surprising that there are often conflicts and contradictions between governmental bodies, even within individual agencies (Crabb ch 11).

In this context, it is vital to take a broad view since virtually all government policies have some urban impact. There is no clear distinction between urban policy and other policy relevant to urban development (Neutze 1978). In practice there is a gradation from urban planning (dealing with, for example, land use zoning, development control and regulation of metropolitan expansion), through policies whose focus is not explicitly urban but which have major impacts on urban change (e.g. housing and transport), to foreign affairs, where any urban influence is indirect and often unintended. It is thus better to consider the urban dimension of public policy than focus simply on urban policy (Neutze 1978), the latter being relatively insignificant except for a brief period in the 1970s. Some examples serve to illustrate the range of government influence.

Amongst the most important are monetary and general economic policies. Measures affecting general financial liquidity, capital inflow, exchange rates and interest rates have major impacts on the nature and pace of urban expansion. For example, there is considerable concern (e.g. AIUS 1980) that federal and state attempts to stimulate and service the 'resources boom', with the vast sums of public and private capital required, will markedly reduce the finance available at reasonable cost for urban development, either private (e.g. housing, business), or public (e.g. transport, other infrastructure). In the face of rising real costs of renting or buying housing, the growing shortage of public housing and the spread of underserviced new suburbs (Dare 1981), this spells major problems for many urban residents.

Federal and state industrial policy, too, plays a prominent role. After underpinning Australian industrialisation since the twenties and playing an important part in postwar economic and population growth (Linge 1979b), protection policy has been an especially significant determinant of Australian urban development. Conversely, the 25 per cent tariff cut in July 1973 was one of many factors reducing the volume of industrial activity and employment in the mid 1970s (Rich ch 5), especially in the inner areas of Sydney and Melbourne. Any future reduction in tariffs and quotas will have adverse impacts on urban areas heavily reliant on the most protected industries, notably Melbourne and Adelaide, and to a lesser extent Sydney (Linge 1979b; Australia. IAC 1981). State government policies also affect industrial development in Sydney. For example, industrialisation policies by Queensland and South Australia probably helped reduce industrial activity in Sydney, as did (in a marginal way) NSW decentralisation policy, while current fostering of energy and resource processing activities in the Hunter region also have important spillover effects, both positive and negative, for the metropolitan area (Rich ch 5).

Defence policy is also important, not so much because of direct military impact on urban areas (for example, through the stationing of personnel there), but more because of the pattern of purchasing and servicing defence equipment. One of the main criteria in awarding contracts to overseas suppliers is the amount of domestic manufacturing likely to eventuate, either through direct Australian participation in production or via offset orders. Similarly, decisions on whether to proceed with indigenous military manufacturing projects often stem as much from industrial production and employment, technological enhancement of local manufacturing facilities, and export opportunities generated as from sheer military necessity (Robinson 1980, 1981). With its concentration of aircraft production and related activities, Melbourne gains more than Sydney from such circumstances, but there are also important benefits felt in Sydney, especially through its supplying firms and naval docks.

Immigration policy, too, has had a critical impact on urban development. Postwar promotion of immigration boosted population and economic activity, especially in the major cities (Choi and Burnley 1974). Some 620,000 overseas migrants settled in Sydney between 1947 and 1971, the largest component of metropolitan population growth (Neutze 1977). In addition to the quantitative effects, immigration brought major qualitative change to the residential geography of the metropolitan area (Badcock 1973; Burnley 1974b, 1980), not least in slowing the rate of population decline in inner areas (Burnley 1974a; Kendig 1979), as well as many other shifts in shopping, cultural, entertainment and eating habits of the population. After a slump in the 1970s (Borrie 1978), which contributed substantially to reduced population growth rates and projections, immigration levels are now again increasing (Jay 1981; Snow 1981). The nature of the urban impact of the latest influx will depend in part on the criteria for immigrant selection, whether family reunion, securing of skills in short supply or humanitarian reasons. In the latter context, refugee policy, a subset of immigration policy, is of considerable significance. For example, large intakes of Lebanese as a result of the civil war in the mid 1970s left many of the refugees with severe adjustment problems, including prolonged unemployment (Burnley and Walker ch 10). Recent immigration of large numbers of Indochinese has brought similar difficulties.

These are merely examples of the range of non-urban policies having important urban effects. Many other components of government policy have more direct and obvious impacts on urban development. 'Transport policy has a direct and strong influence on the inter- and intra-urban pattern of development. Indeed it may have as much influence as land use controls and measures specifically designed to influence the pattern of development' (Neutze 1978:218). Cost and availability of transport, both under substantial but not complete government control, have very important effects on the shape, form and density of cities (Neutze 1977:ch 2), while government attempts to grapple with externally imposed transport changes, such as introduction of containerised goods transport and expansion of domestic and international jet travel, also involve substantial urban change (Rimmer and Black ch 11). Housing policy has similarly important results. Schemes to promote ownership and construction of new properties have contributed to urban sprawl, while construction of public housing has been a significant part of both fringe expansion and inner city residential redevelopment (Neutze 1978). Equally, provision of infrastructure such as water and sewerage lines (see Crabb ch 11) are important in moulding the pattern and regulating the speed and extent of urban expansion. In each of these cases — transport, housing and infrastructure — the impact of government intervention on Australian cities has been explored in detail elsewhere (e.g. Neutze 1977, 1978; Thomson 1979).

## 1.6   Planning Sydney

Urban planning is the most obvious example of government influence on urban development. In broad terms, urban planners have two roles. One is the preparation of plans and procedures to guide future patterns of urban development from the local government level to the metropolitan scale. Their less obvious role, but one forming most of their work, is development control, involving assessment of development applications usually within the context of existing planning instruments. This book is chiefly concerned with the first of these roles, and particularly its metropolitan dimension.

There have been attempts to influence Sydney's development at both metropolitan and local scales throughout the postwar period. In many respects, though, these attempts have been rather ineffectual. Both market forces and other aspects of government policy have had greater impact. At times, both have been in conflict with planning objectives and urban planners have been able to do little to influence either.

The details of Sydney's postwar planning have been widely discussed (Alexander 1981; Harrison 1972, 1974; Sandercock 1975b, Winston 1957). Several authors in this book explore particular aspects (Daly ch 2; Aplin ch 13; Faulkner ch 14). This section summarises the major developments, outlines some of the main environmental conditions influencing them, and indicates the lack of appreciation amongst planners of the nature and importance of the impact of economic processes on urban development.

The first metropolitan planning documents were prepared by the DMR in 1945 (NSW. DMR 1945) and were largely incorporated in the County of Cumberland Planning Scheme (CCC 1948). The Scheme proposed a greenbelt to restrict metropolitan expansion and satellite towns to accommodate growth, both urban management techniques employed in Britain, and an increase in the range of jobs and facilities available in the suburbs (Faulkner ch 14). The County Scheme formed the basis for metropolitan planning for the next two decades.

In 1968 a new and different type of plan, the Sydney Regional Outline Plan, was published (NSW. SPA 1968). In contrast to the County Scheme, it was a strategic plan: it provided a broad outline of future growth corridors with a general indication of the planning of development rather than the detailed prescription of land use zones. It sought to provide an orderly approach to urban development in conditions of rapid population growth. Among its major concerns were to maintain Sydney as Australia's major city, accommodate growth, ensure efficient extension of public utilities to cope with new demands while making best use of existing facilities, ensure an adequate and well located supply of industrial land, retain a strong CBD but decentralise jobs and reduce traffic congestion.

During the 1970s economic, demographic and political conditions changed rapidly, confronting planners with a new range of problems and producing a reassessment of the fundamental nature of metropolitan planning. A long expected Review of the Outline Plan published in 1980 (NSW. PEC 1980) represented one stage of that reassessment. It recognised that the issues confronting planners had widened to include social, environmental and additional economic considerations. Several objectives of the Outline Plan were modified while others were added. These included enhancing the natural and built environments, conserving Sydney's heritage and natural resources, influencing land prices, extending the range of housing types available and managing urban change to make the most effective use of existing resources. This Review is the starting point for metropolitan planning in the 1980s.

There have been major changes in the demographic, political and economic environments affecting urban development. In some ways metropolitan and local planning have evolved to reflect such changes, but all too often adjustment has lagged far behind, and frequently there has been little real recognition of the potential impact of changing conditions. The County Scheme was based on a population projection of 2.3 million (in the context of an expectation that Australia's population would stabilise at 9 million). High birth and immigration rates led the CCC to raise the projection to 3.7 million in 1959 (CCC 1959), while still further acceleration of population growth meant that the Outline Plan was developed on the assumption of a Sydney population of 5.5 million by the end of the century. Recession, a falling birth rate and rapid decline in immigration meant that in the Borrie Report (Australia. National Population Inquiry 1975) Sydney's projected end of century population was reduced to between 3.8 and 4.3 million. In 1980, the Outline Plan Review expected a population of between 3.5 and 3.9 million by the year 2001. However, Sydney's growth rate had already doubled between 1975/76 and 1977/78, and a rising birth rate and return of immigration rates to the level of a decade ago indicate that such figures will be underestimates: Sydney's population seems destined to exceed 4 million before the end of the century. Such marked variations illustrate the hazards of making growth projections and inevitably make metropolitan planning difficult because of the long time horizons involved (Faulkner ch 14). But the implications of these projections have not always been fully recognised in terms of either the physical or social infrastucture required to meet them. In particular, planners have been very slow to employ appropriate methods of translating population growth into expected demand for land and associated investment in water, sewerage and transport (Cardew 1976).

The political environment has likewise undergone many changes. The County Scheme reflected the optimism and idealism of early postwar years (Stretton 1970); it was strongly imbued with a sense of social justice and equity in line with the philosophy of governments of the day (Alexander 1981). Economic efficiency was also seen as desirable but was a secondary objective. In contrast, the Outline Plan was concerned primarily to achieve a more efficient urban structure and efficient accommodation of growth; again this appeared to reflect the ideals of the Coalition state government of the day, as well as the Labor opposition (Alexander 1981). Similarly, the Review reflects the current declared political ethos of efficient use of resources, tempered with a concern for social and environmental issues. Perhaps understandably, planning appears to be more sensitive to political circumstances than to other aspects of contemporary conditions. In extreme cases, planning has been viewed as little more than a desire to legitimate the capitalist system and reinforce the existing order and distribution of wealth (Sandercock 1975b). While sensitivity to political conditions and governmental requirements is understandable, rapid changes in political philosophy or governing party make for major changes in planning priorities or funds available, as evidenced at a federal level by the rise and fall of urban concerns during the 1970s (Faulkner ch 14).

Economic conditions have a major impact on urban development (section 1.3), but this has not been clearly recognised in metropolitan planning. Reflecting prevailing conditions, the Outline Plan implicitly interpreted the economy as prosperous, growing strongly and distributing benefits to all (the latter perhaps one reason for the lack of concern with equity issues); market forces, where recognised at all, were viewed as largely irresistible and adequately reflecting community preferences. But while economic bouyancy was recognised, the Outline Plan was based on little real analysis of the mechanisms underpinning economic change and their impact on urban change. Gradually there has been a growing recognition of the importance of such mechanisms. The interrelation of macroeconomic and urban issues was reflected in the establishment at a federal level of DURD. Later in NSW growing economic problems demanded an increasing awareness of the impact of economic change. Such awareness grew as the 1970s proceeded and meant that the Outline Plan Review recognised phenomena such as the unpredecented level of activity in property development, deterioration of economic conditions in the 1970s, and reduced government funding for urban programs, as well as other changes such as the new planning system in NSW and growing community involvement in planning issues (NSW. PEC 1980).

Despite such growing awareness, those formulating the Review have failed to recognise the crucial importance of issues such as the extent of dispersal of economic activity, rapid change in business organisation, growing significance of the finance sector, major change and rapid expansion of the communications sector, and the full extent of the urban planning conflicts engendered by technological and economic change, for example in the transport field. Each of these has major impacts on the nature of urban development, the lives of Sydney's inhabitants, the performance of business, and so on. Each needs to be examined carefully and its implications fully probed in designing future metropolitan plans. Each is explored in some detail in the ensuing chapters, and some of the planning implications assessed.

# 2 Finance, the capital market and Sydney's development

MAURICE T. DALY

## 2.1 The setting

In 1976 Davis published a list of cities in the 'top league of international investment centres' (Davis 1976). There were many surprises and some paradoxical results. London ranked number one, perhaps not unexpectedly given London's status as an international financial centre for 160 years and the excellence of The City's banking and other services, but certainly remarkable considering Britain's parlous economic condition. Another notable listing was that of Sydney in ninth place. At the same time Citicorp, one of the major forces in the capital market, was describing the land market in Sydney as being on the verge of total collapse, and the price of housing had begun to fall. While Sydney was being seen as a major force in the world network of capital, the very fabric of its property market was falling apart. The property collapse contrasted with the preceding six years of unparalleled, unbridled and seemingly unstoppable growth. Large construction and development companies, which up to 1974 had been recording record profits, fell into bankruptcy and receivership, and the ripple effect of the crash was felt in almost every cranny of the stock and capital markets, leading one major bank and several finance companies into penury. Indeed, the effects of the shake up were felt until 1979 and 1980 when a flurry of buying and selling of shares caused a dramatic restructuring of the ownership of some of Australia's major corporations.

Paradoxically, Sydney's achieving great importance in the international scene and the more dismal aspects of the city's functioning in 1975 were closely related. In fact, the relationship was intimate and typical of the long term nature of Sydney's growth.

Sydney's development has been characterised by frequent and often violent fluctuations, with sudden surges of growth collapsing into periods of stagnation or decline (Daly 1982). The triggers setting off rapid growth have been investments made during major structural change in the Australian economy. Capital to support substantial new developments has never been fully available locally, and throughout its history Australia has been a debtor economy. Overseas funds have been arranged and managed by financial institutions clustered in the cities. No matter whether the new projects have been agricultural, mineral or industrial, Australian cities have played a vital role in their development. As the nerve centre directing the growth of the state, and more recently controlling vital aspects of the national economy, Sydney has grown in response to such investments. The pace of city development has quickened or slowed in response to the magnitude of the capital flows it handled.

Structural changes in the economy, conditioned by external demands and lubricated by external capital, have manifested themselves in the demands on the resources of the cities. In particular, Sydney's CBD has been reconstructed at various times to respond to these new demands. Substantial investments in the city centre have been paralleled by demands of a growing labour force and have produced great pressures on the services and housing of the city. This has often resulted in violent inflation in values, accompanied by a relocation and spread of people and activities. As well, various upsurges of growth have had a critical impact on the problems of managing Sydney's development. Decisions made in haste, under pressure and with an unrealistic view of the future have set the mould for the subsequent decades of recession or slow growth.

## 2.2   The greatest boom: 1968–1974

*Origins*

The decade 1968–1977 embodied all these aspects of Sydney's growth. Between the mid 1960s and the mid 1970s Sydney's heart was rebuilt and a wave of speculation sent the prices of dwellings and land soaring even in the most peripheral suburbs. Large numbers of migrants entered the city and record quantities of capital flowed in from abroad. The state and federal governments committed unprecedented sums to help control and improve urban development, while property financing helped to swell the profits and assets of finance institutions and to reconstruct the Australian capital market. Large institutional investors took a strong entrepreneurial role in developing the city. The combination of big business and government meant that the boom produced was larger and more significant than any which had preceded it. In essence, however, the general pattern was similar to those of earlier years.

It is difficult to pinpoint a time and location at which the boom could be said to have started. Some might go back as far as Jack White's discovery of uranium at Rum Jungle in the Northern Territory in 1949 or to Ampol's oil strike at Rough Range in Western Australia in 1953, because these discoveries ushered in a phase of 'new' mineral developments which at first added 'an exotic touch to the mining scene' (Sykes 1978: 3) but which ultimately led to a new era for the Australian economy. Others might more accurately see the harbinger of boom in Lang Hancock's discovery of iron ore in the Hamersley Ranges in 1952 or in the proving of the Weipa bauxite deposits in 1955, but the point is the same: exploitation of these 'new' minerals progressively increased until by the late 1970s minerals had become firmly established as a major export earner for Australia. Between 1967/68 and 1978/79 the value of mineral exports rose by 673 per cent, whereas the value fo all Australian exports rose by 368 per cent; mineral exports grew from 16.4 per cent of the total value of all exports in 1967/68 to 29.0 per cent by 1979.

The 1970s was then a crucial period of readjustment for the Australian economy. The generally declining manufacturing base, so carefully nurtured for half a century and for long a major engine of national economic growth (Rich ch 5), corresponded with a rise in Australia's role as a supplier of minerals and mineral products to a world suddenly conscious of its resource frontiers. By the early 1980s the very viability of the economy seemed to rest with minerals, and Australia's place in the world had been redefined as a key supplier of energy and basic resources.

If all the costs of establishing Australia's new mineral position could be accounted, the capital requirements of the 1960s and 1970s would probably have reached $20 billion, while some projections into the 1980s see a further $50 billion dollars needed for mineral and mineral-associated developments (such as the growth of the aluminium industry). Australia simply did not have the capital to sustain investments on such scale, nor did it have enough institutions in the capital market sufficiently sophisticated to raise and manage massive investment projects. Much of the capital and expertise came from abroad. Capital inflow increased from $559 million in 1964/65 through $1,112 million in 1967/68 to reach $1,512 and $1,436 million in 1971/72 and 1972/73. Whereas in the early 1960s direct foreign investment in manufacturing had made up two thirds of the total capital inflow, by 1971/72 this proportion had fallen to only 13 per cent; in the five years up to 1971/72 a total of $1,027 million of foreign capital was invested in the mining industries. Foreign capital inflow fell off during the 1970s but revived in 1979, reaching a record peak of over one billion dollars in the single month of October 1980, and continuing through 1981 with almost $5 billion entering Australia in the first six months.

There were major developments in the international financial sphere which paralleled and assisted the changes taking place in Australia. The Eurodollar market, centred in London, developed rapidly during the 1960s and provided bankers with a fund which was largely free of government controls. The market received a great boost as a result of the two big OPEC price increases in the 1970s, and by 1980 banks were holding three thousand billion dollars in 'off shore' locations. Terms offered to borrowers were attractive and, often using syndicates of several banks, very large projects could be funded. In the 1960s Hamersley Iron Pty. Ltd., Mount Isa Mines Ltd., and Comalco of Australia all tapped the Eurodollar market to help finance their developments.

In 1965 the Australian government attempted to steer Australian capital into Australian enterprises by restricting the local funding available for foreign owned firms. Foreign firms therefore sought the help of foreign banks, which in turn were eager to establish themselves in Australia to play some part in Australia's booming economy. By the end of 1966 five new banks had been established, four in Sydney and one in Melbourne. This began a period of rapid growth of foreign banking representation and clustering of such banks in Sydney. The reasons for Sydney being preferred over Melbourne, the long established domestic centre for capital, are unclear. Sydney housed the Reserve Bank and the first of the merchant banks in Australia and it was the international gateway to Australia and the largest city. There was probably an element of historical accident and leadership by example: Bank of America (1964) and Citibank (1965), the two largest American banks, both established in Sydney, thus enticing others to follow. Probably as important as anything were the number of finance companies headquartered in Sydney. Australian banking regulations prevented foreign banks from carrying out normal banking operations in Australia and their direct entry into the Australian market was provided by finance companies, almost all of whom eventually had foreign banks as significant shareholders. By 1972, of the 17 members of the London Accepting Houses Committee, 13 were shareholders in Australian finance companies. By 1971 there were 37 foreign banks in Australia, compared with two in 1965. Equally significant was the growth of merchant banks from none in 1965 to nearly 100 in 1971.

As the size of the Eurodollar market grew, the number of centres linked with the market expanded across the world. A hierarchy of interlinked financial centres emerged, dominated by London but having distinct regional and subregional nodes. Singapore served as the regional centre for South East Asia and parts of the Pacific. It was set up as the centre of the so called Asiadollar market by the direct collaboration of the Bank of America and the government of Singapore in 1968. Sydney became the main Australian link in this system.

Other events conspired to link closely the macroeconomic changes described so far to Sydney's development. Success of Western Mining Corporation's development at Kambalda, accompanied by a rising price for nickel through to 1969, and the promise of enormous profits from the Poseidon venture at Windera set in motion a wild spree on

Australian stock exchanges. Collapse of this boom and declining opportunities presented by manufacturing turned investors directly or indirectly via building societies and finance companies towards real estate. Large quantities of both foreign and domestic capital were sunk into every facet of the urban property market.

Government policies accelerated the movement of investors into the property market. In the first place, government policy helped to swell the volume of overseas funds coming into Australia. Between 1969 and 1971 European rates of interest were falling whilst in Australia the government raised interest rates in an effort to combat rising inflation (ironically, partly caused by the expansion of the Eurodollar market). British developers, with strong lines of credit to the cheaper European funds, were able to enter the Australian property market from 1968 and compete successfully in the areas of office, factory and retail developments. Increases in the mineral exports, moreover, helped to solve Australia's balance of payments problem and by 1971 Australia's external resources had begun to grow to record levels, increasing by 41 per cent in the financial year 1970/71 and reaching an historically high figure of $2,726 million by January 1972. Revaluation of the dollar appeared inevitable but was prevented by pressure from the Country Party, and by September 1972 reserves had grown to $4,401 million. The result was a massive speculative inflow of capital in 1972, variously estimated to be between $1.5 and $2.0 billion (Porter 1974: 3). By then, property was the favoured form of investment.

A second feature of government policy contributing to the property boom was the relaxation of control over the money supply in 1971/72. Whilst the annual growth of the money supply had averaged 8.2 per cent in the six years to 1971/72, growth in 1972/73 was 25.7 per cent. There was more money available than investment opportunities and the real estate market seemed to be the most promising for most investors.

*Effects on the CBD*

One of the first effects of the mineral boom of the late 1960s was to force the pace of office development in Sydney's heart. Over a long period the traditional land uses of the CBD had been declining as manufacturing, wholesaling and retailing joined the flight of population to the suburbs; even service oriented offices had begun to be located in the suburbs, and by the early 1970s both state and Commonwealth governments were applauding the process and promising to accelerate it by legislation and example. But instead of suffering the outright decline which the long term trend suggested, Sydney's CBD in the 1960s revived under the impetus of the mineral developments and their associated capital and professional demands. The CBD assumed a larger, more substantial form than ever before.

Some rebuilding of the heart of Sydney was inevitable because little had been done since the building boom which preceded World War I and the more selective developments of the 1920s (City of Sydney 1980). The CBD of the 1950s comprised buildings accommodating: the storage and distributional roles associated with the port; offices associated with these activities; the banking, insurance and manufacturing headquarters which combined with the government functions in organising the economy; the small scale manufacturing concerns traditionally located in the centre; and the retailing, entertainment and specialist professional services which catered to a metropolitan population. By the 1950s Australia's development as a broadly based manufacturing economy called for higher levels of management and control and this, in turn, stimulated some growth of offices in the city. As population and prosperity grew, organisational and administrative demands of government, finance and professional services grew as well, placing further strains on the accommodation offered in the city's core. Existing buildings, old and often designed for other purposes, were unsuitable for modern developments of office machinery and office organisation.

Redevelopment of Sydney's CBD began in the late 1950s and was led by Australian and foreign firms building offices to suit their new needs and by British insurance companies, which had considerable experience in property development in Britain and sensed great investment opportunities in Sydney. They were right. Sites between Martin Place and Circular Quay procurable in 1958 at $22-33 per square metre, but in the following seventeen years peak prices in this area were to rise an astounding twenty six fold to about $800 per square metre.

Between 1960 and 1965 offices worth $118 million were built in Sydney's core. Then came the major impetus of the mineral boom. British insurance companies were followed by British developers who in turn were trailed by Australian developers and eventually by Australian financial institutions such as life office and superannuation funds: all consorted to turn a needed redevelopment of an aging core into a gigantic bonanza of office construction. Some 210 new buildings were completed in the CBD between 1958 and 1976, 84 of them after 1971. By the end of 1973, half a million square metres of office space was left vacant in the CBD with more than 100,000 square metres empty in North Sydney.

*Effects on the land market*

Through the 1960s there was a broadening of the Australian capital market, which was eventually critical in expanding the scope of the property boom. The official money market, which was not created until 1959, together with the unofficial dealers on that market, provided a source of short term money for investors. Further, finance companies grew from simply providing hire purchase funds for cars and household items into major sources of funds for a wide range of investment projects. They moved strongly into property in the mid 1950s, a move which was rapidly repaid in terms of increased profits. This allowed them to compete aggressively for funds from the public, and between 1968 and 1973 they did consistently better in terms of net receivables than savings banks and building societies: over the period net receivables grew by $2,997 million compared to $1,334 million growth of the savings banks and $2,039 million of the permanent building societies.

Permanent building societies themselves expanded enormously between 1968 and 1973 with annual net receivables increasing by 452 per cent over the period. Stimulus to growth was provided by high wages and buoyant economic conditions in Australia, by the loss of investment opportunities in the stock market with the collapse of the mineral boom, and by the impact of inflation (rising from 2.9 per cent in 1966/67 to 5.4 per cent in 1969/70 to around 14 per cent in 1972/73), which made the low, government regulated rates offered by the savings banks very unattractive. Finance companies were largely responsible for funding the boom in land whilst building societies provided extra money needed to sustain the housing boom. By 1975, of the top 25 finance companies in Australia, nine had more than 50 per cent of their loan portfolio and 14 had at least one third of theirs invested in property. As well, many companies were heavily involved in joint venture operations with developers wherein the financiers put up as much as 100 per cent of the funds, relying on the development companies to supply the expertise. The building societies were obliged under the terms of their charters to invest at least 90 per cent of their funds in property.

In January 1972 the median price of a block of land in Sydney passed $10,000 for the first time. In the financial year 1972/73 the price of developed land in Sydney increased by 42 per cent and by 1974 the median price of land had reached $20,200 per block. Land values inflated faster than any other prices and this was reflected in the contribution of land to the land and house package. In 1950 the median price of land represented only 14 per cent of the median land plus house price. By 1966 it had risen to 38 per cent and by 1974 it briefly became the major element at 51 per cent. Despite fluctuations in prices during the 1970s the proportion of total value contributed by land has remained in the vicinity of 40 per cent.

This boom could not have taken place without free money conditions and the rise of institutions such as finance houses, but there were several other factors which explained the very high prices of blocks of land. These include the limited supply of serviceable land and speculation in home sites or residential lots (Cardew 1979). Sydney's dissected topography aggravated land prices by reducing the amount of easily developed building land and by providing environmentally attractive sites in some areas for which purchasers were prepared to pay substantial premiums.

Pressure on the land market may have been relieved in the 1960s by the granting of strata titles, which gave a boost to home unit building. By 1969/70 multiple dwelling units surpassed single houses as the major proportion of all dwelling commencements. But to a large extent the demand for home units and flats was a product of an increased rate of household formation among householders who typically exhibited a preference for medium density housing (AIUS 1973; Cardew 1980).

Government legislation added to the forces creating higher prices. Developers were required to make roads, kerbs and gutters and to help fund sewerage and water supplies and provide public space on their sub-divisions (Tyler 1973; Wynyard 1970). These costs, probably compounded by the fact that they were funded by money borrowed at high interest, helped to double the price of a developed block of land between 1959 (when the first legislation was introduced) and 1968 (when the boom began).

Another government action influencing land prices was the intro-duction of the Sydney Region Outline Plan in 1968. In many ways this represented a reversal of the planning philosophies underlying the 1951 County of Cumberland Plan. The 1951 Plan attempted to restrict Sydney's horizontal growth by encircling the city with a greenbelt (Figure 1.1), inevitably restricting the amount of land available for development. Planners unfortunately had accepted population esti-mates drastically underestimating the effect of immigration. Very quickly population growth placed severe pressure on land resources, prices rose, and with the connivance of developers the green belt was eroded. The aim of the Sydney Region Outline Plan was to provide enough land to meet projected demand and to do so in an orderly fashion (Rich *et al.* ch 1). Unhappily the timing was sadly amiss, while the understanding of developers' psyches and the land market was woefully inadequate.

One element in the price of land derives from uncertainty about its future use. Each purchaser of land on the urban fringe gambles on the prospect of urban growth proceeding in the direction of his land and on the land being approved for development. Part of the potentially high profits associated with land development derive from the risks involved. The Sydney Region Outline Plan reduced these risks. it detailed for a period of 30 years the location and timing of urban releases and set in motion a scramble by developers to acquire those sites. Stocks of land held by developers grew rapidly from two to three years before the boom to holdings of five, seven or even eleven years by 1973. This competition bred its own mechanism for pushing up the price of land; the apparent inevitability of rising prices spurred developers to 'get in early', and soon sites anywhere within a hundred miles of Sydney were considered worth purchasing. Valuations tended to be based on the last or silliest sales, and finance companies were extremely anxious to fund the whole process; there were no brakes to be applied to the runaway prices. On top of this the government introduced in 1969 a betterment tax, the aim of which was the tax the gains made by landowners because of zoning changes. The 30 per cent tax on the increase in value was added to the price of land paid by developers and was generally regarded as contributing to further price increases.

## 2.3   Cycles of boom and bust

### Dispersal and the changing CBD

The office boom and land scramble represented two extremes of the period 1968 to 1974, but every other facet of the property market was also affected. In the early postwar period Sydney's future was seen to be based squarely on manufacturing. Even in the late 1960s there was unquestioned optimism about the continuing expansion of manufacturing. Consequently, industrial land became a target for speculators as manufacturing rapidly dispersed from the inner city across the metropolitan area. Even though industrial building continued at a relatively high level throughout the 1970s (Cardew and Rich ch 6), the sudden contraction in manufacturing after 1973 meant that some speculative purchasers of industrial land suffered considerable losses.

Some aspects of commerce, particularly retailing, also decentralised. (Cardew and Simons ch 8). With the establishment of the first planned shopping centre at Top Ryde in 1956, a new era of park and drive retailing was established. The traditional dominance of retailing by the CBD was challenged; its share of total retail sales fell sharply. Investment in retailing continued to grow through the 1970s, partly because the boom of 1968-1974 had bred a new type of property investor. Australian developers in the CBD had found themselves hard pressed to compete with British developers and had turned to Australian life offices for finance. Accordingly, major institutions lifted the proportion of their assets in real estate. The AMP Society, for example, had only six per cent of its assets in real estate in 1962 but 20 per cent in 1974, and between 1968 and 1974 investment in property by the AMP Society rose by 191 per cent.

Collapse of the office boom directed institutional investors to other sectors of the property market, and by the mid 1970s building of shopping centres became a favourite target for these investors (Simons ch 8). One result was a disposition for building large centres which introduced a 'lumpiness' into the market and aggravated the tendency for supply and demand to get out of phase and creating special difficulties for planners (Poulsen ch 9). In 1978/79 new retailing space came on to the market in Sydney at a rate four times as great as that of population growth despite a depression in retail sales.

The loss of workers in manufacturing and retailing in the CBD meant a fall in the number of workers there (Alexander ch 3). In addition, the character of the CBD began to alter, reflecting changes in the general economy. Government and big business became the dominant forces. In 1971 workers engaged in public administration comprised 12 per cent of the total workforce of the CBD. Much of the new growth in manufacturing had resulted from investment by foreign companies, and the CBD became the nerve centre housing head offices of the new or expanding companies and the associated plethora of government, financial or professional services called into being by the developments in the economy. Finance and business services came to dominate the CBD; in 1971, 30 per cent of the workers in the CBD were employed in these sectors and by 1976, 56 per cent of total floor space of the CBD was taken up by offices.

## Collapse of the boom

The growth of Sydney, which had seemed inevitable and unremitting in 1970, suddenly slowed in 1973 and with it the confidence of investors in property evaporated. At the same time money became tighter. Foreign capital inflow effectively dried up for real estate investors. In March 1973 a $621 million outflow of capital was recorded, the first outflow for 11 years. On 9 September 1973 Prime Minister Whitlam announced that the Reserve Bank would move to mop up excessive liquidity. Interest rates began to rise almost immediately and by the following June rates in the money market had reached as high as 25 per cent; the long term bond rate in September 1973 had been 7.0 per cent.

The property boom ended abruptly, dramatically. Large companies such as Home Units of Australia, Mainline Corporation and Cambridge Credit crashed. Others struggled through 1975 and 1976 but the fall of the giant Parkes Developments group in early 1977 seemed to spell the complete collapse of the market. In 1977 the average price of a block of land in Sydney ($16,482) and of a house ($35,139) fell below the 1974 median prices and continued falling through the first half of 1978.

Housing completions in Sydney between 1974 and 1978 were more than 25 per cent below the level maintained in the first part of the 1970s. However, in the late 1970s demand began to build up and rents rose. There was a revival of home unit development with a special focus on the inner city suburbs, partly caused by the increased costs of movement within the city. North Sydney residential values rose faster than those of any other areas in 1978/79 with a 42.7 per cent increase. All inner city areas recorded increases with rises of around 30 per cent in both the City of Sydney and South Sydney. The jump in prices in the inner areas corresponded to a revival of capital inflow and an improved performance of the domestic economy, both leading to easier money conditions. The revival spread to the outer suburbs and eventually to the land market. In 1979 and 1980 price increases of between 20 to 40 per cent became common in a number of suburbs. Once again a tightening of money in 1981 worked against the surging market and by June 1981 the Sydney residential property market had plateaued, with prices in some districts falling.

## 2.4  Conclusion

The rise and fall of property values in Sydney throughout the 1970s mirrored the fashion of Sydney's growth over its entire history. Few commentators have recognised how pervasive the pattern has been and fewer still have related this cyclical system to external factors. Alan Hall (1968) was an outstanding exception in drawing attention to the close relationship between the arrival of British capital and migrants and surges of growth in Australian cities in the second half of the nineteenth century. More generally, Thomas (1972), Abramovitz (1961), Easterlin (1961) and others have suggested a systematic relationship between Britain and Europe (as exporters of capital and people) and the New World during the latter half of the nineteenth century and the early part of the twentieth century. Upswings in the economies of nations like the USA, Canada, Argentina and Australia were counterposed to down-swings in the older economies and vice versa. Mineral discoveries, agriculture or manufacturing developments, or even major investments in infrastructure might begin the upswing and, if profits and potential seemed sufficiently great, would attract labour and capital from abroad. The vital significance of the cities in the Australian space economy meant that each upswing would be reflected by buoyant conditions in them.

Sydney's boom and bust sequences of the 1960s and the 1970s followed the pattern of its development from its earliest days; the forces involved have always included an intermingling of local and external factors. The complexity of the forces causing bursts of growth or periods of recession is such that at the peaks and troughs critical decisions have been made which were founded on unreal optimism or unknowing pessimism and which have set the seal on the character of the city's growth for decades.

# 3 Office suburbanisation
## A new era?

IAN ALEXANDER

## 3.1 Introduction

During the halcyon days of economic growth in the 1960s, office skyscrapers became a symbol of progress in all Australian capital cities, but nowhere more so than in Sydney. The then Premier of New South Wales, Sir Robert Askin, probably reflected majority opinion when he described the rapid changes in the skyline around Sydney as 'exhilarating' (quoted in Harrison 1972:95). Office development was seen as a tangible sign of 'progress' and a matter for considerable local and indeed national pride, a somewhat ironic attitude given the amount of construction financed and developed by foreign organisations (Daly ch 2).

The building boom of the 1960s and early 1970s led to a substantial oversupply of office space in Sydney's CBD and nearby North Sydney. Millions of dollars were invested in buildings that remained empty for years and even in the early 1980s a remnant of this surplus remains. This experience soured the 'office development as progress' view. Indeed, the last decade has witnessed increasing community concern over the effects of seemingly uncontrolled office development. Many groups and individuals have pointed to worsening central area congestion, displacement of central area activities and increased lengths of journeys to work as adverse impacts of central office building (e.g. NSW. SPA 1968). Others have seen redevelopment as damaging the amenity of the inner city and reducing its stock of historic buildings.

A solution to these problems, suggested in the 1968 Sydney Region Outline Plan, was the diversion of some future office development to major metropolitan subcentres such as Chatswood, Parramatta and Campbelltown. However, these suggestions drew little support and ran into considerable opposition from developers, councils of the City of Sydney and North Sydney and even from the NSW state government which continued to centralise its own office activity. Only green bans imposed by the Builders Laborers' Federation prevented some of the worst conceived office development schemes from going ahead

**Table 3.1   Composition of the office workforce in the Sydney metropolitan area and New South Wales, 1976**

| Occupation | Sydney | | | % of Sydney office workforce | New South Wales | | | % of NSW office workforce | Sydney as per cent of NSW | | |
|---|---|---|---|---|---|---|---|---|---|---|---|
| | Male | Female | Total | | Male | Female | Total | | Male | Female | Total |
| Professional and technical[a] | 55,218 | 12,154 | 67,372 | 14 | 71,222 | 14,929 | 86,151 | 14 | 78 | 81 | 78 |
| Executive and managerial[b] | 86,742 | 15,244 | 101,986 | 22 | 119,438 | 21,210 | 140,648 | 23 | 73 | 72 | 73 |
| Clerical[a] | 85,087 | 185,018 | 270,105 | 57 | 107,532 | 241,635 | 349,167 | 56 | 79 | 77 | 77 |
| Sales[c] | 18,872 | 2,163 | 21,035 | 4 | 26,262 | 2,734 | 28,996 | 4 | 72 | 79 | 73 |
| Communication[d] | 7,069 | 7,817 | 14,886 | 3 | 9,412 | 11,069 | 20,841 | 3 | 75 | 71 | 73 |
| Office workforce | 252,988 | 222,936 | 475,384 | 100 | 333,866 | 291,577 | 625,443 | 100 | 76 | 77 | 76 |
| Total workforce | 836,196 | 499,919 | 1,336,115 | - | 1,302,594 | 728,378 | 2,030,972 | - | 64 | 69 | 61 |
| Office as per cent of total workforce | 30 | 45 | 36 | - | 26 | 40 | 31 | - | - | - | - |

*Notes:* [a] Includes only the following occupation groups: architects, engineers and surveyors, law professionals, draftsmen and technicians, other professional and technical
[b] All workers
[c] Includes only the following occupation groups: insurance, real estate salesmen, valuers, manufacturers' agents, commercial travellers
[d] Includes the following occupation groups: telephone and telegraph operators, postmen and messengers
*Source:* 1976 Census

(Sandercock 1975b). Thanks to their efforts, reinforced in the early 1970s by the emerging oversupply of office space and the economic downturn, areas such as The Rocks and Woolloomooloo were saved from the wreckers' hammers.

Yet despite the 40 per cent increase in central office space brought about by the 1965-1975 development boom, there was only a small increase in central employment levels. In fact by the mid 1970s the number of central office jobs showed signs of a decline. In the light of these trends, what are the policy issues?

## 3.2 Office job growth in a regional context

Sydney provides an outstanding example of the tendency for office activity, concerned with the production, processing and exchange of information (Goddard 1975:1), to concentrate in large urban areas. Over three quarters (76 per cent) of the NSW office work force was located within the Sydney Statistical Division in 1976 (hereinafter the Sydney metropolitan area), whereas the area contained only 66 per cent of the total state workforce and 63 per cent of its population (Table 3.1). Office jobs comprised 31 per cent of the NSW workforce in 1976, while their share within Sydney was 36 per cent, having increased from 33 per cent in 1966.

Office jobs have grown faster than other jobs for some time, particularly in Sydney; the trend was accentuated in the slower growth environment of the 1970s. Although the rate of office job growth was reduced, office jobs in Sydney accounted for 67 per cent of metropolitan employment growth between 1971 and 1976, compared to their 56 per cent share in the 1966-1971 intercensal period. Attention has recently focused on the growing impact of computer and microprocessor technology on job availability: office activity, with its accent on paper work and information transfer is particularly susceptible to automation. Hence office workers, especially those in clerical occupations, are at considerable risk of being displaced by the introduction of new technologies in the office sector. Some observers predict that very substantial proportions of jobs in industries such as banking and insurance will be displaced by machines in the decades ahead (Jenkins and Sherman 1979).

To date, however, automation within the office sector has not meant *overall* job loss. Clerical jobs, which compose the bulk of the office workforce (Table 3.1), grew at 2.5 per cent per annum between 1976 and 1979 compared to a rate of 3.8 per cent over the previous 15 years. A similar reduction in job growth occurred in administrative and executive office jobs. However, the overall national rate of office job growth between 1976 and 1979 (2.5 per cent per annum) continued to

**Table 3.2  Changing distribution of office-type jobs in the Sydney metropolitan area, 1971–1976[a]**

| Region[b] | 1961 | | | | 1971 | | | | 1976 | | | |
|---|---|---|---|---|---|---|---|---|---|---|---|---|
| | Professional and executive | Clerical | Total office-type | % of Sydney office-type jobs | Professional and executive | Clerical | Total office-type | % of Sydney office-type jobs | Professional and executive | Clerical | Total office-type | % of Sydney office-type jobs |
| Central area[c] | 74 | 116 | 190 | 58 | 86 | 136 | 222 | 47 | 88 | 129 | 217 | 41 |
| Inner ring[c] | 29 | 18 | 47 | 14 | 43 | 33 | 76 | 16 | 47 | 35 | 82 | 15 |
| *Middle suburbs* | | | | | | | | | | | | |
| West | 15 | 12 | 27 | 8 | 22 | 21 | 43 | 9 | 26 | 25 | 51 | 10 |
| South West | 7 | 6 | 13 | 4 | 13 | 12 | 25 | 5 | 14 | 13 | 27 | 5 |
| *Outer suburbs* | | | | | | | | | | | | |
| South | 11 | 5 | 16 | 5 | 16 | 11 | 27 | 6 | 19 | 15 | 34 | 6 |
| Outer South West | 2 | 1 | 3 | 1 | 5 | 3 | 8 | 2 | 7 | 6 | 13 | 3 |
| Outer West | 7 | 4 | 11 | 3 | 14 | 10 | 25 | 5 | 20 | 15 | 35 | 7 |
| North | 9 | 4 | 13 | 4 | 17 | 10 | 27 | 6 | 23 | 14 | 37 | 7 |
| North East | 4 | 2 | 6 | 2 | 9 | 6 | 15 | 3 | 11 | 8 | 19 | 4 |
| Fringe | 2 | 1 | 4 | 1 | 6 | 4 | 10 | 1 | 8 | 6 | 14 | 2 |
| Total[d] | 160 | 170 | 330 | 100 | 300 | 246 | 476 | 100 | 263 | 266 | 529 | 100 |

*Notes:* [a] Includes those not stating workplace; these workers, comprising between 2 and 6 per cent of the total, have been reallocated in the same proportion as those stating workplace.
[b] Locations of regions are shown in Figure 3.1
[c] Due to LGA boundary changes between 1961 and 1971, figures for these dates are not directly comparable with those for 1971 and 1976. However, textual comparisons between 1961 and 1971 incorporate adjusted 1971 figures. 1976 data on an LGA basis do not permit the adjustment of 1976 figures.
[d] Totals may not add exactly due to rounding.

*Source:* Journey to work data from 1961, 1971 and 1976 Censuses.

be above that of the workforce as a whole (1.9 per cent per annum).

This does not mean that office job growth will continue inexorably or that some jobs have not already been lost to office automation: the number of typists and stenographers, for example, declined slightly during the 1970s but was offset by growth in other clerical jobs. It appears that the introduction of technologies such as word processors, computerised filing and accounting systems and automatic bank telling services is making inroads into both the recruitment and replacement rate of clerical labour (ACTU 1979). With further reductions in the real cost of new technologies, such trends are likely to accelerate and this will eventually lead to a decline in the numbers of clerical jobs. The Myers Committee (Australia. Report of the Committee of Inquiry into Technological Change in Australia 1980) takes the view that any job loss due to technological change will be more than offset by job growth resulting from improved productivity and increased demand for new products and services. This view, however, is based on neoclassical economic analysis and has been hotly contested (Windschuttle 1979).

In any event, reductions in office job opportunities will have adverse effects on young females, many of whom have traditionally sought jobs in the office sector. This is particularly true in the banking and insurance industries: for example, the AMP Society has already reduced the number of base grade employees, although it has increased the number engaged in computer operations (Encel and Walpole 1980). This can only add to already critical unemployment problems among this group. It is likely to further discourage the return of women to the labour force.

## 3.3   Changing patterns of office location in Sydney

Until recently the pattern of office development and job concentration in Sydney has been remarkable for its high degree of centralisation. Jobs are more centralised in Sydney than in Melbourne and to a greater extent than in many US or European cities (Thomson 1977:72). However, this pattern of centralisation started to break down in the 1960s. Despite the central building boom, the bulk of office job growth in the decade occurred in suburban locations (Alexander 1976a, 1978, 1979a). More recent data suggest that office job dispersal accelerated considerably in the 1970s, a pointer to the emergence of a new era in Sydney's evolving office job pattern.

In 1976 Sydney's central area, here defined to include the CBD core and the surrounding 'frame' in North and South Sydney (Figure 3.1), accounted for 41 per cent of the region's office-type jobs (defined in Appendix 3.1) and 49 per cent of clerical jobs. Fifty five per cent of office-type jobs and 62 per cent of clerical jobs were located within ten

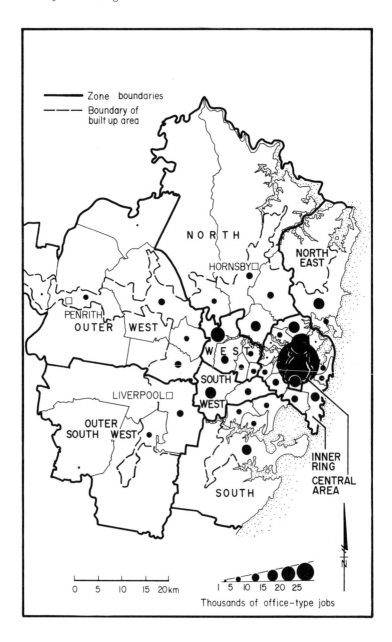

**Figure 3.1    Distribution of office-type employment by LGA in the Sydney metropolitan area, 1976**

kilometres of the city centre, that is within the inner city area defined in Figure 3.1. This pattern is far more centralised than that of non-office jobs, of which only 39 per cent were located within the inner city area in 1976.

Despite the continuing concentration of office jobs, the pattern of central dominance has decreased markedly in recent years. The proportion of office-type jobs located within the central area declined from 58 per cent in 1961 to 41 per cent in 1976 (Table 3.2). Conversely, the proportion of office-type jobs located in the outer suburbs increased from 16 to 29 per cent of the total. Even more significant is the fact that between 1971 and 1976 there was a reduction in the number of central office jobs, from 222,000 to 217,000. The decline was sharpest in the City of Sydney and South Sydney where the number of office-type jobs fell by five per cent and 13 per cent respectively; in North Sydney the number actually rose (by 37 per cent) but insufficiently to offset the decrease in the City and South Sydney. The overall decline is attributable to a significant reduction in the number of central clerical jobs which more than offset a continuing expansion of professional and executive jobs. This marks a clear reversal of previous trends, for during the 1960s the number of central clerical jobs rose strongly and accounted for one quarter of the metropolitan increase.

The recent reduction in clerical jobs appears to reflect a tendency towards relocation and subregionalisation of routine office jobs, a trend which seems likely to accelerate as office automation proceeds. Computerisation of office functions facilitates greater fragmentation of office operations (see section 3.6). A further reason for the increasing significance of suburban office jobs is the 'hidden' element of office employment, that is office jobs located not in office buildings as such, but in premises attached or ancillary to activities such as factories, warehouses, shops, schools, hospitals and the like. Proliferation of these activities in suburban areas has led to a concomitant increase in suburban office activity. Even in 1971 there were around 30,000 office jobs located in Sydney's major suburban industrial areas at Parramatta-Auburn, Fairfield-Yennora, Blacktown, Ryde, Lane Cove, Artarmon and Botany. At the same date there were only around 25,000 office jobs located in the major suburban office centres shown in Figure 3.5, with a large proportion of these being accounted for by Parramatta (5,400) and Chatswood (3,100).

More recent data assembled by Cardew (1981b) confirm the growing significance of office activity in industrial areas. A sample of 90 industrial establishments in Sydney established since 1970 showed that a quarter of the firms used more than 20 per cent of floorspace for office purposes. This can result in up to 50 per cent of jobs in 'industrial' establishments being in office occupations, particularly in modern scientifically oriented industrial areas such as North Ryde, located

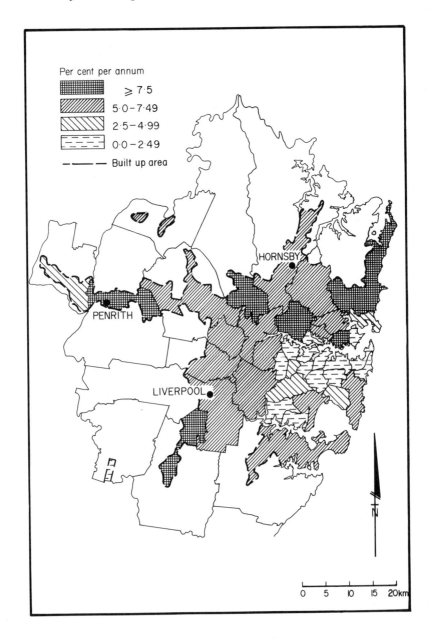

**Figure 3.2    Growth rate of office-type employment in the Sydney metropolitan area, 1961-1971**

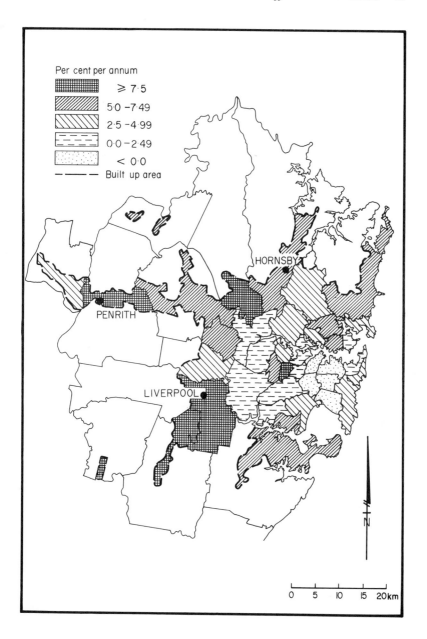

**Figure 3.3 Growth rate of office-type employment in the Sydney metropolitan area, 1971–1976**

adjacent to Macquarie University. In other words, a large and increasing number of office jobs in Sydney are located in suburban areas outside traditional office buildings (Cardew and Rich ch 6).

At a metropolitan scale, this trend was undoubtedly a contributor to the recent acceleration of office job dispersal (Figures 3.2 and 3.3). While all central and inner LGAs recorded employment growth in the 1960s, all except those on the North Shore showed declines in jobs or very slow growth between 1971 and 1976. Meanwhile, office employment in most middle and outer suburban LGAs continued to grow rapidly within the context of reduced overall growth. In sum, the 1970s saw a marked acceleration of office employment suburbanisation, particularly in clerical jobs, with suburban areas absorbing 90 per cent of office job growth compared to their 55 per cent share during the 1960s.

## 3.4    Job location, balance and work journey trends

Despite the increased rate of office job dispersal, significant imbalances in the distribution of office jobs remain. In 1976 only in the central and western sectors did the number of office-type jobs exceed the number of resident workers in these occupations (Figure 3.4). There were particularly heavy job deficiencies in southern and northern suburbs. Office job opportunities are still more unequally distributed than other jobs in comparison to the resident workforce. The Gini index compares equality of distributions on a scale from 0 to 100; the higher the index the greater the inequality (Smith 1977:165). On an LGA basis the 1976 index was 37.6 for office-type jobs and 24.1 for all jobs within Sydney. Inequality of total job distribution fell by 30 per cent between 1971 and 1976, but the reduction in office job inequality was only 16 per cent. These figures reflect the high proportion of office-type workers that continue to rely on central area jobs: 49 per cent of clerical workers and 33 per cent of professional workers, compared with 30 per cent of the total workforce.

Nonetheless, it is clear that the accelerated rate of office job dispersal évident in the 1970s has facilitated an increase in the proportion of office workers finding jobs within the sector of the metropolitan area in which they live. Concomitantly, the reduction in the proportion of office job trips to the central area has been matched by an increase in cross-suburban journeys. This continues a trend evident during the 1960s and appears to result both from increased use of the car for work journeys and from spatial mismatches between home and job locations (Aplin ch 13; Manning 1978). Within the office workforce, cross-commuting is far more prevalent among professional/executive workers than among their clerical counterparts. This is probably a reflection of

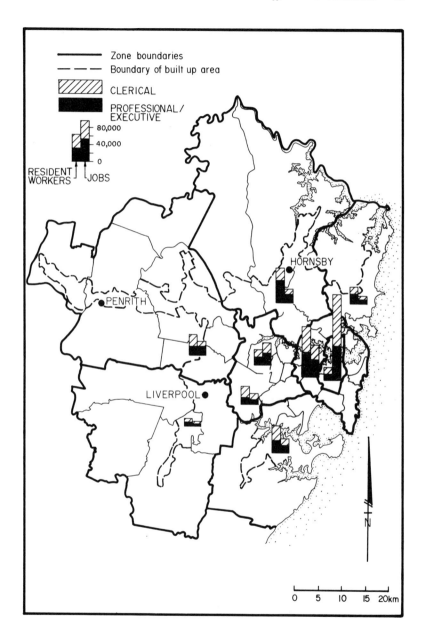

**Figure 3.4    Distribution of office-type employment and office-type workers by zones in the Sydney metropolitan area, 1976**

higher income and car ownership levels among the former group on the one hand and their relatively strong residential concentration on the North Shore on the other (Figure 3.4).

## 3.5   Changing office development patterns

Although the pattern of office building does not correspond with the distribution of office activity, the two are clearly associated; in any case the changing pattern of office development is of interest in itself. The pattern of suburbanisation evident among office jobs is also present to an extent in office building patterns, despite the record building boom of the 1970s, which saw a total of $790 million invested in central area office buildings completed between 1970 and 1978. While the central area monopolised Sydney's office development in the 1960s, accounting for no less than 89 per cent of the value of investment in office buildings, the proportion dropped to 77 per cent in the 1970s. But in contrast to the pattern of job suburbanisation, much of the non-central growth in office investment occurred in the inner ring area, rather than in the middle and outer suburbs. The inner ring's proportion of office building doubled from four per cent in the 1960s to eight per cent in the 1970s. Elsewhere, only the western suburbs recorded a significant increase in its share of total development, from two per cent in the 1960s to five per cent in the 1970s, largely due to developments at Burwood and Parramatta. Both these centres have seen an influx of financial offices which are heavily dependent on clerical labour, a large pool of which resides in surrounding areas (Figure 3.4).

Thus, there has been a marked but spatially restricted spread of office development away from the central areas in the 1970s. Clearly, however, the centre has dominated metropolitan office building patterns over the past two decades, since it accounted for 81 per cent of the total value of completions.

## 3.6   Development of office activity in suburban centres

While the preceding analysis has given some idea of the acceleration of office suburbanisation within Sydney in recent years, it has said little of the type and location of office activity that has developed in the suburbs. Results of an enumeration of private sector office establishments located in Sydney's major suburban centres at 1975 and 1979 (Tables 3.3 and 3.4) throw some light on this question, although it is recognised that a good deal of office activity has grown outside these centres in industrial areas and the like. The surveys were identical in method, with the 1979 survey covering several additional centres. The

**Table 3.3** Numbers of private sector office establishments[a] in Sydney suburban centres, by type of market area served, in 1975 and 1979

| Market area served | Local/district | | Metropolitan/state | | Interstate/national | | Total | |
|---|---|---|---|---|---|---|---|---|
| | 1975 | 1979 | 1975 | 1979 | 1975 | 1979 | 1975 | 1979 |
| *Centre* | | | | | | | | |
| Chatswood | 117 | 190 | 91 | 143 | 28 | 32 | 236 | 365 |
| Parramatta | 155 | 285 | 24 | 47 | 2 | 5 | 181 | 337 |
| Burwood | 103 | 104 | 15 | 23 | 1 | 3 | 119 | 130 |
| Bondi Junction | 121 | 138 | 11 | 24 | 1 | 1 | 133 | 163 |
| Ryde | 6 | 26 | 4 | 14 | 0 | 3 | 10 | 43 |
| Gordon-Pymble | 1 | 2 | 9 | 11 | 5 | 5 | 15 | 18 |
| Bankstown | 116 | 153 | 8 | 20 | 0 | 0 | 124 | 173 |
| Hurstville | 120 | 132 | 11 | 18 | 0 | 0 | 119 | 150 |
| Liverpool | 129 | 162 | 14 | 16 | 0 | 0 | 143 | 178 |
| Blacktown | 41 | 86 | 5 | 9 | 0 | 0 | 46 | 95 |
| Brookvale | b | 31 | b | 17 | b | 0 | b | 48 |
| Epping | b | 27 | b | 5 | b | 2 | b | 34 |
| Campbelltown | b | 91 | b | 5 | b | 0 | b | 96 |
| Hornsby | b | 59 | b | 3 | b | 1 | b | 63 |
| Manly | b | 71 | b | 4 | b | 0 | b | 75 |

*Notes:* [a] For a note on establishments included see Alexander (1976a)
[b] Not available as these centres were not surveyed in 1975
*Sources:* 1975-based on field survey in October 1975; see Alexander (1976a:194)
1979-follow up field survey in October 1979

**Table 3.4  Composition of non-local firms in Sydney suburban centres in 1975 and 1979[a]**

| Type of activity | No. establishments | | % of establishments | | Change in No. establishments 1975–1979 | |
|---|---|---|---|---|---|---|
| | 1975 | 1979 | 1975 | 1979 | No. | % |
| Manufacturing, mining and service industry | 39 | 92 | 17 | 22 | +53 | +136 |
| Distribution, transport and publishing | 38 | 94 | 17 | 23 | +56 | +147 |
| Finance | 12 | 17 | 5 | 4 | +5 | +42 |
| Building and development | 21 | 31 | 9 | 8 | +10 | +48 |
| Professional and business services | 119 | 177 | 52 | 43 | +58 | +49 |
| *Total* | 229 | 411 | 100 | 10C | +182 | +79 |

*Note:* [a] Excludes centres not surveyed in 1975
*Source:* As for Table 3.3

office establishments are classified according to the market area they serve. The methodology is detailed in Alexander (1976a), but essentially involves a three tier division into those serving: (1) local (suburban) or district markets; (2) metropolitan and/or state markets; and (3) national and interstate or overseas markets.

At both dates, the vast majority of establishments were of a local or district serving nature (Table 3.3). However, between 1975 and 1979 there was a limited dispersal of non-local offices away from the two centres that dominate the pattern, Chatswood and Parramatta. Ryde, Gordon-Pymble, Epping and Burwood all had a significant share of non-local establishments by 1979 (Figure 3.5). A number of these firms have relocated from the central area, continuing the earlier pattern. This is significant since, while rent savings were a major inducement to relocation before 1975, the oversupply of central office space substantially reduced the rental gap between central and suburban locations.

Relocation has not been indiscriminate, however, since all centres with a significant number of non-local offices are located in inner and middle suburban areas and several are on the North Shore; centres located in outer suburbs have a very small number of non-local establishments. This is indicative of the limited spatial mobility of company head offices: while an increasing number are prepared to locate away from their traditional central locations, they overwhelmingly prefer to remain within easy access of contacts in the central area and to be close to executive residential areas.

The composition of non-local firms has altered over the period (Table 3.4). There has been a particularly rapid growth of firms in the manufacturing and distribution sectors. By 1979 they accounted for 45 per cent of total establishments, compared to their 34 per cent in 1975. While the financial, building/development and professional/business service firms also increased in number, their share of the total fell. This pattern continues earlier trends: between 1965 and 1975, manufacturing and distribution firms were by far the most spatially mobile within the office sector (Alexander 1976a:202-3; Cardew and Rich ch 6).

Additional data from the 1979 survey, not recorded in the tables, also indicate a rapid growth of subregional offices of state and federal government agencies and an increased presence of area offices of private sector finance and banking firms (as opposed to local branch offices entirely dependent on the central head office). Both of these components represent a significant augmentation of office activity in suburban centres and a further strengthening of the suburbanisation of administrative office activity (see Langdale ch 4 for the decentralisation of banking functions).

This trend appears to have been assisted by the accelerated auto-

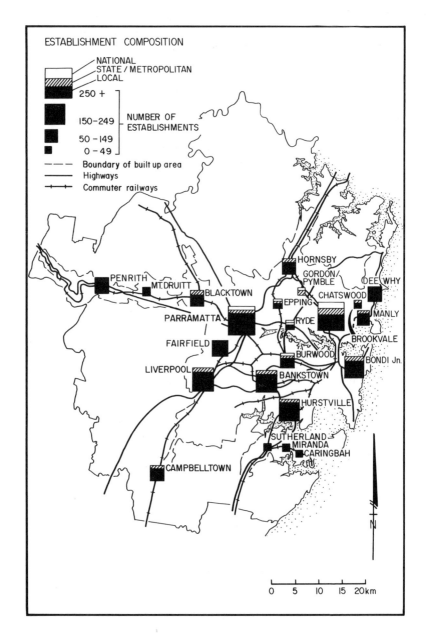

**Figure 3.5   Distribution of private sector office establishments by market area served, 1979**

mation evident within the office sector. A number of banks, finance and insurance companies established data processing offices in subcentres in the early 1970s: this was facilitated by potential rental savings and increasing use of telecommunications for data transmission. Further dispersal of administrative activity in the late 1970s is an extension of this development. This is in accord with the scenario proposed by Nilles *et al.* (1976), who linked increasing office automation with the dispersal or 'fragmentation' of office organisations. The ultimate extension of this idea is the development of home based offices and local neighbourhood work centres, from which office workers telecommunicate rather than travel to a central workplace. But while this may be technically feasible, it is unlikely to become widespread in the short term, given the important social function of traditional workplaces and the continuing relatively high cost of short distance telecommunication in comparison with travel (Langdale ch 4; Pye 1977). In any case, while the home based office has intuitive appeal from a transport/energy saving point of view, it must also be recognised that any benefits brought about by such a system will be offset by the reduction of office job opportunities that appears certain to accompany increasing automation.

## 3.7 Implications for planning

Limited dispersal of office jobs and office activity evident in the 1960s accelerated markedly in the last decade. The 1970s saw a decline in central office jobs, accompanied by rapid suburbanisation. Growth of non-local office establishments in suburban centres accelerated partly as a result of further relocation from the central area. In addition, there are indications of a growth in both public and private sector subregional offices in major subcentres and some industrial areas. This has reinforced the importance of clerical and routine office job concentrations in the suburbs, although even with the 1971-1976 central area decline these jobs remain highly centralised. However, if job numbers in the clerical sector start to decline as automation proceeds, this will further reduce the importance of the central area for clerical jobs. The most vulnerable industries, banking and insurance, are still highly concentrated in central or near central locations.

Since 1976, a good deal of the then 30 per cent surplus office space in the central area has been absorbed (Jones Lang Wootton 1980). However, this does not mean that the growth of central office jobs has resumed, since (a) a high proportion — 40 per cent in 1976 — of the office vacancy was in newly constructed buildings, many of which have since been filled by tenants vacating older buildings which are now empty, and (b) there has been a continuing trend towards more office floorspace per worker (Neutze 1977:98). In fact, whilst the surplus was greatest, generous lease agreements led to very low employment densities which could be increased when demand subsequently rose.

Dispersal of office activity within the region accords, in principle, with the aims of the Sydney Region Outline Plan of 1968. Ironically, it appears that dispersal has occurred in spite of rather than because of the plan. The SPA, while responsible for the Plan's implementation, had few direct powers to encourage growth of office activity in suburban centres in preference to the city centre. In the only area where it did have power, the vetting and approval of local government land use plans and codes, it did not act with sufficient determination. The SPA allowed the City of Sydney scheme, after years of controversy, to be gazetted in 1971 without any codes to control building bulk and size. When the Council adopted a floorspace ratio code, following the preparation of its Strategic Plan (City of Sydney 1971), it turned out to be something of a paper tiger and was too late to have any effect on the office building boom. While the SPA moved to encourage the North Sydney Council to lower floorspace ratios in the office development area in 1975, this was also too late to have any effect on the office building boom.

The SPA and its successor, the PEC (now the Department of Environment and Planning), also prepared reports calling for rapid expansion of office employment in two of its nominated suburban office centres, Parramatta (NSW. PEC 1978) and Campbelltown (NSW. SPA 1973). The latter plan called for a new city to 'perform some of the metropolitan centre's functions thus relieving some of the development pressures and movement problems of the latter' (NSW. SPA 1973:20) and proposed some 15,000 metropolitan-type office jobs in the new city centre at Campbelltown (Faulkner ch 14). Similarly the 'prime objective for Parramatta city centre is to increase office employment to a long term level of around 50,000 to give those office workers in the western subregion the choice of working closer to where they live' (NSW. PEC 1978:2). Laudable as these objectives may be, the difficulty is that without some positive intervention it is highly unlikely that office employment in these centres will reach anything near projected levels, especially for Parramatta: 50,000 is a very large workforce for a single centre. Chatswood and Parramatta are the only 'natural' suburban office centres within Sydney to have attracted a significant number of non-local office functions. But forecasts made in the early 1970s suggested that even in 1985 the combined total office jobs in these two centres would be only around 20,000, compared with over 200,000 in the central area (Australia. Cities Commission 1975). This assumed implementation of plans formulated by the Whitlam government between 1972 and 1975 for the dispersal of at least 5,000 Commonwealth government office jobs to Parramatta. With the shelving of these plans, along with most other urban initiatives, by the Fraser government in 1976, even these modest aims went by the board.

Other centres nominated for office expansion in the Outline Plan — Blacktown, Mt. Druitt and Penrith — contain an insignificant number of non-local office establishments. Centres in inner and middle suburban areas and those close to executive residential areas (e.g. Ryde, Epping and Gordon-Pymble) have attracted more office activity of this type. In addition, many office jobs were located in areas outside subcentres altogether, such as industrial zones. Suburban office employment is therefore now scattered over a wide array of locations.

In theory, means are available to achieve a greater concentration of suburban office jobs. A system of office development or employment location licencing, or one of site tax penalties and incentives, could be used to steer development to desired centres and to prevent it elsewhere. Whether such systems would work in practice, however, is problematic given the weakness of resolve at state government level and Sydney's long history of the defeat of planning measures by powerful financial interests. Nowhere are these interests stronger than in the office development industry, which not only has strong political connections and sympathisers in local councils and at the state government level, but also is prepared to campaign publicly against the spectre of so called 'socialism' should planning proposals run contrary to its interests (Sandercock 1975a).

Even assuming that office development could be steered to 'desirable' suburban locations, is such a policy really in the overall public interest? It has been shown elsewhere (Alexander 1980a) that the policy of subcentre office development was originally adopted on rather subjective grounds. It was simply assumed that the benefits of office dispersal, seen as shorter work journeys, reduced central congestion and development pressures and greater suburban work opportunities, would outweigh any social costs. However, it is likely that with current transport facilities, office dispersal would be accompanied by a dramatic shift from public to private transport for work journeys (Alexander 1980b). Whereas almost three quarters of the CBD office workforce uses public transport for work trips, it is likely that one quarter or less would do so were their offices located in subcentres. The switch would result not only in short term revenue losses for the operators of Sydney's ailing public transport system but also in heavy suburban road congestion and considerable increases in cross-commuting and petrol consumption for work journeys (trends already apparent). Public transport users, largely those with no alternative means of travel, would also be considerably disadvantaged in terms of average travel times. These disadvantages would offset the benefits of improved job access, shorter work journeys for the majority of workers and reduced central congestion (Aplin ch 13).

It is apparent therefore that unless accompanied by a concerted program of suburban public transport improvement — only feasible where jobs are concentrated in a limited number of subcentres — office dispersal can create as many problems as it solves. The need for improvements in public transport services to key subcentres has been recognised in several studies, including the Outline Plan itself and the subsequent Sydney Area Transportation Study (NSW. SATS 1974b). A detailed study of options for improving public transport services to Parramatta was undertaken in the early 1970s following a federal government offer to upgrade rail services to the centre as a supplement to its own office job dispersal program. The study recommended the construction of a new rail system focusing on Parramatta and connecting it more effectively to its potential labour catchment area (De Leuw Cather 1976). But because of the change of federal government in 1975 and opposition from the then Liberal NSW government, the twelve volumes resulting from the study joined innumerable others gathering dust on public authority shelves. Very little has been done since to upgrade public transport services to Parramatta or any other major subcentre. In the meantime, road congestion and parking problems in the subcentres have become progressively worse.

Thus, office suburbanisation is not only proceeding in an unplanned way, resulting in a scatter of suburban job opportunities rather than their concentration in key centres, but it is also giving rise to considerable increases in suburban cross-commuting, suburban road traffic, congestion and parking problems. Workers may benefit in terms of reduced travel time but the community is bearing a high cost, especially given the increasing financial problems of the public transport system and impending liquid fuel shortages. The office suburbanisation process within Sydney, desirable as it may be in principle, seems to be generating many additional social costs without providing the full range of benefits of which it is capable.

If greater net benefits are to be drawn by the community from the accelerated office suburbanisation which is now apparent and if those benefits are to be more equally distributed, then several government initiatives are required.

(1)   Immediate upgrading of public transport services to a small number of strategically located subcentres and limitation of parking space within these centres;

(2)   Control of new office development within the central area and within non-designated subcentres;

(3)   Control of the expansion of office activity attached to other activities within industrial zones or other areas poorly served by public transport;

(4)   Selective dispersal of governmental office employment to centres where they are closer to the homes of a majority of employees

and encouragement of private sector dispersal along similar lines using financial incentives if necessary.

Such initiatives would require considerable commitment of funds and political will from the government. At present, such commitments are not fashionable, for the accent is on expenditure restraints and modest government intervention in the market place. But fashions do change and change they must if office suburbanisation within Sydney is not to further complicate the region's already severe planning problems.

## Appendix 3.1   Definition of office jobs

The definition of office jobs is a complex task, particularly given the nature of available data. Accepting that office jobs are primarily concerned with the collection, processing and exchange of information, it is possible to arrive at a reasonable Census based definition (Alexander 1979a:3). However, such a definition requires detailed occupational data (relating for example to specific occupations such as typists, architects and the like) which are not readily available for small areas.

Hence the term 'office-type jobs' (following Armstrong 1972) is used at several points in this chapter. This encompasses all jobs classified in the Census as professional, technical, clerical and administrative/executive. It thus includes all white collar jobs except sales jobs.

# 4 Telecommunications in Sydney
## towards an information economy

JOHN V. LANGDALE

## 4.1 Introduction

The Australian economy, in common with those of other industrialised countries, is increasingly dominated by information industries (Lamberton 1977; OECD 1981). The major functions of such industries are the collection, storage, analysis and transmission of information, which represent substantial components of such diverse activities as banking, education, printing and data processing. Rapid technological change in the electronics, computer and telecommunications industries has been a critical factor in the growth of the information economy: in particular, increasing diversity of telecommunication services and falling costs have allowed organisations to interconnect computers, computer terminals and office equipment in different locations (Langdale 1979b).

These trends represent the emergence of an information economy, which functions at a variety of geographical levels ranging from the international to the local. Large cities, functioning as key decision making centres and control points in the domestic and international economy, have particularly strong communications linkages.

The term information economy has been applied to describe the growing use of electronic and computer equipment in providing services, as well as to the substitution of electronic means of communication for travel and for conventional mail (Nora and Minc 1980; Porat 1978). The emergence of the information economy is having an impact on the structure and functioning of cities. It is also influencing the number and skills of employees in information occupations as well as the geographical distribution of jobs.

Meier (1962:13) has argued that cities evolved primarily to facilitate human interaction. Circulation of information, goods and people via communications and transportation networks has permitted rapid growth of cities (Gottman 1970). Most studies of urban circulation systems have focused on movement of goods and people to the neglect of communications flows. However, the most rapid growth in linkages within and between cities is via telecommunications. In contrast, growth in transportation linkages is likely to be constrained by rising levels of traffic congestion and automobile pollution as well as by increasing energy costs.

The business communications area represents a major growth component in telecommunications: organisations are deriving substantial benefits in adopting equipment for information storage, manipulation and transmission. In contrast, it is unlikely that private subscribers will use the wide range of information technologies in the next decade because of high costs of upgrading connections to millions of telephone subscribers and the relatively high cost of much computer and telecommunications equipment. More importantly, it is questionable whether private users would want to access a large amount of information available in data bases or would want to process such information using computers.

Greater diversity and lower charges for telecommunications services have resulted in a reduction in the friction of distance as a barrier to national and international linkages; this has promoted growth of national and international economies. However, such developments have contributed to the dominance of major metropolitan cities over the rest of the economy by facilitating centralisation of control in public and private organisations. At an international level they have assisted in centralisation of control in headquarters of transnational corporations located in major US, European and Japanese cities. At a national level firms in Sydney and Melbourne have extended their control over the rest of Australia, although the extent of this dominance has in turn been diminished by the growth of foreign control over the Australian economy (Rich ch 5).

These developments have also had an important influence on the nature of linkages at an intraurban level. Adoption of information technologies has allowed firms to improve contacts between head offices located in the CBD and suburban branch offices. In addition, some small and medium sized firms are acquiring computer and office equipment with communications capabilities, which allows them to connect with firms offering specialised services, such as computer service bureaux.

This chapter examines the geographical patterns of telecommunications linkages for Sydney as well as the impact of new telecommunications services. Sydney's external communication linkages are of considerable importance in its economic role, since it is Australia's preeminent international gateway as well as being the dominant node in the web of national economic transactions. At an intraurban level geographical linkages of telephone and specialised business telecommunications services are examined. Three broad areas of communications intensity are identified: the heaviest is the CBD; this is surrounded by an inner communications core of lower intensity which stretches from Chatswood in the north to Mascot in the south and Newtown in the west; the rest of the metropolitan area has activities of a much lower communications intensity, apart from regional business centres such as Parramatta and Liverpool.

## 4.2 External linkages

Sydney's pattern of external communications reflects its role as a state, national and international city. As Australia's largest city, it is not surprising that Sydney has the largest volume of international telecommunications traffic. However, the extent of its dominance is greater than might be expected from a consideration of relative population sizes. For example, Sydney Telephone District (02 area code) attracted 40 per cent of telephone traffic coming into Australia in September 1980 and the Outer Sydney District (04 area code) attracted a further 3.6 per cent. In contrast, Melbourne received only 23.3 per cent of traffic. The extent of Sydney's dominance is even greater for business oriented services. For outgoing international telex traffic in March 1981, over 50 per cent of traffic originated in Sydney, compared with 30 per cent for Melbourne and 14 per cent for all other capital cities.

Several factors account for Sydney's dominance in international telecommunications. It has an important role as an international financial centre and much of the overseas capital being invested in Australia is funnelled through Sydney (Daly ch 2). The financial market is a heavy user of telecommunications, since participants require immediate access to information on commodity markets and stock exchanges as well as to any information on economic and political events which may affect the capital market.

Sydney has a high proportion of all head offices of transnational corporations in the Australasian region. In many cases there are intense communications linkages between the Australian subsidiary and corporate headquarters located in the USA, UK or Japan, with information on production and inventory levels as well as financial data on Australian operations being transferred overseas. In addition, many head offices of Australian firms are located in Sydney and have widespread national and international linkages. For example, most Australian banks have extensive international financial transactions. Other firms generating substantial international flows of information are computer service bureaux, which primarily link up with large computer facilities in the USA. Australian Associated Press (AAP) is also a major receiver and transmitter of information, although the predominant flow of international news is towards Australia.

There are significant geographical variations within the metropolitan area in the volume of international telecommunications linkages.

Clearly, the CBD has the most important international connections: it functions as a gateway between other countries and the rest of Australia. Most of the headquarters of international and Australian firms are located there and, as we have already seen, it is these firms which have heavy international communications linkages.

Suburban areas show significant variations in the volume of international connections. An indication of the importance of international linkages to people in various parts of Sydney is given by the proportion of total subscribers with international subscriber dialling (ISD) access. Areas with a high penetration rate include high status areas in the Eastern Suburbs (Rose Bay and Potts Point) and the North Shore (Killara and Pymble). In addition, areas with relatively large numbers of migrants (Ashfield, South Sydney and Petersham) have high ISD penetration rates.

Sydney is also a focal point for national telecommunications traffic. It originates or receives approximately one third of the total intercapital city telephone traffic; Sydney and Melbourne together account for almost two thirds of the total. Over half the traffic that Sydney originates or receives is with Melbourne. The large flows between the two cities come as little surprise given their predominance in the national economic system, aspects of which are discussed elsewhere (Rich *et al.* ch 1; Daly ch 2; Rich ch 5). The linkages are also related to the complementary economic structures of the two cities: Melbourne has the headquarters of large mining companies while Sydney has a more diverse range of economic activities (Taylor and Thrift 1980:277). Sydney has relatively strong flows with Brisbane, reflecting the close economic linkages between the two states; this results from the relatively large distances from Brisbane to other capital cities. Perth is strongly connected to Sydney, a surprising result given the importance of mining in Western Australia and Melbourne's predominance as the headquarters' location for large mining firms (BHP and CRA). This pattern of Sydney's dominance is also repeated for telex traffic. It is possible that Sydney's diversified industrial and commercial structure and financial strength combined with its preeminent position as an international communications gateway city has resulted in its dominance over traffic with Perth.

Sydney dominates much of the telephone traffic within NSW. However, its influence is limited in border areas by Melbourne in the southern Riverina, Adelaide in the Broken Hill area, and Brisbane on the far North Coast (Langdale 1975:127). Within the rest of the state, regional centres such as Wagga Wagga, Tamworth, Newcastle and Dubbo dominate their surrounding regions and restrict the extent of Sydney's influence.

Sydney's external role as a focus for traffic is being enhanced by technological change in telecommunications, which is likely to result in further reductions in charges for long distance calls and closer integration of organisations located in Sydney with the international and domestic economies. Such changes have important implications in terms of the growth and location of various industries and will be considered in detail in section 4.5.

## 4.3 Intraurban linkages

There are three major geographical components in intraurban telecommunications linkages. The most important communications focus is the CBD, the business and cultural heart of the city. The inner suburban core is less important as a receiver and generator of communications but contains a number of communications intensive activities, such as administrative offices, computer service bureaux and newspaper publishing firms. Inner suburban centres (North Sydney, St Leonards, Redfern and Newtown) represent secondary peaks in the spatial distribution of telecommunications traffic. Finally, outer suburban areas are characterised by low communications usage of residential subscribers; regional, community and local business/retail centres are the only focal points for communications.

### Telephone traffic

One perspective on the geographical extent of dominance of various centres is provided by ranking the three largest destinations for telephone traffic from each telephone exchange and mapping the resulting pattern (Figures 4.1 and 4.2). The CBD was the most important destination for telephone exchanges in an area north to Wahroonga, west to Parramatta and south to Blakehurst (Figure 4.1). Local calls occupied second rank within this area. For outer suburban areas local calls were the most important flow from each exchange with flows to the CBD generally occupying second rank. This reversal of linkage pattern with increasing distance from the CBD reflects the diminished importance of the CBD for peripheral suburbs. There is a marked contrast to the north of the city between the North Shore and the Manly-Warringah area in terms of the extent of the CBD's dominance. The CBD's area of influence extends along the northern rail line as far as Wahroonga. In contrast, its influence is less dominant in the Manly-Warringah area, a district which has relatively poor access to the city centre (Aplin ch 13).

Liverpool and Parramatta are important regional communications foci; both are major commercial and retail centres and are able to dominate surrounding regions because they are a considerable distance from the CBD and from competing regional suburban centres. Black-

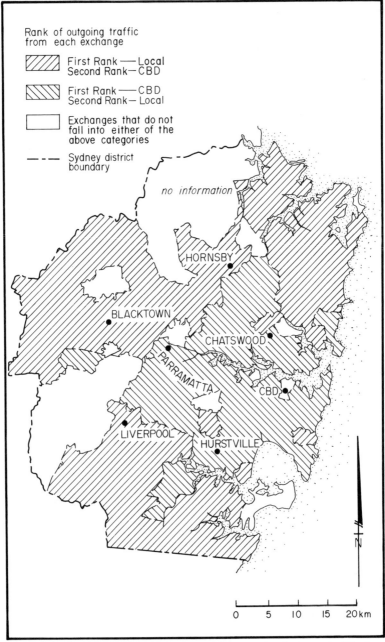

**Figure 4.1    First and second rank destinations of telephone traffic from exchanges, June 1979**

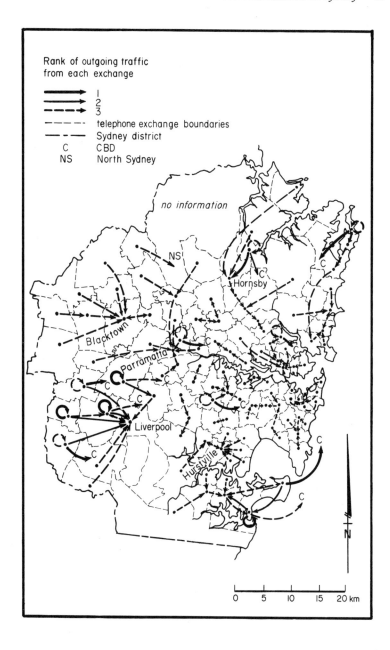

**Figure 4.2 Rank of telephone traffic from each exchange, June 1979**

town dominates the outer western suburbs, although to a lesser extent than do the other two centres.

North Sydney is a moderately important regional centre to the north with St Leonards-Crows Nest forming a subsidiary focus. The concentration of offices in the North Sydney-St Leonards area accounts for the importance of these two destinations. This area represents a northwards extension of the CBD; offices in these centres are primarily serving an international, national or city wide role rather than a specific local function (Alexander ch 3). Thus these centres and others in the inner suburban core do not show up strongly as communications foci for a surrounding region.

## Business telecommunications services

A somewhat different perspective on the pattern of intraurban linkages is provided by a consideration of business services. They include such services as external extensions, private data and telex lines. This group of services has grown rapidly, increasing by over 12 per cent in 1978/79. External extensions are used primarily by an organisation wishing to link a branch office directly to its main switchboard. Private lines are used by a variety of organisations which want to ensure an uninterrupted and secure connection between two offices. For example, an increasingly important use of private lines would be for telemetry applications, wherein a bank or security company connects offices to a security centre. Private data lines are used to link parts of computer networks. They may be lines connecting computer terminals to a central computer or, in other cases, lines directly linking computers.

Once again the CBD emerges as the communications focus of Sydney with just under half of the total originating and terminating services (Table 4.1). This concentration of services reflects the high communications intensity of organisations located in the CBD. Many public and private organisations have several offices within the CBD which require external extensions and private data and telex lines for efficient operation. In addition, there are numerous computer communications networks linking financial and economic information providers, such as the Sydney Stock Exchange and AAP/Reuters services to stockbrokers, banks and commodity traders as well as to head offices of large companies in the CBD.

Private data lines provide an indication of the size of computer communications networks within the metropolitan area. The largest number of data lines connect offices within the CBD, reflecting the concentration of computer networks linking the head and administrative offices in the downtown area (Figure 4.3). The CBD has strong linkages with the inner suburban zone. North Sydney and, to a lesser extent, Kensington are prominent destinations, both accommodating large computer service bureaux. North Sydney has a major concentration of information intensive activities, having the head and regional offices of numerous computer and office equipment firms. However, high office rentals are encouraging a northwards extension of such activities and the St Leonards-Crows Nest area is emerging as a secondary concentration. There are signs of a further northward extension of this zone; in 1981 Digital Equipment Corp. opened its Australian head office in Chatswood, employing over 250 people and operating a statewide bureau service.

The next most important linkage from the CBD is to Mascot (Figure 4.3). These data lines link airline companies' computers in the CBD to terminals in the freight and passenger areas at Kingsford Smith Airport. In addition, there are numerous freight forwarders in the Mascot area with links to the CBD. Transport companies (especially in air transport) are progressively introducing computer communications networks to link offices in different parts of Sydney with interstate and international offices in order to speed delivery of bills of lading, insurance and customs forms. The Customs Bureau has also established a nationwide computer network to facilitate the processing of forms and has offices in the CBD and airport area.

**Table 4.1  Number of originating and terminating business telecommunications services lines, September 1979[a]**

|  | Originating lines | | | Terminating lines | | |
|---|---|---|---|---|---|---|
|  | rank | number | % | rank | number | % |
| CBD | 1 | 18,173 | 44.8 | 1 | 19,337 | 47.7 |
| North Sydney | 2 | 1,624 | 4.0 | 2 | 1,473 | 3.6 |
| St Leonards | 3 | 1,389 | 3.4 | 5 | 904 | 2.2 |
| Redfern | 4 | 1,306 | 3.2 | 7 | 861 | 2.1 |
| Newtown | 5 | 917 | 2.3 | 4 | 925 | 2.3 |
| Bankstown | 6 | 904 | 2.2 | 8 | 644 | 1.6 |
| East | 7 | 896 | 2.2 | 6 | 880 | 2.2 |
| Mascot | 8 | 790 | 1.9 | 3 | 1,053 | 2.6 |
| Parramatta | 9 | 741 | 1.8 | 9 | 539 | 1.3 |
| Potts Point | 10 | 676 | 1.7 | 10 | 449 | 1.1 |
| Remaining Exchanges |  | 13,153 | 32.4 |  | 13,504 | 33.3 |
| *Total* |  | 40,569 | 99.9 |  | 40,569 | 100.0 |

*Note:* [a] The most important types of services in this category are external extension, private lines and data lines (see text for details). Only intraurban services are included. A service is taken to originate from an exchange if the head office of the organisation is located within the exchange area boundary. The terminating exchange is the destination point of the particular line

*Source:* Unpublished Telecom figures

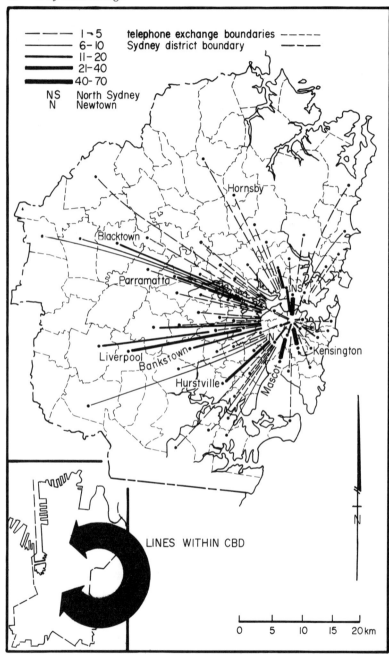

**Figure 4.3    Number of private data lines from the CBD, June 1979**

There are a number of moderately large data linkages from the CBD to outer suburban business/retail centres, such as Parramatta, Liverpool and Blacktown, as well as smaller linkages to community and local shopping centres. These data lines link head or regional offices in the CBD with branch suburban offices of private organisations (banks, building societies and travel agents) and public organisations (TAB, police stations and Telecom offices).

North Sydney and St Leonards are the major originating exchanges for private data lines in the suburban area. Aside from lines within their respective exchange area boundaries, both have their largest number of lines back to the CBD. In addition, both centres have a large spread of relatively small linkages to suburban areas, reflecting the widespread distribution of customers to their computer service bureaus. Other inner suburban exchanges (Newtown and Kensington) show a similar pattern, although the size and geographical range of linkages is substantially reduced.

Outer suburban locations have far fewer private data lines and are generally the terminating or branch office ends of a line. These lines reflect the fact that stores and offices in suburban retail centres are being increasingly linked into computer communications networks as more organisations adopt information systems. The geographical distribution of private data lines thus provides an indicator of the nature of the emerging information economy.

## 4.4  Impact of telecommunications

Emergence of the information economy has led to greater diversity of telecommunications services available to users. Many of these have been grouped under the broad heading of electronic mail and include such services as telex, facsimile, communicating word processors and computer communications systems (Langdale 1979a, 1979b).

Two basic types of electronic mail systems can be recognised. The first is found in large firms or government departments which have sufficient internal communications demand to install their own intra-organisational systems to handle electronic mail (Figure 4.4). In contrast, small businesses and private individuals with insufficient demand to justify purchasing this equipment must rely on a public agency or commercial bureau. Commercial bureaux offer computer and facsimile services between major cities. In addition, Telecom and Australia Post operate a joint facsimile service between capital cities, which uses Australia Post's courier service for delivery. This service provides a two-hour pick up and delivery between capital cities. Furthermore, international facsimile transmission services are available to major overseas cities.

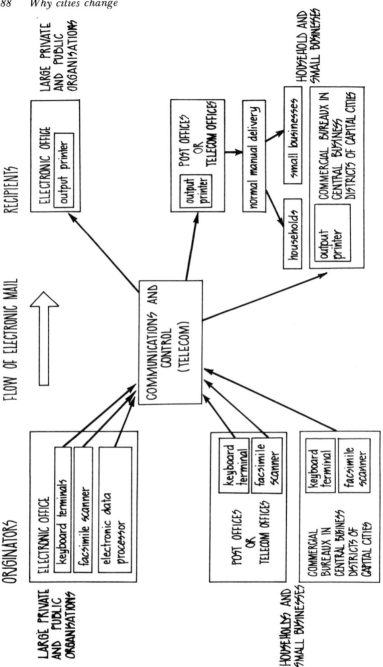

**Figure 4.4   A possible future electronic mail system**

Banking provides an example of large organisations which are adopting intraorganisational electronic mail systems. Central records of customers' accounts are stored in a bank's head office computer with terminals located in head and branch offices. In addition, computer communications systems have been used to transfer general and accounting information between banks' head offices and suburban branches.

Adoption of these information technologies has reduced the overall rate of employment growth in banks. For example, the Commonwealth Banking Corporation pointed out that while full time staff numbers in Australia have grown by over 9,500 from 1966 (the start of computerisation of operations) to 1979, there had been a saving of approximately 2,000 positions due to the introduction of computer technology. The bank also stated that the overall percentage of staff in branch office locations had remained constant at around 67 per cent; however, the number required to deal with 'back office' or bank administrative matters had decreased, and most growth in staff numbers was in the area of direct customer service (Commonwealth Banking Corporation 1979:20).

These technologies may lead to either a reduction or an increase in the decision making capability of suburban branches. The possibility of increasing the degree of decentralisation of decision making stems from the ability of the branch manager to access on-line information held in the bank's computer data base. However, most banks are still establishing on-line computer networks. A number have set up area or regional offices, which have greater decision making responsibility than the normal suburban branch office. For example, the ANZ bank has established nine area offices in the Sydney metropolitan area, each controlling several branches. At present, the ANZ does not have an online system, but it is likely that in the near future the decision making capability of its area managers will be enhanced by a computer communications network.

Similar developments have been taking place in other organisations and are having important impacts on consumer service oriented organisations found in suburban shopping centres. A number of firms, such as building societies, supermarket chains and department stores have adopted or are in the process of adopting such systems. For example, retailing chains such as Grace Bros. have already installed point of sale terminals in all stores, which are linked to a central computer which in turn is linked to head office and warehouse terminals. Such a computer communications system improves inventory control and reduces labour costs of checking inventory and manually filling in order forms. It also allows head office to monitor turnover of various products in all stores and may assist them in examining the impact of an advertising campaign promoting certain products. It is likely that most, if not all, retail chains will have adopted such systems in the near future.

The department store chain, Myer Emporium, is also investigating the possibility of using a videotex system to allow consumers to order goods from their home. The basis of videotex is that a user has a modified television set which allows information to be retrieved from a computer data base. Any type of information could be stored in the data base, but Myer is investigating the possibility of displaying information (including pictures, prices and dimensions) on retail goods. Once the consumer orders the goods and pays using an account number or by Bankcard, the retailer would arrange delivery. Clearly, widespread adoption of such a system by retailers and users would have a major impact on the nature of suburban shopping centres and the volume of shopping trips. Consumers could compare prices and quality of products in different stores without having to travel to the stores.

Public organisations with extensive suburban branch networks (TAB, police and Telecom) are also adopting electronic mail techniques. The TAB has an extensive computer communications system linking betting offices throughout the state to a central computer in Ultimo, with results from horse, trotting and dog racetracks throughout the country fed into the system. Punters place their bets either by visiting a suburban branch office or, if they have established an account with the TAB, by using a telephone betting service. Introduction of the computer communications system has significantly reduced labour requirements despite a rapidly growing turnover. A study commissioned by the Myers Committee on Technological Change of the effects of computerisation in the South Australian TAB found that significant job losses resulted from the introduction of such systems (Russell 1980:189–235).

A possible future development is that a videotex service could provide a racing form guide for punters at home and they could also place their bets using this service. AAP has a computerised data base which contains the complete racing form of every racehorse in Australia. At present, only a brief summary is printed in the racing guide of daily newspapers. However, a punter using a videotex terminal could access the entire track history of the horse; perhaps with better availability of information the ability of punters to pick winners would be improved.

While most electronic mail systems are intraorganisational in character, some are interorganisational (Langdale 1979b). Several industries (securities, travel and newspapers) rely extensively on information sharing between firms; applications of information technologies are having a substantial impact on their linkage patterns and employment levels. We have already seen that economic and financial information is provided by the Sydney Stock Exchange and AAP/Reuters to various firms, largely located in the CBD. AAP also distributes local and international news to newspapers throughout Australia, which in turn store the information in their computer data bases for subsequent editing.

The major newspaper groups in Sydney also control television stations, and in the future they are likely to use videotex systems to distribute information to homes and offices. Thus, much of the collection, processing and distribution of information by media conglomerates could be by electronic means, which are likely to have a significant impact on the volume of trips generated within Sydney.

Newspaper publishing has traditionally been a labour intensive process, concentrated in the inner suburban core. However, progressive automation of the entire information collection, processing and distribution process has led to substantially reduced employment levels (Smith 1980). For example, adoption of computerised typesetting at John Fairfax and Sons from 1976 led to over 400 employees becoming redundant (Souter 1981:563). Further reductions in employment are likely as newspaper proprietors strive to maintain profitability in the face of increasing competition from electronic means of communication.

Aside from their intraurban impact, adoption of information technologies is having employment implications at an international and national level. For example, a trend in the telecommunications and computer industries is to centralise maintenance operations. One factor which precipitated work bans imposed by telecommunications technicians in industrial disputes in 1978 and 1979 was a Telecom proposal to centralise maintenance staff for new electronic local telephone exchanges. Electronic switching equipment will require fewer technicians and will deskill many of those employed in local telephone exchanges, since much of the fault diagnosis can be done from a central location. A similar trend is occurring in the data processing industry, and it is likely that increasing numbers of computer engineers will be centralised in Sydney or Melbourne rather than in maintenance centres throughout the country. In addition, as international telecommunications charges fall, there is increased scope for computer fault maintenance to be centralised in the USA. An additional impact of reduced international and national telecommunications charges is that processing of data could be done more cheaply at larger and more centralised computing installations located in Sydney and Melbourne or, potentially, in the USA. These trends would encourage a centralisation of employment in Sydney and Melbourne as well as a loss of jobs to the USA.

Adoption of electronic mail systems is having an increasingly important impact on the volume of conventional international, national and intraurban mail flows. While the volume of international mail is relatively small, adoption of electronic mail methods would virtually eliminate present lengthy delays in receiving mail. The greatest volume of linkages are intraurban in character, with 64 per cent of Sydney's originating mail also terminating within the metropolitan area. Generally, there is only a short delay for most intraurban mail delivery, and therefore, there is less urgency for electronic mail on intraurban routes. However, many organisations are progressively adopting information technologies in all offices. Once a sufficient number have adopted compatible machines, there is little point in using conventional mail methods even for intraurban deliveries. Thus, widespread adoption of the electronic office is likely to accelerate the substitution of electronic for physical distribution of mail.

The potential market for electronic mail is largely confined to business and government mail. In a sample survey in March/April 1976 for the Sydney metropolitan region, approximately 46 per cent of the total number of standard letters were sent between business and/or government offices (Table 4.2). Many businesses and government departments are not in a position to use electronic mail methods. However, adoption of such systems will widen as technological change further reduces cost of machines and telecommunications transmission charges.

An additional future development is that electronic mail systems could be extended into the area of business and government mail sent to private residences. A business firm could generate each 'letter' through its own computer and transmit it on-line to terminals located in post offices (Figure 4.4). Mail would then be converted to hard copy and hand delivered to homes by Australia Post. Business and government mail to private residences accounts for 24 per cent of the total volume of mail in the Sydney metropolitan region, although it is likely that only a small percentage of mail would be sent in electronic form (Table 4.2). Such a system would reduce the role played by Australia Post to that of receiving messages and delivering the hard copy to residences.

It is unlikely that the mail originating from private homes (30 per cent of the total) will be sent in electronic form in the near future.

Table 4.2    **Percentage distribution of standard letters between major user groups: Sydney metropolitan area, March/April 1976**

| To | Private | Business | Government | Total |
|---|---|---|---|---|
| *From* | | | | |
| Private | 16 | 11 | 3 | 30 |
| Business | 16 | 34 | 3 | 53 |
| Government | 8 | 6 | 3 | 17 |
| *Total* | 40 | 51 | 9 | 100 |

*Source:* Unpublished Australia Post survey

However, it is possible that if videotex systems are widely adopted, messages could be sent to other residences using a modified television set as the display device and a simple keyboard for inputting information.

## 4.5 Conclusion

Continued advances in telecommunications technology and growing demand for information transmission are expanding the volume of Sydney's external and internal linkages. At an international level, improved telecommunications services are promoting international commerce by facilitating the interconnection of Sydney's industries to the international system. Furthermore, moves to deregulate the financial sector are likely to increase the volume of international financial transactions and enhance Sydney's role as an international financial centre (Australia. Committee of Inquiry into the Australian Financial System 1981). However, reduced costs of international information transfer will minimise the degree of protection from international competition for Australian information industries and may lead to fewer jobs for Australian computer engineers and technicians.

Similar trends can be identified at a national level. Improvements in telecommunications services may lead to both a decentralisation and a centralisation of economic activity. Decentralisation could be enhanced by improved information availability in peripheral locations, allowing firms access to the same information that is available in Sydney and Melbourne. However, as in the international situation, improved telecommunications may lead to a centralisation of information industries in dominant cities — namely, Sydney and Melbourne.

Expansion of electronic mail services will have a significant impact on the growth of telecommunications as against transportation for both intraurban and interurban linkages. While there has been much speculation as to the possibility of office workers working at home by using computer terminals to link up with the 'office', it is not likely that this type of substitution of telecommunications for transportation will take place on any significant scale in the immediate future, if at all (Alexander ch 3; Albertson 1977). Firms are adopting information technologies to improve operating efficiency. Many wish to minimise labour costs by substituting capital for labour. In achieving these aims firms are using telecommunications to connect head and regional offices to branch plants and offices; consequently, the volume of telecommunications linkages is likely to rise rapidly and there may be some substitution of telecommunications for transportation. However, the primary reason for adopting information technologies is not related to a desire to save transportation costs.

Emergence of the information economy is leading to significant changes in the nature of urban linkages and the pattern of land use. However, because many of the changes are taking place in the business sphere rather than in the more readily observable domestic area, most people are unaware of their significance. We have seen that the growth of electronic mail is having a major influence on information flows. The impact of the geographical separation of offices on the nature of their operations is being reduced and firms have greater choice in the configuration of their operations. New forms of information technologies are giving firms the option of increasing or decreasing the degree of centralisation of their office employment and the relative power of head office as against regional and branch offices. It is difficult to say whether these technologies have led to an overall loss or gain in the number of jobs, because the indirect effects resulting from firms adopting information technologies are extremely difficult to trace through the economy. What is clear, however, is that the emergence of the information economy is increasing the pace of change in the nature of cities. Sydney is becoming more and more reliant on its 'electronic highways' for the efficient functioning of its internal and external relations.

# 5 Structural and spatial change in manufacturing

DAVID C. RICH

## 5.1 Introduction

Manufacturing is an important part of Sydney's economy. In 1971, it provided 360,000 jobs, 27.9 per cent of all employment in the metropolitan area (Table 1.1). Almost 50,000 of these jobs were lost by 1976, so that, with the expansion of tertiary and quaternary activities, the sector's share of employment fell to 23.2 per cent. This decline was by far the largest contractionary element in the metropolitan economy. Coincidentally, it closely matched, though does not fully explain, the massive increase in unemployment in the period (Table 5.1). Crudely, then, we can suggest that if manufacturing had maintained its 1971 employment, there would have been no increase in unemployment in Sydney by 1976. Of course, matters are not as simple as this, but it does illustrate the significance of the decline of manufacturing: the collapse of manufacturing employment was at the root of the rapid growth of unemployment in Sydney during the 1970s.

Manufacturing change is a major feature of economic trends in contemporary Sydney. Such change can only be understood in the light of trends in Australian industry as a whole and its place in the international economy. This chapter thus focuses on Sydney's position in the Australian industrial system. Spatial and economic changes occurring within the Sydney metropolitan area are examined in the next chapter.

**Table 5.1  Levels of employment and unemployment in Sydney, 1971 and 1976**

|  | 1971 | 1976 | 1971–1976 change | |
|---|---|---|---|---|
|  |  |  | no | % |
| Total employment | 1,293,490 | 1,336,118 | 42,628 | 3.30 |
| Unemployed in labour force | 18,869 | 67,787 | 48,918 | 259.25 |
| Total labour force | 1,312,359 | 1,403,904 | 91,545 | 6.98 |

*Source:* 1971 and 1976 Population Censuses

Five themes underline the discussion. The first is the changing role of manufacturing in the Australian economy, with its declining overall importance on the one hand and a gradual swing from producing consumer goods towards raw materials processing on the other. Second, this has been accompanied by important shifts in the location of industry, involving relative declines in Sydney's and later Melbourne's previously overwhelming shares of output and employment. While production has become more dispersed, the two major cities have come to exercise growing control over the national economy, a function of the increasing importance of very large corporations and financial institutions; this forms the third theme. The fourth is that given the importance of Sydney and Melbourne as control and production centres, they can be characterised as twin cores around which the rest of the economy is articulated. The final theme is that these apparently disparate trends are all closely related elements in a complex mosaic often referred to as 'structural change'.

To develop these themes, this chapter outlines the changing fortunes of manufacturing over recent decades (section 5.2), presents some evidence of the dominant positions of Sydney and Melbourne (section 5.3) and investigates geographical shifts of manufacturing (section 5.4). Discussion builds mainly upon data on employment and value added (effectively, the net value of output) available from the annual Census of Manufacturing since 1968/69. Earlier trends are outlined but, because of major definitional differences, the relevant data are not directly comparable with post-1968 figures. Sydney's boundaries follow the post-1976 Statistical Division, thus incorporating the former Outer Sydney Statistical Division.

## 5.2   The national context

Australian manufacturing has faced considerable pressures in the last two decades. Coinciding with an upsurge of minerals production and an expanding tertiary sector, these have brought a decline in the relative importance of manufacturing. Nevertheless, it still plays a vital role, providing over one fifth of all jobs and net output, attracting substantial capital investment and contributing over half of all exports (Australia. BIE 1981a).

Four phases of postwar industrial change can be recognised. Manufacturing boomed after the Second World War. Employment increased by over 40 per cent, from 0.8 million to 1.14 million, between 1947 and 1961. Industrial expansion was a major component of economic growth (Kasper 1978), so that manufacturing constituted a growing proportion of all economic activity, with its shares of output and employment reaching about 29 per cent by the early 1960s. Besides its direct impact on the level of economic activity, manufacturing also created sizable indirect growth impulses through its growing demand for goods and services from other sectors (Linge 1977).

The second phase emerged in the early 1960s and continued until mid 1974. Manufacturing generally maintained its postwar expansion, though sometimes at a reduced rate, so that by 1973/74 it provided 1,338,000 jobs in 37,100 establishments; during that year it paid $14.4 billion in wages and salaries, had a turnover of $62.7 billion and contributed a value added of $26.4 billion (1979/80 prices). Manufacturing was still a substantial component of the economy, but it was a slowly declining component as its growth was outstripped by other sectors (Australia. BIE 1981a). In part, this simply reflected more rapid expansion in demand for services than for goods, while rapid expansion of minerals production was another factor, but manufacturing itself faced a range of increasingly severe competitive pressures.

Many factors contributed to the deteriorating position of Australian manufacturing. There was growing competition in both domestic and international markets (Australia. IAC 1977; Bernasek 1978), affecting an ever larger range of goods. On the one hand, rapidly growing high technology industries such as computers, telecommunications equipment and electronics were increasingly dominated by the USA, Western Europe or Japan, with Australian production either insignificant or falling ever further behind world trends (Australia. Department of Industry and Commerce 1980a). On the other hand, industrialisation of many Asian countries brought growing competition, at first mainly in simple products such as clothing and footwear, but soon extending into other goods as these countries turned quickly to modern capital and skill intensive production. At the same time, overvaluation of the Australian dollar, due largely to surpluses built up in the minerals boom and refusal by the Country Party to countenance currency adjustments (Daly ch 2; Walsh 1979), made exports more difficult to sell and imports more difficult to compete against. Australia's competitive position was similarly weakened by more rapid escalation of labour costs (Wilde 1981a) and slower productivity increases (Kasper 1978) than in many other countries. At the same time, manufacturing was in many cases less efficiently organised than elsewhere, for example because of the loss of scale economies resulting first from the small size of the domestic market and second from spatial and commercial disaggregation of production to supply that market (Linge 1978). Indeed, Australia's entire industrial structure was in many ways artificial, being the product of protective decisions made by successive federal and state governments for short term electoral or political reasons (Linge 1979a). Added to all this, rapid changes in technology and business organisation often worked to Australia's disadvantage. For example, internationalisation of production (Hamilton and Linge 1981), together with the

high level of foreign ownership and control of Australian manufacturing (Wheelwright 1971; Hickie 1981) and its subordinate position
in the world industrial system (Wilde 1981b) made the country
increasingly vulnerable to alterations in the investment policies of
international business. Because of the poor competitive conditions
available in Australia, these changes often involved companies switching resources to other countries or into other sectors of the domestic
economy, especially mining and related activities.

These pressures were at first ignored or hidden by high levels of
demand and rapid growth in the domestic and international economies
(Linge 1979b). Gradually, though, the difficulties became more
apparent. They were compounded by additional changes such as the 25
per cent tariff cuts in 1973 and the Borrie Report's lower estimates of
population growth (Australia. National Population Inquiry 1975)
which meant sharply reduced projections of market expansion. Matters
came to a head when these long term difficulties became intertwined
with the severe effects of the world recession that started in 1974
(Stilwell 1980).

The third phase thus dates from mid 1974. After a decade of relative
decline, manufacturing moved into a period of absolute contraction.
Between mid 1974 and mid 1978, 170,000 jobs were lost in manufacturing, a decline of 12.7 per cent. Most other indicators point to a

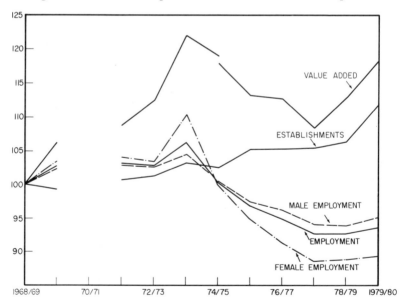

**Figure 5.1 Changes in the level of activity in Australian manufacturing,
1968/69-1979/80, as a percentage of 1968/69 levels**

similar downturn (Figure 5.1) and no major subdivision of manufacturing escaped some contraction. Collapse of manufacturing employment growth has been a major cause of increased unemployment in Australia generally (Australia. BIE 1979a), just as in Sydney. The combination of industrial decline and a generally depressed economy made it doubly difficult to absorb labour displaced from manufacturing. Not only was displacement rapid but also the ability of other sectors to take on additional employees was reduced by slack demand for their products and services. Further, the tertiary and quaternary sectors were, in contrast to previous experience, unable to provide sufficient jobs for all wanting them because of rapid technological change and the increasing substitution of capital for labour on the one hand and government policies to cut public sector employment growth on the other.

The depths of the industrial recession were reached in 1977/78 and the period since then — the fourth phase — has seen a slow and tentative recovery of manufacturing (Figure 5.1). Revival has been most marked in terms of net output; even so, value added has yet to regain the level reached in 1973/74. Employment has made only a very slow recovery from recession levels.

Several factors fuelled recovery. During the late 1970s, Australian industry became increasingly competitive (in terms of price) in international markets because of a decline in the value of the currency and wage inflation below that in many other countries (Australia. IAC 1980a). For similar reasons, together with continuing high levels of protection and generally bouyant consumer demand, domestic sales of many products have been high. Equally, the beginnings of the much vaunted 'resources boom' contributed to manufacturing expansion directly by increasing the volume of resources processed and indirectly by raising demand for the capital equipment necessary to achieve this.

Each of these mechanisms is fragile, however, so that continued industrial expansion is by no means assured. For example, sustained debate on protection policies indicates that few industries can rely on present arrangements continuing unaltered. As one illustration, new protection arrangements announced in December 1981 for the motor vehicle industry for the 1985–1992 period are likely to benefit the largest companies, but encourage others to cease production and aggravate employment losses in component supplying firms.

Similarly, continuation of the 'resources boom' is problematic, because of weak international demand for many products and rapidly rising costs, resulting from very high international interest rates and sometimes unproven technology: already, several projects in the aluminium industry have been delayed or abandoned. In any case, benefits of resource developments to the Australian economy may be limited because of the modest employment and tax revenue generated, substantial repatriation of profits and high propensities to import capital equipment.

Industrial recovery since 1977/78 has been highly selective. Not only has output increased far more than employment, but also many industries have received little benefit. Five of the 12 two digit ASIC industries continued to lose employment between 1977/78 and 1979/80. Of these, food, beverages and tobacco, previously one of the most expansionary industries (Rich 1981a), and the long troubled clothing and footwear also suffered real declines in value added. Greatest expansion was in basic and fabricated metal products, reflecting the importance of resource based developments, and in paper and publishing. Recovery of the manufacturing sector has, then, been uneven, with restructuring and rationalisation continuing despite a return to somewhat more prosperous conditions.

## 5.3    Core and periphery in the Australian industrial system

What part does Sydney play in Australian manufacturing? It is important to consider Sydney alongside Melbourne because jointly they dominate most aspects of the economy. This is not simply a question of their share of productive activity, substantial though that is (section 5.4). Rather, it involves the control of economic events in most parts of the country that is exerted from the two cities. In part, this reflects the growing significance of multifunctional, multilocational businesses (Linge 1977). The Australian headquarters of almost all such enterprises are in Sydney or Melbourne, after several decades of retreat from other state capitals and industrial centres (Taylor and Thrift 1980, 1981a). Of the 100 largest companies listed on domestic stock exchanges in 1978 — thus ignoring some important unlisted companies (Taylor and Thrift 1981d) — 52 were based in Sydney and 38 in Melbourne (Table 5.2), with four in Brisbane, five in Adelaide and one in Perth.

**Table 5.2    Polarisation of control in the Australian space economy: location of the headquarters of the 100 largest listed companies, 1953-1978**

| Year | No. firms with headquarters in | | % of shareholders' funds (1953 and 1963) or market capitalisation (1973 and 1978) | | % of profits | |
|---|---|---|---|---|---|---|
| | Sydney | Melbourne | Sydney | Melbourne | Sydney | Melbourne |
| 1953 | 37 | 50 | 38.8 | 50.9 | 27.7 | 60.0 |
| 1963 | 44 | 47 | 36.9 | 55.2 | 38.0 | 53.1 |
| 1973 | 50 | 39 | 33.4 | 57.0 | 33.7 | 59.3 |
| 1978 | 52 | 38 | 38.1 | 53.7 | 40.2 | 51.6 |

*Source:* Taylor and Thrift (1981a Tables 2 and 3)

Of the 42 of these 100 whose primary interests lay in manufacturing, 39 were headquartered in Sydney or Melbourne (Table 5.3). Melbourne retains a disproportionate share of headquarters of the very largest firms, especially mining companies (Fagan *et al.* 1981). Sydney based companies are much more diverse, with manufacturing, finance, trading, transport and communications concerns all represented (Taylor and Thrift 1981c, 1981d). Although these are rather smaller than Melbourne companies, they have been much more dynamic and growth oriented in recent times. Among both manufacturing and non-manufacturing firms, the proportion of activity controlled from Sydney has been rising, especially during the 1970s (Tables 5.2 and 5.3). On most indicators, Sydney thus appears to have taken over Melbourne's former position of commercial leadership and dominant control centre (Taylor and Thrift 1981c, 1981d), though Melbourne undoubtedly still plays a vital role.

Corporate headquarters in Sydney and Melbourne control the operations of branch establishments scattered across the country; though these establishments may have a measure of autonomy in routine matters, strategic decisions generally remain firmly the responsibility of head offices. Because of the size and importance of major firms, the pattern of dominance and subservience at the establishment level carries through to the respective regional economies. Moreover, the major corporations also influence smaller independent businesses, for example through their purchases of raw materials and intermediate goods, so further reinforcing the pattern of domination.

Given these characteristics, a convenient shorthand description of the Australian space economy is that it has a core-periphery structure (Wilde 1980). Sydney and Melbourne form twin economic cores, around which activity in the rest of the country — the periphery — is articulated. But, of course, matters are not as simple as this. For one thing, this characterisation ignores the role of government. The actions of the Commonwealth government must add Canberra as a subsidiary focus of control for some purposes, even though many of its instrumentalities operate from Sydney (e.g. Reserve Bank) or Melbourne (e.g. Telecom). State government powers and policies add further elements to the picture: for example, the Queensland government has tried to block the increasing dominance of Sydney and Melbourne by resisting the takeover of indigenous firms by externally based concerns.

Another pertinent factor is Australia's perennial position as a net importer of capital. Around 40 per cent of inward investment went into manufacturing in the mid 1970s, though in the mining boom of the late 1960s the figure was about 30 per cent (Australia. BIE 1981a), a level probably being repeated today. The major economic roles of Sydney and Melbourne are reinforced by their accommodation of the main financial institutions handling much of the capital inflow. The implica-

**Table 5.3   Location of headquarters of manufacturing firms within Australia's largest 100 companies, 1953-1978**

| | No. manufacturing firms in largest 100 businesses | No. with headquarters in | | Mean size, in $million of shareholders' funds (1953 and 1963) or market capitalisation (1973 and 1978) | | Mean profitability, in $million at current prices | |
|---|---|---|---|---|---|---|---|
| | | Sydney | Melbourne | Sydney | Melbourne | Sydney | Melbourne |
| 1953 | 59 | 22 | 29 | 11.0 | 9.1 | 0.8 | 1.2 |
| 1963 | 58 | 24 | 29 | 31.2 | 35.4 | 2.7 | 2.4 |
| 1973 | 43 | 21 | 17 | 101.1 | 123.0 | 7.5 | 9.1 |
| 1978 | 42 | 21 | 18 | 105.8 | 251.3 | 12.1 | 14.0 |

*Source:* Taylor and Thrift (1980, 1981a)

**Table 5.4   Distribution of Australian manufacturing, 1978/79**

| % Australian total located in | Establishments | Male employment | Female employment | Total employment | Value added |
|---|---|---|---|---|---|
| Sydney | 28.11 | 26.95 | 32.14 | 28.27 | 28.70 |
| Melbourne | 26.36 | 26.85 | 34.43 | 28.78 | 27.38 |
| Rest of Australia | 45.53 | 46.20 | 33.43 | 42.95 | 43.92 |

*Source:* Calculated from : ABS *Manufacturing establishments: details of operations by industry class, Australia 1978/79*; ABS *Census of manufacturing establishments small area statistics by industry, NSW 1978/79*; and ABS *Manufacturing establishments: small areas statistics, Victoria, 1978/79.*

tions for patterns of dominance of interactions between these agencies and large industrial firms is an intriguing but largely unexplored area, although the simultaneous growth in Sydney of new financial institutions (Daly ch 2) and of its control over Australian industry may well be significant and certainly underscores the growing importance of the city.

Direct foreign investment by transnational corporations, often without resort to external financial institutions, is a major mechanism for capital transfer into and out of Australia and is important because of the degree of control that passes to the investors (Taylor and Thrift 1981b). Around one third of manufacturing (and probably more if overseas holdings through nominees are included) is subject to external control (Australia. BIE 1981a), adding an important qualification to the domestic core-periphery pattern identified earlier. Australia itself is in a subordinate, if not wholly dependent, position in the international industrial system, a position that can be characterised as semiperipheral (Taylor and Thrift 1981c; Wilde 1981a). Any control exerted by Sydney or Melbourne is thus not wholly autonomous. Rather, they act in some respects as points of interaction with the global industrial system and serve as the agencies through which that system manipulates Australian industry. But even this is a simplification. First, the extent of overseas ownership or control is much higher for Melbourne based firms than those in Sydney (Taylor and Thrift 1981c). This suggests that Sydney has a greater degree of autonomous control; this is despite its strong overseas links, for example through its financial institutions, and its role as Australia's dominant communications gateway (Langdale ch 4). Second, for some foreign based transnationals (admittedly a minority), Australian activities are such a major part of global operations that it is inaccurate to view their organisation as one of dominance and subservience: there is a complex two way interaction with neither Australian nor overseas components wholly dominant (Taylor and Thrift 1981b). Third, although Australia is a substantial net importer of capital, it has generated investment in manufacturing overseas during the last decade, especially in the Pacific Basin (Sorensen and Cooper 1981; Taylor and Thrift 1981c). Australia thus acts as a dominant country with respect to some of the truly peripheral countries of the region, adding further complications to both its international position and the domestic pattern of dominance and subservience.

Finally, even though overseas holdings through nominees hide the true picture, the majority of Australian manufacturing is probably still owned indigenously. Most loan and equity stock is not held directly by individuals but by financial intermediaries such as banks, life insurance offices, pension funds and finance companies (Mills 1981a; Reserve Bank of Australia 1979). While some of the smaller institutions, such as credit unions, are based outside of the core, most of the larger ones have their headquarters in Sydney or Melbourne. They generally attract investment capital from right across Australia, so that the bulk of capital generated indigenously is funnelled through Sydney or Melbourne and on to property development and resource extraction and processing schemes (Mills 1981b). Even though such bodies generally avoid day to day intervention in the activities of the companies in which they invest, they often play a vital role in reorganisation or rationalisation of firms, especially in takeovers and mergers (Crough 1981); this represents another element in the dominance of the core. Again there are complications. Many of the institutions, insurance companies in particular, are partly foreign owned, while the likely liberalisation of the financial system after the Campbell Inquiry will probably increase the part played by foreign finance houses in the Australian economy.

In broad outline, then, Sydney's role — along with that of Melbourne — is reasonably clear. The two cities jointly exert a dominant influence over considerable sections of the economy. But, without destroying the picture, closer investigation shows that the situation is much more complex.

## 5.4    Manufacturing in Sydney from the 1940s to the 1980s

Just as Sydney and Melbourne are the dominant control centres, so too they are the major concentrations of production and employment. Each accommodates around 28 per cent of Australian manufacturing (Table 5.4). Sydney accounts for a substantial proportion of each of the country's 12 two digit ASIC manufacturing industries: it contributes more than one fifth of national employment in every case except basic metal products (involving smelting, refining and initial processing). With more than 46 per cent of all employment and value added, Sydney is especially significant as a centre of chemicals production and related activities. It also accounts for more than one third of national activity in paper and printing, in other machinery and equipment (production of such things as photographic, scientific and electrical equipment, and agricultural and industrial machinery), and in other manufacturing (including leather, rubber, plastics, jewellery and sports goods).

Whereas economic control is becoming more centralised, production and employment are becoming progressively more dispersed. Further, while there are indications that Sydney is outpacing Melbourne as a control centre, industrial growth has been slower than in Melbourne for much of the postwar period. These apparently paradoxical trends are evident from a comparison of employment and value added changes in Sydney with those in Melbourne, the rest of Australia (the periphery) and the country as a whole (Tables 5.5, 5.6 and 5.7). Three main features are evident.

First, like Australia as a whole, Sydney, Melbourne and the periphery all registered expansion until the early 1970s, contraction in the middle of the decade and some recovery subsequently. But industrial change is inherently uneven geographically, so that correspondence between regional and national trends was by no means exact.

Most pervasive of these changes has been the growing importance of the periphery. This trend was particularly marked during the 1970s, so that Sydney and Melbourne accounted for 60.7 per cent of manufacturing employment in 1968/69 but only 56.3 per cent in 1979/80. Surveys of recently completed or committed major manufacturing projects indicate that Sydney and Melbourne are jointly attracting less than one quarter of new investment (Table 5.8); even allowing for the many problems with such data, the differential expansion of the periphery seems destined to accelerate in the 1980s.

Third, there has also been a significant shift of balance within the core. In the 1940s, Sydney was unquestionably Australia's premier industrial centre, with almost one fifth more manufacturing employees than Melbourne (Table 5.5). Subsequently, expansion has been greater in Melbourne, so that its manufacturing employment surpassed that in Sydney by 1973/74. Melbourne's especially rapid growth had run its course by the mid 1970s, though, and since then rates of change have been broadly similar in the two cities.

Why have these changes occurred? The erosion of Sydney's pre-eminence is particularly intriguing. Despite some speculation in the literature (Linge 1979b; Rich 1981a), the reasons are not entirely clear. One possibility is that differences in industrial mix explain the phenomenon: particular industries might have had similar growth rates in the two cities but with Melbourne having a disproportionate emphasis on the nation's growth industries and Sydney an excess of sluggish performers. The evidence suggests this was not the case. If anything, the situation was reversed, with Sydney having more than its

**Table 5.5  Employment change in Australian manufacturing, 1947-1966[a]**

| Area | 1947 employment | 1947-1966 change | |
|---|---|---|---|
| | | no. | % |
| Sydney | 262,124 | 128,110 | 48.9 |
| Melbourne | 221,764 | 146,678 | 66.1 |
| Rest of Australia | 315,246 | 238,203 | 75.6 |
| Australia | 799,134 | 512,991 | 64.2 |

*Note:* [a] Sydney and Melbourne statistical divisions are as defined in 1966. Manufacturing is as defined before the introduction of the ASIC system in 1968. These data are thus not directly comparable with others used in this chapter.
*Source:* Linge (1979b) Table 4

**Table 5.6    Employment change in Australian manufacturing, 1968/69-1979/80[a]**

| Area | 1968/69 employment | Change in period 1968/69-1973/74 no. | % | 1973/74 employment | Change in period 1973/74-1977/78 no. | % | 1977/78 employment | Change in period 1977/78-1979/80 no. | % |
|---|---|---|---|---|---|---|---|---|---|
| Sydney | 396,617 | +393 | +0.10 | 397,010 | −68,601 | −17.28 | 328,409 | +593 | +0.18 |
| Melbourne | 369,030 | +29,034 | +7.87 | 398,064 | −63,231 | −15.88 | 334,833 | +1,162 | +0.35 |
| Rest of Australia | 495,630 | +47,675 | +9.62 | 543,305 | −38,169 | −7.03 | 505,136 | +10,068 | +1.99 |
| Australia | 1,261,277 | +77,102 | +6.11 | 1,338,379 | −170,001 | −12.70 | 1,168,378 | +11,823 | +1.01 |

*Note:* [a]The definition of manufacturing was modified in the revision of the ASIC system in 1977/78, reducing registered manufacturing employment in Australia by about 1,500 (0.13 per cent).
*Source:* Calculated from various issues of: ABS *Manufacturing establishments: details of operations by industry class, Australia*; ABS *Manufacturing establishments in local government areas, statistical subdivisions and statistical divisions, NSW*; and ABS *Manufacturing establishments: small area statistics, Victoria.*

**Table 5.7    Changes in the value added by Australian manufacturing, 1968/69-1979/80[a]**

| Area | 1968/69 value added | Change in period 1968/69-1973/74 no. | % | 1973/74 value added | Change in period 1973/74-1977/78 no. | % | 1977/78 value added | Change in period 1977/78-1979/80 no. | % |
|---|---|---|---|---|---|---|---|---|---|
| Sydney | 6,697.4 | +1,197.3 | +17.88 | 7,894.7 | −994.1 | −12.59 | 6,900.6 | +265.4 | +3.85 |
| Melbourne | 6,243.9 | +1,494.6 | +23.94 | 7,738.5 | −923.9 | −11.94 | 6,814.6 | +155.0 | +2.27 |
| Rest of Australia | 8,687.5 | +2,056.4 | +23.67 | 10,743.9 | −990.9 | −9.22 | 9,753.0 | +1,725.4 | +17.51 |
| Australia | 21,628.8 | +4,748.3 | +21.95 | 26,377.1 | −2,908.9 | −11.03 | 23,468.2 | +2,145.8 | +9.14 |

*Note:* [a]Value added is expressed in $million, at 1979/80 values. The definition of manufacturing was modified in 1977/78, raising registered value added in Australia by about $0.7 million (0.003 per cent). Similarly small changes resulted from a revised definition of value added, introduced in 1978/79.
*Source:* As Table 5.6.

**Table 5.8 Major investments in manufacturing industry[a]**

| Area | Projects completed June 1980–June 1981 | | | | Committed projects at June 1981[a] | | | |
|---|---|---|---|---|---|---|---|---|
| | No. projects | % of projects | cost ($million) | % of total cost | no. projects | % of projects | estimated cost ($million) | % of total estimated cost |
| Sydney | 7 | 17.1 | 100.1 | 16.3 | 14 | 11.0 | 792.9 | 10.4 |
| Melbourne | 4 | 9.8 | 41.2 | 6.7 | 16 | 12.6 | 910.9 | 11.9 |
| Rest of Australia | 30 | 73.2 | 472.7 | 77.0 | 97 | 76.4 | 5,950.3 | 77.7 |
| Australia | 41 | 100.0 | 614.0 | 100.0 | 127 | 100.0 | 7,654.1 | 100.0 |

*Note:* [a] 'Committed' projects are those where any one or any combination of the following applies: construction is proceeding or is expected to commence shortly; company board approval (either final or in principle) has been given; or studies have established economic viability, markets or contracts have been secured and the project is expected to proceed shortly. These figures thus include some projects that may not go ahead. Most projects involving expenditure of less than $5 million are excluded. The Table thus gives only a very approximate guide to the pattern of investment.

*Source:* Australia. Department of Industry and Commerce. *Major manufacturing and mining investment projects*, Australian Government Publishing Service, Canberra (December 1980 and June 1981 editions).

share of what nationally were growth industries and Melbourne less (Rich 1981a). On average, then, similar industries have expanded more rapidly in Melbourne (or contracted more slowly) than in Sydney for much of the postwar period. The clothing and footwear industry provides a good example. The industry is heavily concentrated in Sydney and Melbourne, with 26.2 and 47.1 per cent respectively of national employment in 1978/79. It has experienced heavy competition and rapid decline (Australia. Department of Industry and Commerce 1980b, 1980c), but contraction has been consistently much more severe in Sydney than in either Melbourne or Australia as a whole (Table 5.9). Within Sydney, much of the industry has been located in four inner LGAs; these have suffered even more than Sydney as a whole, especially in the early 1970s, with disastrous consequences for local employment, particularly for recent immigrants (Burnley and Walker ch 10).

Industrial mix provides little understanding of Sydney's experience. A more useful, though still partial, explanation lies in the activities of multiplant firms. Rising costs and increasing competition, merger and takeover activity, or technological change have led many firms to concentrate their Australian production on fewer sites. Both Sydney and Melbourne have at times benefited from this rationalisation, but in many other cases Sydney has been a net loser. One example comes from the tyre industry, which in the early 1970s had six manufacturers operating ten Australian plants, while by 1979, five producers operated seven plants: among the closures, 800 jobs were lost at Drummoyne (Sydney) when Dunlop ceased production there, concentrating its manufacturing activities in Melbourne (Dawson-Grove 1979). Another example is the abandonment by General Motors-Holden of its Pagewood plant, with a direct loss of 1,200 jobs. Further, closure of British Leyland's car assembly plant at Zetland is one of several cases where

**Table 5.9    Percentage changes in employment and value added in the Australian clothing and footwear industry**

| Area | 1968/69-1973/74 | | 1974/75-1978/79[a] | |
|---|---|---|---|---|
| | employment | value added | employment | value added |
| Sydney | −22.2 | + 3.3 | −14.5 | −6.2 |
| Inner Sydney[b] | −28.6 | c | −15.4 | c |
| Melbourne | −10.3 | + 10.7 | −10.6 | −0.7 |
| Rest of Australia | + 10.4 | + 50.6 | −5.7 | + 4.3 |
| Australia | −10.0 | + 14.5 | −10.4 | −1.1 |

*Notes:* [a] Data for the period 1974/75-1978/79 *exclude* establishments employing fewer than four people.
[b] The LGAs of Leichhardt, Marrickville, South Sydney and Sydney.
[c] No data available.
*Source:* As Table 5.6.

Sydney has suffered from the international rationalisation of production. Multiplier effects have enlarged the impact of such closures, contrasting with the spinoff from major developments in Melbourne, such as the Altona petrochemical complex (Linge 1979b).

Rationalisation and other activities of large firms, by themselves, are not explanations of Sydney's deteriorating position: we need to consider why Melbourne has been more attractive to many businesses. The industrial land market is one factor (AIUS 1970; Solomon 1975). Industrial land and its development are much more expensive in Sydney than elsewhere in Australia. Melbourne has more industrial land than Sydney accessible simultaneously to the city centre, the metropolitan area and interurban road links; it is thus an attractive place from which to serve both local and national markets. In addition, there are indications that large national companies dealing in industrial land have favoured Melbourne in their marketing policies.

State and local governments have probably reduced Sydney's attractiveness, so impeding its industrial development. For example, much of the land zoned for industry was poorly located or otherwise unsuitable (Cardew 1981a) and thus unattractive to potential developers. Planning procedures may well be such that development approval can be obtained less readily and less quickly than outside of NSW. Finally, the vigorous industrial promotion campaigns waged by other states (Linge 1967), combined with more rapid market growth elsewhere, almost certainly meant that Sydney and NSW lost industrial investment.

There is evidence that Sydney's manufacturing has been less competitive than that in Melbourne (Rich 1981a, 1981b). In 1968/69, labour productivity was higher in Melbourne than in Sydney in 30 of the 48 four digit industries for which data are available. Productivity variations between plants in the same industry can occur because of differences in capital intensity or technology, scale of production, capacity utilisation and behavioural factors relating to the ability and attitudes of management and labour (Pratten 1976; Salter 1966). Whatever its origins, Sydney's inferior productivity undoubtedly represents a competitive disadvantage to the firms involved, perhaps contributing to their lower growth (and even survival) rates, and is thus a factor in Sydney's slow aggregate expansion.

From another perspective, Sydney's inferior productivity is a symptom of its changing position in the Australian industrial system, a reflection of low levels of investment and an aging capital stock. After decades of growth when it was the focus of the country's industrial expansion, Sydney had reached industrial maturity, accompanied by reduced rates of expansion, by the 1960s. Starting from a lower postwar base, Melbourne's industrial boom peaked later, but it too had run its course by the mid 1970s. By the end of the decade, Melbourne's productivity advantage had virtually disappeared, perhaps reflecting inadequate investment in recent years. Current investment data (Table 5.8) provide little sign of immediate revival in its industrial fortunes, while the city's considerable reliance on heavily protected industries means that any moves to reduce protection will probably have serious consequences there (Australia. IAC 1981).

Melbourne seems to be following the path traced earlier by Sydney. Industry specific factors are one contributor: for example, the car industry, once an important growth stimulus and still a mainstay of Melbourne's economy, has stagnated since 1974 in the face of general recession, import competition (albeit heavily restricted), higher petroleum prices and generally depressed demand. Government action, too, may have helped stifle Melbourne's industrial expansion in the 1970s. After the vigorous growth promotion of the Bolte era, the Hamer government was apparently more concerned with social and environmental goals. Government regulation of business and the authority of statutory bodies expanded much more rapidly in Victoria than in other states in the 1970s (Chapman 1981; Robinson 1981a). Rightly or wrongly, Victorian businessmen came to see themselves as restricted by red tape and over-regulation. A self defeating spiral of declining business confidence and low investment set in (Robinson 1981b). By 1980, businessmen were lobbying the state government for more active support and less restraint on industry, while in 1981 one of the country's major institutional investors, the AMP Society, warned of dire consequences if this did not happen.

The industrial fortunes of Sydney and Melbourne have long been vital features of Australia's industrial geography, but increasingly the key phenomenon is expansion of manufacturing in the periphery. This has occurred during most of the postwar period, accelerating somewhat in the last decade, but it has involved evolutionary rather than rapid change. In 1968/69, 39.3 per cent of manufacturing employment was located outside of Sydney and Melbourne, while by 1979/80 this had reached 43.7 per cent. Not all areas of the periphery have benefited (Queensland's bouyancy contrasts with continuing stagnation in Tasmania, for example) and within the periphery, industry remains concentrated in small areas, notably the state capitals. Two industry groups accounted for much of the peripheral growth in the 1970s (Rich 1981a): food, beverages and tobacco throughout the decade, and basic metal products in the early and late 1970s.

One reason for industrial growth in the periphery in the early postwar period was construction of plants to serve expanding regional markets. Many firms found it advantageous to divide production between several states because of long distances between major centres, the poorly integrated rail system and high costs of internal goods transport, as well as the industrial promotion activities of state governments. Interfirm competition meant that markets were often divided commercially as well as spatially, so that factories were generally far smaller than the minimum efficient scale. They were able to survive because of tariff protection, but growing competitive pressures led to the massive rationalisation of production seen in the 1970s (Linge 1978; Wilde 1981a).

Government actions have also contributed to industrial dispersal (Linge 1978). The Commonwealth government lacks constitutional power to intervene directly in industrial location decisions, but for decades there has been intense competition between state governments for a share of available investment (Linge 1967). Governments still compete for industry by offering cheap power to major energy users, payroll tax reductions and relaxing planning and environmental controls. Such policies are significant elements in industrial dispersals, even within NSW and Victoria, as current developments in the Hunter Valley testify. The benefits of such policies (e.g. increased employment and income generated in peripheral locations) and the disadvantages (e.g. inefficient fragmentation of production) are not relevant here. The point is that governments play a significant part in the relative growth and decline of Sydney and Melbourne.

Many other factors are involved. Changing organisational structures and competitive strategies adopted by firms in response to constraints and opportunities facing them are major considerations. For example, in the brewing industry falling profits and growing competition in the 1970s produced complex responses including both geographical dispersal of production and financial concentration of ownership (Fagan 1981a).

Exploitation of raw materials is another factor, but this can only be understood in terms of strategies adopted by large firms in the light of worldwide competitive conditions. The aluminium industry has long been an important contributor to peripheral growth, with most bauxite mining, alumina refining and aluminium smelting occurring well away from Sydney or Melbourne. The recent surge of interest in the industry will, if sustained, accentuate the trend. This interest stems not simply from Australia's position as a stable, low cost supplier of bauxite and alumina, nor from its ability to provide relatively cheap energy needed for smelting, but from a complex interaction of these factors with others such as government willingness to embrace the internationalisation of production by the industry and finance necessary infrastructure, the ability of local capital markets to supply much of the funding, and the existence of a westernised economy with a skilled workforce and a large information processing sector. But even this complex of issues only became relevant when major aluminium producers were forced to consider relocating production capacity from industrial countries by worldwide recession, falling profits resulting from rising costs and over-capacity, and especially because of sharp rises in energy costs in these countries (Fagan 1981b). The growth of industry in Australia's peripheral regions is thus a highly complex phenomenon, resulting not just from domestic economic and political considerations but also from the country's changing role in the international industrial system.

Accelerating exploitation of mineral and energy resources means that expansion in parts of the periphery will be an increasingly visible feature of Australia's industrial geography in the 1980s. The basic metal products industry will be in the forefront of the trend, even if some of the more extravagant claims for aluminium production prove unfounded. As the decade progresses, activities in the chemical, petroleum and coal products group, especially those related to energy production, are likely to strengthen the trend. While petroleum refining will remain concentrated in capital cities, petrochemical plants may be established to utilise hydrocarbons, for example from South Australia's Cooper Basin or even the North West Shelf. Further ahead, coal to oil or (later still) shale to oil conversion projects may mean massive investment in non-metropolitan Queensland, NSW and Victoria. Many of the proposed schemes are problematic. Not all will proceed, whether because of capital costs, depressed world demand, technological difficulties, infrastructure weaknesses or — especially important for synthetic oil schemes — water shortages. But others will, so that the periphery will contain more of Australia's industry, especially capital intensive, technologically advanced activities.

The core will not be unaffected by these developments. Construction of mining and processing projects will require much capital equipment, including earth moving machinery, industrial and electrical machinery, and pumps (Australia. BIE 1981b), and there will be continuing demand for inputs during subsequent operations; most of these needs will be met by firms in or near the main cities, or by imports. Minerals, energy and related activities will increase personal and governmental incomes and, to the extent that this flows through to consumer demand, increase sales of the core based consumer goods industries. But there will also be adverse effects for the core, such as competition for labour, bidding up of wage rates especially in engineering and technical fields, and possible shortages of investment funds as capital seeks more profitable outlets in the new industries. Many established industries can thus expect little if any relief from competitive pressures, and their problems are likely to be worsened by increased imports stemming from a rising exchange rate (the result of growing mineral exports) and, perhaps, decreased protection. More generally, metropolitan areas may lose out in terms of public investment as governments divert more of their investment funds to meet the infrastructure requirements of expanding peripheral industries. Both manufacturing and the population at large may suffer in the cities: the power shortages of the winter of 1981 are merely a harbinger of things to come.

## 5.5   Conclusion

Australian manufacturing is undergoing considerable change and Sydney's industry is by no means insulated from these events. Sydney has lost its preeminence as Australia's main industrial city and, though it retains a substantial role as a centre of employment and production, it seems destined to decline further in relative, if not absolute, terms. On the other hand, there is clear evidence, not only from manufacturing but also from the financial (Daly ch 2) and information (Langdale ch 4) sectors that Sydney is at the very least maintaining its position as one of two centres of control of Australian business, and there are signs that its position is becoming more entrenched.

   In these terms, the outlines of industrial change in Sydney are clear, but the processes are much more difficult to disentangle. It is evident, though, that to understand them, it is vital to consider them in a national context and then in turn to interpret Australian phenomena in terms of world events: discussion here has thus necessarily ranged far from Sydney's boundaries. Explanation of industrial change in Sydney must probe a complex interweaving of processes, at all geographical scales from the global to the local. To understand Sydney's changing industrial role we must consider issues as apparently diverse as growing financial concentration of ownership and control of all types of business at both national and global levels, internationalisation of production and capital, technological change, the world mineral and energy supply situation, world recession, industrialisation of many Pacific Basin countries, and attempts by Australian governments to attract international capital into local resource exploitation in the face of growing pressure on the traditional manufacturing base, together with corporate and entrepreneurial reactions to these events, and the changing structure of the domestic economy that results. In the face of such a multitude of issues, considerations such as the price or quality of industrial land in Sydney or the nature of local development control procedures, though important in their way, can be seen as they really are: small elements of a complex web of industrial change.

# 6 Manufacturing and industrial property development in Sydney

RICHARD V. CARDEW and DAVID C. RICH

## 6.1 Introduction

The last decade has witnessed a transformation of Sydney's industrial areas. Not only have there been marked changes in their appearance, their function and in the corporate and financial organisation of the firms located there, but also new districts, predominantly in the middle and distant suburbs have been opened up for industrial development, while others, especially in the inner city, have come to be used less intensely or turned over to other uses.

Industrial change in Sydney has been a product of a complex inter-weaving of processes operating at global, national and local scales. International economic restructuring, combined with a variety of domestic pressures, have brought substantial changes in the volume, nature, organisation and spatial distribution of industry in Australia (Rich ch 5). These external mechanisms have interacted with internal influences, such as land supply, urban planning and other forms of government regulation, to produce a series of changes in Sydney's industrial geography.

This chapter focuses on four important features of recent trends. First is the diversification of activity in industrial zones. Far from being confined to production, activities present include growing proportions of storage, distribution and office activities. These additional functions have appeared in response to the greater flexibility and increasing quality of industrial buildings on the one hand and the changing structure of business on the other. Second, manufacturing, and to a lesser extent other occupants of industrial premises, have become progressively more dispersed within the metropolitan area, paralleling the dispersal of production from Sydney to other parts of Australia (Rich ch 5). Third, a significant factor promoting and facilitating each of these changes has been a revolution in the financial sector which altered the capital structure of business and channelled large amounts of foreign and domestic money into industrial property development. Finally, planning, principally development control, and other forms of

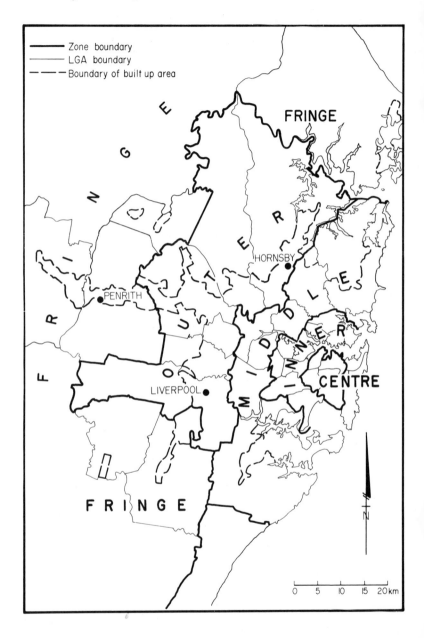

Figure 6.1    Five zones used to examine the changing distribution of industry in the Sydney metropolitan area

government regulation have been important factors influencing both the spatial pattern and the physical form of new industrial building. In turn, many of the changes in the industrial system have important and largely unrecognised implications for the planning system.

Industry is in constant flux, but the period of rapid change began during the boom conditions of the 1960s and continued unabated — in many respects even accentuated — during the recession of the mid 1970s. There is every indication that it has continued during the faltering industrial recovery of the last two or three years, but for reasons of data availability discussion concentrates on the period between the late 1960s and the late 1970s. Statistical data refer, unless otherwise stated, to the Sydney Statistical Division as enlarged in 1976 to include outlying areas such as Gosford-Wyong, but the main focus is on trends in the contiguous built up area. Much of the discussion of spatial changes refers to five concentric groupings of LGAs (Figure 6.1).

## 6.2  Diversification and dispersal

By the 1960s there were two major concentrations of manufacturing in the Sydney metropolitan area (Logan 1963), one in the central area south and west of the CBD and the other in the mid western suburbs. The former had emerged as an industrial area in the nineteenth century (Linge 1979c), while the latter was essentially a postwar phenomenon (Linge 1979b; Logan 1963). In 1968/69 these concentrations were represented by two groups of contiguous LGAs, each LGA having more than 20,000 manufacturing jobs. Sydney, South Sydney and Marrickville together provided 128,200 jobs in manufacturing, while Auburn, Bankstown and Parramatta offered 81,500. Six of the 45 LGAs thus contributed 53 per cent of all metropolitan employment in manufacturing, and 44 per cent of all manufacturing establishments. Already, though, there had been quite substantial dispersion of activity away from these two concentrations, both to adjacent LGAs and increasingly to the more peripheral northern, outer western and southern suburbs; as yet, there was relatively little industrial development in the outermost parts of the metropolitan area.

Manufacturing has become increasingly dispersed since the late 1960s in Sydney, as in many other cities (Kain 1975; Wood 1974). The two innermost of the five concentric zones suffered losses of employment (Table 6.1) and establishments (Table 6.2) between 1968/69 and 1978/79 while the two most peripheral zones experienced net gains. The middle suburban zone, containing Logan's second major industrial concentration, lost employment despite a significant increase in the number of establishments.

Most LGAs shared the same experience as their respective zones, at

**Table 6.1  Changes in the zonal distribution of manufacturing employment in the Sydney metropolitan area, 1968/69-1978/79**

| Zone | Employment | | | Employment change | | | % change | | |
|---|---|---|---|---|---|---|---|---|---|
| | 1968/69 | 1973/74 | 1978/79 | 1968/69-1973/74 | 1973/74-1978/79 | 1968/69-1978/79 | 1968/69-1973/74 | 1973/74-1978/79 | 1968/69-1978/79 |
| Centre | 164,613 | 140,633 | 105,136 | −23,980 | −35,497 | −59,477 | −14.57 | −25.24 | −36.13 |
| Inner | 70,954 | 67,962 | 51,663 | −2,992 | −16,299 | −19,291 | −4.22 | −23.98 | −27.19 |
| Middle | 119,571 | 128,839 | 111,366 | +9,268 | −17,473 | −8,205 | +7.75 | −13.56 | −6.86 |
| Outer | 31,411 | 43,985 | 44,273 | +12,574 | +288 | +12,862 | +40.03 | +0.65 | +40.95 |
| Fringe | 10,432 | 15,591 | 17,292 | +5,159 | +1,701 | +6,860 | +49.45 | +10.91 | +65.76 |
| Metropolitan area | 396,981 | 397,010 | 329,730 | +29 | −67,280 | −67,251 | +0.01 | −16.95 | −16.94 |

Source: ABS *Manufacturing establishments; summary statistics of operations in local government areas and statistical divisions and subdivisions, New South Wales*, ABS, Sydney (various issues)

**Table 6.2 Changes in the zonal distribution of manufacturing establishments in the Sydney metropolitan area, 1968/69-1978/79**

| Zone | Establishment | | | Establishment change | | | % change | | |
|---|---|---|---|---|---|---|---|---|---|
| | 1968/69 | 1973/74 | 1978/79 | 1968/69-1973/74 | 1973/74-1978/79 | 1968/69-1978/79 | 1968/69-1973/74 | 1973/74-1978/79 | 1968/69-1978/79 |
| Centre | 4,080 | 3,432 | 3,061 | −648 | −371 | −1,019 | −15.88 | −10.81 | −24.98 |
| Inner | 2,106 | 1,899 | 1,736 | −207 | −163 | −370 | −9.83 | −8.58 | −17.57 |
| Middle | 3,114 | 3,462 | 3,541 | +348 | +79 | +427 | +11.18 | +2.28 | +13.71 |
| Outer | 837 | 1,212 | 1,449 | +375 | +237 | +612 | +44.80 | +19.55 | +73.12 |
| Fringe | 405 | 549 | 805 | +144 | +256 | +400 | +35.56 | +46.63 | +98.77 |
| Metropolitan area | 10,542 | 10,554 | 10,592 | +12 | +38 | +50 | +0.11 | +0.36 | +0.47 |

*Source:* See Table 6.1

least in the direction of change. All LGAs in the central and inner suburban zones lost manufacturing employment, while in the two outer-most zones only Colo failed to increase employment. Within the middle suburban zone employment trends were more varied as a consequence of a net decline in the mid western suburbs and growth in the newer industrial areas of Warringah and Sutherland. The same general pattern is evident for manufacturing establishments, but there is rather more variability around the respective zonal averages: for example, three LGAs in the inner suburbs attracted small net gains.

Dispersal of manufacturing continued throughout the period as the area of greatest net growth migrated from the outer suburban zone out to the metropolitan fringe after 1973/74. There was no sign of any easing of the trend to dispersal, despite the transition from bouyancy to recession in the national economy in 1973/74.

We have, then, a picture of industrial activity becoming more dispersed within the Sydney metropolitan area. This picture is, however, incomplete for two main reasons. First, the data refer to *net* changes in the distribution of manufacturing. Overseas work (e.g. Gudgin 1978; Struyk and James 1975) demonstrates that net changes conceal much larger gross shifts in the industrial components of change, such as factory openings, closures and relocations. Further, the mechanisms influencing the spatial patterns of change are likely to be different for each of these gross components. Ideally, analysis should focus on each component separately, but unfortunately appropriate data for a full investigation are unavailable in Australia.

Second, activities occupying industrial land and buildings are becoming increasingly diversified. The data used so far relate to manufacturing (i.e. production), but this is not the only activity present in industrial areas. Other functions, particularly storage (warehousing) and business administration (office work) are becoming more common both as ancillary functions within factories and as separate establish-ments. In 1973 only 65 per cent of occupied industrial land in Sydney accommodated manufacturing (Solomon 1975). No more recent data are available, but it seems certain that this percentage will have declined. For example, the value of new warehouse construction has risen substantially relative to that of factory building (Table 6.3). Consequently, to understand the processes of industrial dispersal, comprehend the pattern of industrial land use and evaluate the planning implications of recent events, one must consider the totality of industry and not focus exclusively on the production process itself.

For these reasons it is desirable to examine the gross components of change in the total range of industrial activity. Information is not available for a complete investigation, but data on the value of new industrial buildings indicate the location of gross additions to the stock of industrial activity resulting from plant openings and relocations, as well as from expansion *in situ*. Separate figures are available for factories and for other industrial buildings. The latter category is dominated by warehouses (but also includes post offices, service stations and the like). Because modern industrial buildings are designed to serve as either factories or warehouses, with the ultimate use often unknown at the time of construction, there is merit in considering the two categories in tandem.

Overall, industrial building activity clearly became more dispersed in Sydney in the 1970s (Table 6.4). The centre and inner zones each registered declining shares of new building, while the three peripheral zones all attracted growing proportions of a falling volume of investment. The pattern was much the same for factory construction viewed in isolation, except that only the two outermost zones obtained growing shares of new building. For other industrial building the pattern was somewhat different. The centre suffered a massive drop in construction

**Table 6.3   Value of industrial building completions in the Sydney metropolitan area, 1968/69-1979/80[a]**

| Year | Manufacturing | | Other industrial building | | Total industrial building ($million) |
|---|---|---|---|---|---|
| | Value ($million) | % of total industrial building | Value ($million) | % of total industrial building | |
| 1968/69 | 199 | 78.7 | 54 | 21.3 | 253 |
| 1969/70 | 186 | 74.4 | 63 | 25.2 | 250 |
| 1970/71 | 195 | 56.0 | 153 | 44.0 | 348 |
| 1971/72 | 187 | 57.5 | 138 | 42.5 | 325 |
| 1972/73 | 160 | 55.2 | 130 | 44.8 | 290 |
| 1973/74 | 192 | 66.2 | 98 | 33.8 | 290 |
| Subtotal 1968/69- 1973/74 | 1,119 | 63.7 | 637 | 36.3 | 1,756 |
| 1974/75 | 148 | 63.5 | 85 | 36.5 | 233 |
| 1975/76 | 85 | 50.3 | 84 | 49.7 | 169 |
| 1976/77 | 96 | 47.8 | 105 | 52.2 | 201 |
| 1977/78 | 77 | 51.0 | 74 | 49.0 | 151 |
| 1978/79 | 98 | 57.6 | 72 | 42.4 | 170 |
| 1979/80 | 123 | 55.7 | 98 | 44.3 | 221 |
| Subtotal 1974/75- 1979/80 | 627 | 54.7 | 519 | 45.3 | 1,146 |
| Total 1968/69- 1979/80 | 1,746 | 60.2 | 1,156 | 39.8 | 2,902 |

*Note:* [a] 1979/80 values are used throughout; they have been converted from current dollar terms using the implicit price deflator for non-residential building and construction, obtained from ABS (1980) *Quarterly estimates of national income and expenditure, June Quarter 1980*, ABS, Canberra, p8.
*Source:* ABS *Building, New South Wales*, ABS, Sydney, for each year

**Table 6.4  Value of industrial completions by zone in the Sydney metropolitan area, 1968/69-1979/80[a]**

| Zone | Manufacturing | | | | Other industrial building | | | | Total industrial building | | | |
|---|---|---|---|---|---|---|---|---|---|---|---|---|
| | 1968/69-1973/74 | | 1974/75-1979/80 | | 1968/69-1973/74 | | 1974/75-1979/80 | | 1968/69-1973/74 | | 1974/75-1979/80 | |
| | $million | % Sydney total | $million | % Sydney total | $million | % Sydney total | $million | % Sydney total | $million | % Sydney total | $million | % Sydney total |
| Centre | 205 | 18.3 | 81 | 12.9 | 263 | 41.3 | 142 | 27.4 | 468 | 26.7 | 222 | 19.4 |
| Inner | 151 | 13.5 | 71 | 11.3 | 92 | 14.4 | 85 | 16.4 | 243 | 13.8 | 156 | 13.6 |
| Middle | 414 | 37.0 | 226 | 36.0 | 149 | 23.4 | 165 | 31.8 | 563 | 32.1 | 391 | 34.1 |
| Outer | 243 | 21.7 | 167 | 26.6 | 97 | 15.2 | 76 | 14.6 | 340 | 19.4 | 423 | 21.2 |
| Fringe | 107 | 9.6 | 82 | 13.1 | 35 | 5.5 | 52 | 10.0 | 142 | 8.1 | 133 | 11.6 |
| Metropolitan area | 1,119 | | 627 | | 637 | | 519 | | 1,756 | | 1,146 | |

*Note:* [a] 1979/80 values are used throughout: see Table 6.3 note a
*Source:* See Table 6.3

in both absolute and relative terms, while the outer zone also experienced a small decline. The other three zones all increased their shares of activity, with the largest increase being in the middle zone, particularly in Auburn-Parramatta. Here there was a real increase in the value of construction (in constant dollar terms) in the second period, despite an 18.5 per cent decline in other industrial building in Sydney as a whole and in contrast to the zone's declining share of factory building. The fringe zone also attracted an increased share of other industrial building, largely because of the high level of activity in Gosford-Wyong, an area somewhat divorced from the main metropolitan market.


## 6.3   Processes of dispersal

Metropolitan dispersal of manufacturing is one element of the much wider phenomenon of structural economic change (Linge 1979b). Changes in the distribution of industry should be seen as part of the response of industrial firms to alterations in the constraints and opportunities posed by their operating environment. Consequently, any attempt to understand dispersal must look first at the mechanisms triggering locational change and only secondly at the factors influencing the nature of the change.

Many environmental stimuli are insufficiently potent to generate perceptible change in the activities of the firm or to invoke responses that are not overtly spatial (Lloyd and Dicken 1977 ch 8). For example, investment in new technology by John Fairfax and by Tooth's have not affected the location of newspaper or beer production in Sydney, although in both cases employment levels changed, contributing to the declining level of industrial employment in the centre. Other stimuli trigger reactions with clear geographical dimensions. Changing production technology, development of new products, increased competition in established markets and altered government policy are all environmental changes that might lead to a reevaluation of a firm's pattern of production. A changing level of demand is perhaps the most important single stimulus to locational change (Keeble 1968; Logan 1966). On the one hand, installation of new capacity to satisfy increased demand often requires the establishment of a branch plant or a transfer to larger premises. On the other, excess capacity in periods of falling demand may, like attempts to maintain sales by increasing efficiency of production, lead to closure of the least efficient establishments. By way of illustration, the obsolescence of gravure printing and its replacement by offset methods led to the closure of the Sungravure magazine printing operation at Rosebery in mid 1981 and the loss of 375 jobs in the central zone. Similarly, both British Leyland and GM-H have closed car plants in the centre (at Zetland and Pagewood respectively) in response to increasing competition, declining profitability and changing production methods. Further, Unilever's decision to satisfy growing demand and adopt new technology led to a transfer of detergent production from Balmain to Minto in the Macarthur Growth Centre in the late 1970s.

The net effect of these changes is the decline of manufacturing in central areas and its relative or absolute growth in peripheral districts. While the balance of the components of industrial change — factory openings, closures, transfers etc. — varies with the prevailing economic climate, manufacturing continues to disperse in either bouyant or depressed market conditions (section 6.2). These shifts occur in the first place in response to changing environmental conditions, but their exact nature reflects an evaluation of the various locational options open to individual firms. The issues influencing such an evaluation have been widely discussed (e.g. AIUS 1970; Daly and Webber 1973; Logan 1963, 1966; Webber and Daly 1971) and in many ways parallel those affecting the distribution of wholesaling (Nugent *et al.* ch 7). Three groups of factors seem to be important.

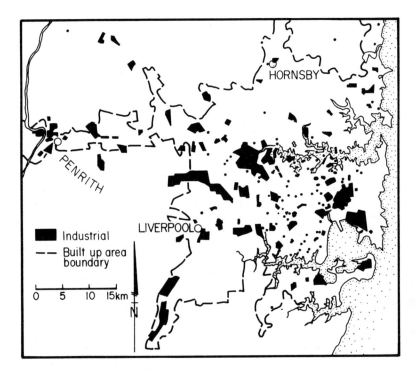

**Figure 6.2    Zoned industrial land in the Sydney metropolitan area, circa 1980**

The first relates to the supply of land and buildings: firms are forced to look towards the periphery when searching for sites suitable for modern industry. Industrial land is scattered over a wide area (Figure 6.2) with numerous small zones and four major areas, the central industrial district, Auburn-Parramatta in the mid western suburbs, Holroyd-Fairfield further south west, and Campbelltown on the metropolitan fringe. Successive increments of industrial investment have progressively used up land in more accessible districts, so that the supply of vacant industrial land is heavily concentrated in the middle, outer and fringe zones (Table 6.5). Of the land nominally available in the central and inner zones, the bulk is currently devoted to other, non-conforming, uses or is attached to the premises of existing businesses. Except in Botany, very little exists in the form of free standing allotments and most of that consists of small plots, while some of the Botany land is unsatisfactory because of the high water table (NSW. PEC 1980a). Even in more peripheral areas some of the vacant zoned land is less than ideal for industrial uses, reflecting in part the tendency to relegate industry to land that is unsuitable for other uses (for example, disused quarries, flood liable land and areas traversed by large service easements).

As a consequence of the chronology of development, central areas are unattractive to many businesses because of the age, quality and cost of the building stock and the congested environment within which it exists. Many of the buildings are cramped and multistoreyed and thus technologically obsolete given increases in the preferred scale of production and the adoption of modern techniques more suited to large, single storey premises. The costs of the property are often high relative to the facilities offered, not so much because of competition for it, but more because of the unrealistic expectations of owners, even when the premises have been vacant for some time. Reconstruction to meet contemporary needs is inhibited by the small sites, congestion, the high costs of rebuilding relative to the development of new sites elsewhere, and in some cases by zoning restrictions. It is therefore not surprising that new firms are generally drawn to more peripheral areas or that businesses operating in the centre often seek to leave it in search of more congenial surroundings. However, such relocation is not effortless. For small firms the capital required to move may be substantially above the levels which their financial structures can service. In addition, while firms with leasehold tenancies can relocate readily, owner occupiers often find disposal of premises difficult and less remunerative than anticipated. Another inhibiting factor is the valuation of property in the shareholders' reports of public companies. Values were often struck during the property boom of the early 1970s and in the later recession were frequently well above the prevailing market. The disincentive to adjust values and alter a company's asset structure was such that firms

**Table 6.5  Distribution and use of zoned industrial land in Sydney, 1972[a]**

| Zone | Land zoned for industry (hectares) | Zoned land unused by industry | | Components of unused land | | | | Unused land as per cent of unused land in four zones |
|---|---|---|---|---|---|---|---|---|
| | | | | Vacant land | | Non-conforming land use | | |
| | | hectares | as % of land zoned for industry | free standing allotments (hectares) | attached to existing industry (hectares) | available to market (hectares) | not available to market (hectares) | |
| Centre | 1,430 | 359 | 25.1 | 70 | 162 | 81 | 46 | 8.4 |
| Inner | 986 | 320 | 32.5 | 57 | 195 | 56 | 12 | 7.5 |
| Middle | 3,243 | 1,555 | 47.9 | 713 | 703 | 85 | 55 | 36.2 |
| Outer | 2,678 | 2,060 | 76.9 | 1,567 | 386 | 89 | 18 | 48.0 |
| Total (four zones)[a] | 8,337 | 4,294 | 51.5 | 2,406 | 1,446 | 311 | 131 | 100.0 |

*Note:* [a]Comparable data are not available for all LGAs in the fringe zone.
*Source:* Calculated from material in Solomon (1975), Appendices P and Q.

commonly awaited the return of market prices to book values before contemplating disposal of the property and relocation to the suburbs.

Changes in the supply and market relations of firms, largely associated with developments in transport, form a second group of factors. Historically, the central zone was attractive because it contained the major local sources of inputs and markets, as well as the main transport terminals providing access to sources and markets outside the metropolitan area. Dispersal of potentially linked activities, such as wholesaling (Nugent *et al.* ch 7), across an enlarged metropolitan area means that the central zone is now eccentrically located and much less attractive than hitherto. The rise of trucking as the predominant mode of freight transport has freed firms from locations near major transport terminals and reduced spatial variations in transport costs in the metropolitan area (although congestion in the centre and the remoteness of the fringe influence the cost and quality of transport services). Containerisation of a high proportion of external freight flows (Rimmer and Black ch 12) has likewise increased the locational flexibility of firms. Supply and market linkages are thus somewhat less of a constraint upon industrial location than in the past, but access and transport considerations mean that for many purposes Parramatta-Auburn-Silverwater (approximately Logan's second major concentration of manufacturing) is perhaps the prime location.

The residential proclivities of entrepreneurs, management and labour are a third influence on manufacturing location. The rapid postwar dispersal of population in Sydney has both encouraged and facilitated industrial decentralisation (Webber and Daly 1971) by providing large pools of labour away from the central zone. In particular, rapid population growth in the west and south west of the metropolitan area seems to have been a significant locational attraction in times of near full employment. Even now, with much higher unemployment, the supply of skilled labour is often larger away from central areas. Similarly, relocation of a plant from the centre may be welcomed by existing staff for reducing the length of journeys to work, offering a more pleasant working environment, or opening up attractive residential areas for management, although there might be adjustment problems in some cases (Faulkner ch 14). On the other hand, residential patterns and preferences may act as a brake upon more radical locational change. For example, moves to the metropolitan fringe might be resisted by management or secretarial staff because of limited commercial, social and cultural amenities available there (Linge 1979b) and a middle suburban location adopted instead.

In several respects, the processes influencing dispersal of wholesaling (discussed by Nugent *et al.* ch 7) are similar to those affecting manufacturing. In both cases, relocating firms are influenced by availability of space and seek new building forms with large clear spaces, as well as reasonable access to suppliers and customers. Accessible locations are more important to wholesalers than to manufacturers (perhaps explaining the rather greater dispersal of the latter group), especially to minimise the costs of distribution to intrametropolitan markets.

## 6.4   The industrial property market

Dispersal of industry can thus be viewed as part of the response to changing environmental conditions by users of industrial space. Important though this perspective is, it neglects the vital impact of those influencing the supply of industrial space, especially premises suitable for the increasingly important light industries. These are the individuals and firms operating in the industrial property market, including developers, agents, builders and professional consultants such as architects, surveyors, engineers and planners who produce the space and act as agents for transactions in that space. They are a diverse group, and include: small speculative builders of factory units, architecture/planning consultants expanding into development as planning legislation forces more substantial design before planning approval, small and large and local and overseas property developers and firms whose initial or primary activities are outside the property sector. Their responsibilities range from constructing premises to meet specific user requirements to the development of large projects where the task is effectively to assemble investment packages for clients. In the latter case, industrial property is built for sale to investors, such as pension funds, insurance companies and foreign finance houses, who then generally lease the premises back to the developer for subleasing to avoid the inconvenience of managing the investment.

The rise of widespread investment, especially institutional investment, has been one of the major changes in the industrial property market since the mid 1960s, coinciding with and facilitating industrial dispersal and the modernisation of industrial property. No longer seen as an unattractive high risk investment, the market became a prime target for investment by financial institutions. This did not happen because returns were exceptionally high: indeed, yields were generally a moderate 9-10.5 per cent. Rather it occurred because for much of the 1970s investment opportunities in other property sectors such as housing, offices and retailing were not available or became unattractive (through oversupply of property and/or low returns), and because investors sought to diversify their portfolios to guard against the effects of periodic but not necessarily synchronised slumps in the various property sectors. The new trend also had advantages for users of industrial property. Leasehold tenancies meant that modern premises were available, capital was not unnecessarily tied up in buildings, and changing space needs could be satisfied easily and cheaply, benefits often not available to the owner occupier.

These funds ensured a ready supply of new industrial buildings, typically of single storey clear span construction with light frames and ceilings over heavy load bearing floors. Ample provision is made for office and showroom space, usually amounting to 20 per cent of floorspace and sometimes exceeding 40 per cent. Such property is highly flexible, being suited to both light manufacturing and warehouse use, hence encouraging the diversification of activities in industrial areas. The financial sector thus had a substantial impact on the supply of industrial property and on the opportunities for establishing new plants or relocating old ones. But it was a differential impact in that, because of the scale of investment, it was concentrated in a particular sector of the market: most investment of this type involved sums of $0.5 to $2 million on buildings of between 2,000 and 5,000 square metres. Firms requiring larger premises have generally funded their own developments or needed purpose built accommodation. Small premises have also been somewhat neglected. Factory units, the industrial equivalent of home units and generally of between 100 and 500 square metres, presented greater financial risks to investors, were more difficult to manage and generally involved smaller investment packages. Construction of new units was hindered in some areas by planning regulations that were more stringent than those for buildings for single occupany. Small units have therefore been in short supply.

Participants in the property market play an important role in directing the geographical pattern of industrial investment and development. Property developers and agents are often more sensitive to the locational opportunities and constraints outlined in the previous section than users of industrial space because their business involves continual reassessment of the relevant factors for a succession of clients, whereas most industrial firms make locational decisions very infrequently. Developers and agents thus acquire an awareness of the factors which differentiate between zoned industrial areas: positive aspects like accessibility to major transport routes and labour, and the size and shape of land parcels; and negative features such as drainage and easement problems with the land, difficulties with local authorities and more stringent planning regulations. Their perceptions of and reactions to these factors thus help to mould the industrial geography of Sydney.

For example, several of the larger property developers have seen the outer boundary of the middle zone as the limit to most demand for industrial land. This view was a product of the market they served, predominantly institutions investing in high quality warehouse space with substantial provision for office accommodation. Smaller developers of factory units or more modest enterprises have looked further afield to Blacktown, Prospect or Liverpool. There has been a reluctance to develop in more peripheral districts, but shortage of land has forced all groups to look increasingly to more distant areas.

Similarly, the central industrial area, especially Leichhardt, Marrickville and South Sydney, is not seen to have the locational primacy that proximity to the CBD or transport terminals might suggest. It is congested, poorly served by major roads and has a long standing reputation for noxious industries. Pockets of highly resilient, in some cases expanding and gentrifying, residential areas are virtually impenetrable by industry because of high residential property prices, despite industrial zoning. Likewise, overvaluation has inhibited redevelopment of existing industrial premises. But the main deterrents for developers relate to planning: delays in receiving planning approval (up to eight months in a few cases, compared to the statutory limit of 40 days), restrictive development conditions and the effect of Ordinance 70.

## 6.5   Industrial property development and government regulation

This last point illustrates the important role of government regulation in influencing the behaviour of developers and industrial firms alike. In this context, the effect of Ordinance 70 has been particularly severe. This is a nationally standardised and very detailed ordinance, mainly concerned with fire regulations. It includes discretionary clauses allowing considerable variation in interpretation by each local authority, but these are used very cautiously by council officers for fear of personal accountability at law. It can be invoked either on a change of occupancy or during occupancy to require installation of a range of safety systems. These impositions tend to be most severe on the older, cheaper buildings in the central and inner zones. The Ordinance can substantially increase renovation costs and restrict expansion into adjacent properties in such areas. It thus encourages dispersal by forcing small relocating manufacturers to move to newer property in outer suburbs.

Planning regulations affecting site coverage (the proportion of the site covered by buildings), setbacks, provision for parking, permissible uses and landscaping all differentiate between industrial areas, on the one hand helping to create prestige industrial/commercial estates such as North Ryde, while on the other rendering many of the small businesses in areas such as Dee Why, parts of Rydalmere and Smithfield illegal. These development controls are a primary tool of planning used by local authorities, but despite their significance they are formulated arbitrarily. For example, the requirement for car parking varies by a factor of three across the metropolitan area and by as much as two between adjacent LGAs. With an opportunity cost of between $1,500 and $4,500 per car parking space, the arbitrariness of these standards can lead to expensive imposts (Cardew 1981a) and are of some significance in industrialists' and developers' appraisals of potential sites.

In some cases, especially North Ryde and partially in Lane Cove West and Frenchs Forest, these development standards have helped to create and then sustain a prestige image for industrial areas. In such cases, prices for industrial space can be very high. The highest rentals for industrial floorspace are in the lower North Shore industrial area straddling North Sydney and Willoughby, followed by North Ryde and Lane Cove. Both the geographical centre, a prime location for warehouses, and the central industrial area command lower prices. Indeed, with the exception of the areas mentioned, the price surface for industrial floorspace is a plateau for the central, inner and middle zones, and then a gentle gradient toward the periphery (Figure 6.3). Values in this plateau and its areal extent reflect the market for warehouses, while the gradient in distant areas identifies a peripheral manufacturing zone.

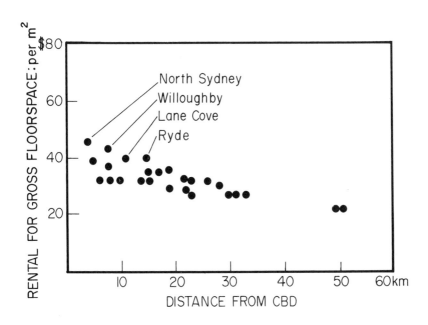

**Figure 6.3  Industrial floorspace rentals by LGA in the Sydney metropolitan area 1978**

## 6.6    Structural change, industrial zones and urban planning

The evolving distribution of industry in Sydney has been a product of the interaction of industrialists, industrial property developers and the planning system. Changes in the organisation and technology of manu-facturing and wholesaling as well as in their locational requirements are vital elements in understanding industrial dispersal, but property developers have also played a very important role, first by obtaining and channelling funds for a large amount of industrial building (much of it, by necessity, suburban), and second because of their generally much clearer appreciation of the locational constraints and opportunities (partly imposed by the planning system) facing industry. Property developers have accelerated the tide of dispersal, but they have tended to direct the flow to specific locations, such as the mid western suburbs in the case of warehousing.

In addition to encouraging and facilitating dispersal, industrialists, developers and planners have also been responsible for changing the character of industrial areas by modernising buildings, consolidating the various activities of particular firms on a single site, and diversifying the activities present in each district. Modernisation of the stock of industrial buildings is a continuing process, but it was particularly rapid in the 1970s. This resulted from the surge of capital investment in industrial property, stricter and more widespread enforcement of planning controls, altered requirements because of changes in the organisation and technology of manufacturing and wholesaling, and the growing initiative and interest of developers.

These factors were also responsible for a tendency for different sections of particular firms to amalgamate on one site, and thus for given areas to accommodate a greater range of economic functions. Before the 1970s, there was a gradual expansion of ancillary functions in manufacturing establishments. Just as scale economies and techno-logical changes encouraged consolidation of production facilities, so some firms found organisational and financial benefits in locating some of their other functions on the production site. Some larger firms moved sales and accounting staff to the factory complex. A few firms (such as Upjohns and Bristol Myer) moved their entire organisation, others whole divisions, to landscaped suburban sites. Developers began to offer carpeted, airconditioned offices in new buildings and other features to make occupation attractive to management. Planners also sought to improve the appearance of industrial zones by requiring buildings to be set further back from roads and sites to be extensively landscaped. They also demanded ample parking provision, placed limits on advertising and restricted the use of less attractive building materials. Industrial premises became more acceptable, and sometimes very attractive, working environments for management and clerical staff. Similarly, modern manufacturing processes in brighter and more spacious buildings improved conditions for production and warehouse staff.

These trends accelerated rapidly in the 1970s. Depressed demand, increasing competition and the many other pressures experienced by industry in the 1970s (Linge and McKay 1981) have encouraged more firms to rationalise not only their production capacity but also their ancillary functions. Amalgamating the various activities on a suburban site has been one favoured way of achieving this. The surge of capital available for industrial property development has helped many firms finance this sort of rationalisation, in many cases freeing up much needed funds from the disposal of owner occupied premises.

One of the more striking symptoms of these changes is the increasing volume of office activity present in industrial zones. The consolidation of office functions, often derived from the CBD, with manufacturing, storage and distribution in the suburbs gathered momentum in the 1970s. The industrial building activity between 1971 and 1976 was sufficient to accommodate more than 30,000 office employees, around 60 per cent of the total metropolitan increase in office-type jobs in the same period (Cardew 1981b). This helps explain the quite staggering rate of dispersal of office jobs throughout the metropolitan area in the last two decades (Alexander ch 3). It has also resulted in the more prestigious industrial estates, such as North Ryde, becoming as much commercial areas as industrial districts. In North Ryde, for example, 27 per cent of floorspace and 50 per cent of employment is devoted to office activities.

There have thus been dramatic changes in the industrial geography of Sydney, with a rapid dispersal of activity, modernisation of premises, consolidation of different functions and a marked trend to diversification of industrial areas. The planning system has been one of several agents bringing about these changes, but the events themselves have important implications for local and metropolitan planning.

## 6.7  Conclusions

The extent of the diversification and dispersal of industrial activity in the last decade or so has not been widely appreciated and as a result the implications for a number of important social issues have yet to be fully assessed. Among these are the transport links between the relatively declining central industrial area and port complexes on the one hand and the expanding industrial zones of the middle and outer suburbs on the other (Rimmer and Black ch 12); the relative disadvantage of both inner and outer zones in terms of employment (Burnley and Walker ch 10); the scope for overcoming the imbalance; and the future uses of industrial land, particularly in the central industrial area.

The suburbanisation of warehousing and outer suburbanisation of manufacturing accord with the general pattern of population growth in the metropolitan area. They do not, however, provide enough new employment opportunities in peripheral areas to match demographic increases, resulting in rising unemployment (Burnley and Walker ch 10) and longer journeys to work (Aplin ch 13; Faulkner ch 14). Planners have sought to speed the dispersal of employment yet they have been ignorant of its pace. Moreover, they have had limited impact except through measures designed to achieve objectives unrelated to dispersal, such as restrictive building and planning controls, limiting use of inner area properties, and creating lower than necessary densities of industrial land use in middle and outer areas.

The supplanting of manufacturing by warehousing in inner and middle industrial zones, often associated with considerable office employment, has created a further dilemma for planners. The distinction between classes of industrial land uses is made less clear, prices for floorspace are raised, and opportunities for manufacturing to return are severely limited. There are also many instances in which residential use at medium to high density could pay more for the land than industrial use. Pressure for back zoning is increasing in line with the Department of Environment and Planning's urban consolidation policy. But should planners allow the stock of industrial land in these areas to be eroded? The implications of this paper suggest that market forces will not protect industry, and by implication its protection should be justified on the externalities associated with its continuing existence in these areas, including employment, and energy costs associated with goods vehicle movement.

# 7 Organisational and locational change in Sydney's wholesaling industry

ELLIS NUGENT, DAVID C. RICH AND
PETER L. SIMONS

## 7.1 Introduction

Marketing is a vital part of modern western economies. It is the means by which the production and consumption of goods and services are linked so that supply and demand are matched in time and space. This role means that marketing is a key determinant of the economic geography of western countries, for example in permitting the geographical specialisation of production while allowing a dispersed demand to be satisfied, and thus in fostering the massive urban growth of the last century. It is a major contributor to living standards and has become intimately intertwined — almost synonymous — with the western way of life. Equally, it is an important source of jobs. In Australia the 1976 Population Census showed that 1,044,000 people, or 18.0 per cent of all employed, worked in wholesale and retail trades; the comparable figures for Sydney were 258,000 and 19.3 per cent (Table 1.1). Even this understates its importance because it ignores many working in transport, storage, advertising and finance who contribute to the marketing process.

Wholesaling is a central element of marketing as well as being one of the primary functions of major mercantile cities such as Sydney. A rather neglected area of economic activity, wholesaling repays investigation because it has undergone dramatic restructuring in recent decades, affecting the functions performed, the methods used and the number, size and location of enterprises involved. The changes have come about in response to continual modifications of the operating environments of wholesaling firms. Alterations in the nature, volume and geographical distribution of demand, introduction of new products, increasing competition between firms, government actions and developments in the technology of storage and transport have all stimulated adjustments by the businesses concerned.

As one example, the rural recession of the late 1960s and early 1970s reduced Australian demand for agricultural machinery by almost half and brought major organisational and locational changes in the distribution channels for such equipment (Wadley 1979). Similarly, recent restructuring of whitegoods manufacturing, involving concentration of ownership and attempts to achieve scale economies, have provoked fears amongst wholesalers and retailers of the consequences of reduced competition between suppliers, and are being followed by many changes in the distribution networks for these products (AFR 5 Aug 1980).

Perhaps the most pervasive changes in wholesaling, though, have resulted from a restructuring of the entire marketing process. Since the Second World War, direct trading has become a principal means of channelling goods from manufacturer to retailer, displacing the independent wholesaler who formerly linked the two. Many wholesalers have survived, but generally only by changing their methods and adjusting their activities to perform different functions. Reorganisation of marketing thus provoked major changes in wholesaling.

Allied with this reorganisation of wholesaling have been important locational changes. Traditionally identified with locations near sea ports and on the fringe of the CBD (Vance 1970), wholesaling is now becoming a suburban phenomenon. The transformation was prompted by the reorganisation of marketing practices and the adoption of new methods of storage, stock control and transport, whereby the low rise warehouse on a spacious site is more attractive than the congested multistorey premises hitherto occupied in the inner city. Orientation to increasingly suburbanised retailers and other sources of demand and the locational flexibility engendered by the almost universal adoption of trucking have further facilitated the dispersal.

This chapter examines first the organisational changes among Sydney's wholesalers, focusing on the impact of direct trading (section 7.2), second the major locational changes that have occurred since the mid 1960s (section 7.3) and finally the factors determining the location of wholesaling enterprises in Sydney (section 7.4). Official statistics are not suitable for investigating these issues; for example, the Wholesale Census has been conducted only once, so that temporal trends cannot be identified. The discussion therefore relies upon surveys of consumer goods wholesalers in the mid 1960s and again in the late 1970s by Simons and a more detailed study by Nugent (1977) of hardware wholesaling, which in many respects is representative of the industry generally.

## 7.2   Direct trading and organisational changes in wholesaling

The most significant trend in marketing since the Second World War, with enormous implications for wholesaling, has been the expansion of direct trading. During the 1950s and early 1960s, the larger retailing and manufacturing firms grew rapidly in two ways. First, through horizontal integration they expanded into lines apparently unrelated to their existing business and, second, through vertical integration they took over the wholesaling function or some part of it. Vertical integration resulted in an increase in direct trading between manufacturers and retailers, a consequential decline in the importance of the traditional manufacturing-wholesaling-retailing channel of distribution, and an apparent reduction in the importance of the wholesaling function. Marketing of groceries was first to be affected, but direct trading soon spread to electrical goods, pharmaceuticals and hardware; other commodities were affected later but to a lesser extent.

One explanation of the growth of direct trading is that it is more efficient, particularly for large organisations. By eliminating the wholesaler, large retailers and manufacturers are able to obtain economies of scale associated with large scale goods movements and to divide between them the often quite substantial margin that formerly went to the wholesaler. Turning such cost savings into a price advantage was probably a significant benefit to large retailers during the period when direct trading increased because of rapid changes in the location and character of the market (see Cardew and Simons ch 8) occurring at the same time.

However, the interest of manufacturers in vertical integration is related more to the fact that direct trading avoids a key disadvantage of the traditional mode of distribution. This is the inability of wholesalers to devote sufficient sales effort to the products of any one manufacturer because they handle a wide range of goods, often from many different producers. In contrast, direct trading allows manufacturers to exert greater control over the pattern of distribution and particularly over the retail outlets handling their goods. Greater control leads to increased sales effort, which can be crucial in advanced economies where the basic problem is normally to sell goods rather than produce them. Hence, control of marketing is more important than cost savings in the adoption of direct trading by manufacturers seeking to maintain a competitive edge and/or their share of the market.

Only after the expansion of direct trading was it realised that the decline in wholesaling was more apparent than real. The wholesaling function had not been eliminated, as many people thought. Control had simply moved into new hands. Facilitating functions, in particular, could not be avoided: retailers and manufacturers had either to provide their own storage, transport and finance or to subcontract these functions.

Just as the wholesaling function was not diminished by the expansion of direct trading, so many independent wholesalers were able to survive and even thrive, despite encroachment on their activities. They achieved this by changing their modes of operation and by expanding into new fields. In consequence, wholesaling has undergone major reorganisation in recent decades.

The traditional type of wholesaling enterprise had no formal ties with either suppliers or customers, bought from manufacturers (or their agents) and sold primarily to retailers but also to a variety of other outlets. Characteristically, they carried a wide range of merchandise and held substantial stocks of each product in all its varieties and sizes. Consequently, inventories were large and tended to emphasise non-perishable, non-fashionable goods, while turnover rates were low. These wholesalers conventionally owned the products they sold, manufacturers being paid promptly while customers were given 30 to 60 days credit and a variety of other services. Most wholesalers employed travelling salesmen, although selling through a showroom was important in some instances. Because of these methods wholesalers' margins were quite high, though less than the retailers' mark up in most cases.

Direct trading meant that wholesalers' largest retail customers were lost. Inevitably, the impact on traditional wholesaling firms was severe. Their reactions had two distinct phases. First responses were essentially negative. In the belief that direct trading was a temporary phenomenon, wholesalers looked for internal cost reductions and prepared to wait for better times. They cut costs by reducing stocks, placing 'hand to mouth' orders with suppliers and continuing to use obsolete equipment and buildings in the inner city. The net effect was to reduce the quality of their service, strengthen the move to direct trading and generally weaken the position of the wholesalers. They responded to the growing threat by cutting costs even further and refusing to handle the goo .s of manufacturers selling directly to retailers. The consequence of these negative reactions was a cumulative reduction in the wholesalers' ability to compete with direct trading.

Positive reactions to direct trading began in Sydney in the early 1960s among grocery wholesalers and continued in the 1970s in other commodities. They took a number of forms. The simplest was to opt out. Some wholesalers were able to sell their business to a manufacturer or retailer looking for an established firm as part of a vertical integration strategy. Others simply closed the business and sold off the assets.

Just as manufacturers and retailers tended to integrate vertically, so many wholesalers reacted to increasing competition by taking over functions formerly carried out by separate firms. Thus, a minority of Sydney's hardware wholesalers now concentrate exclusively on that task (Table 7.1). Many have chosen to combine the roles of wholesaler and importer. One advantage of this strategy is greater security of supply: foreign manufacturers are less likely than domestic suppliers to take over distribution once the wholesaler has promoted a commodity and established it in the market. Another attraction is that imported products are often more competitive in quality and price than Australian produced goods.

Other firms combine the role of wholesaler and manufacturer's agent. These differ from wholesaler-importers mainly in handling products of domestic rather than overseas manufacturers. From the manufacturer's perspective, commissioning wholesaling agents rather than attempting to market goods direct to retailers has a range of advantages. They can tap the expertise of many wholesalers, secure specialised sales promotion in a predefined area, and so concentrate on the often more profitable production activities. There is strict control over selling costs because the agent's commission is usually three to five per cent of gross sales; no sales means no cost to the manufacturer and no income to the agent. In turn, the arrangement allows wholesalers to function with minimal stocks, for example by organising deliveries direct from manufacturer to retailer, a major cost saving given the high interest rates of recent years.

Small retailers have also been subject to increasing competition from large concerns (Cardew and Simons ch 8). One response has been to form voluntary chains to obtain economies of bulk buying. In turn, wholesalers have emerged specifically to supply such groups: ten per cent of hardware wholesalers are of this type. Some are wholesaling cooperatives, owned by the retailers and selling exclusively or primarily to shareholders, while others were established by formerly independent wholesalers to buy for a group of retailers. In either case, various methods are used to minimise costs. Retailers are usually required to purchase most of their merchandise through the wholesaler concerned, order quantities above some minimum threshold and accept deliveries on specified days, thus enabling the wholesaler to forecast demand more easily and plan the most economical distribution of goods. Wherever possible, shipments are made direct from the manufacturer to the retailer. In any case, the storage time of goods is minimised, to reduce investment and carrying costs, and the warehouses are used more as sorting points than storage facilities (Guirdham 1972:113). Frequently, a common brand name is used for goods sold to customers in the group, so that retailers benefit from economies of advertising (Bellin 1976:7).

**Table 7.1   Functions performed by hardware wholesalers in Sydney, 1977**

|  | No. | % of total |
|---|---|---|
| Specialist wholesaler | 19 | 37.3 |
| Wholesaler-importer | 22 | 43.1 |
| Wholesaler-manufacturer's agent | 7 | 13.7 |
| Wholesaler-retailer | 3 | 5.9 |
| *Total* | 51 | 100.0 |

*Source:* Nugent (1977)

Other independent wholesalers sought to remain competitive by specialising in a limited range of goods. More than one third of hardware wholesalers reported that their product range became more specialised between 1965 and 1977. Such a strategy allows small firms to gain some of the benefits of bulk buying, while at the same time providing a wide choice of goods within the area of specialisation. This helps wholesalers build a good reputation and attract customers. The result of this trend is that only 20 per cent of Sydney's hardware wholesalers, including all the cooperative and group buying enterprises, still handle extensive ranges or 'full lines' of hardware products (over 26,000 lines in one case), including household hardware, kitchenware, cutlery, crockery and glassware, tools, electrical appliances, gardening products, paint, plumbing and building supplies, and locks. One third of hardware wholesalers carry a smaller range of these general hardware products but specialise in specific categories. The largest single group, the remaining 47 per cent, specialise in a narrow range of items, although they may still handle a large number of different lines.

Many wholesalers responded to changing conditions by drastic modernisation and cost cutting. Some of these changes involved revised selling methods and an altered relationship with retailers: for example, sales are often on a cash only basis, deliveries are either not offered or paid for by the customer, and customers are permitted to come to the warehouse to make up their own orders. More visibly, many wholesalers have invested heavily in modern goods handling techniques and computerised stock control procedures, and have begun to use new single level warehouses. Such investment, encouraged by the activities of industrial property developers (Cardew and Rich ch 6), has had the corollary of a change in location for many wholesalers. It is to the question of locational change that attention now turns.

## 7.3    Locational change in wholesaling

In the mid 1960s wholesaling was heavily concentrated in the inner areas of Sydney (Simons 1966), as it was in most other major cities. In 1963, 74 per cent of Sydney's consumer goods wholesalers were located in the City of Sydney LGA. The activity dominated land use along the western side of the CBD in a long established wholesaling district (Figure 7.1), which alone contained 26 per cent of all concerns, including the main concentration of hardware wholesalers. There were also significant numbers within the CBD itself (29 per cent) and in other parts of the City of Sydney (19 per cent). Wholesalers had adopted such locations to obtain easy access to a wide market area within Sydney, to the main transport and port facilities nearby and hence to suppliers and markets outside the metropolitan area. Such firms were particularly

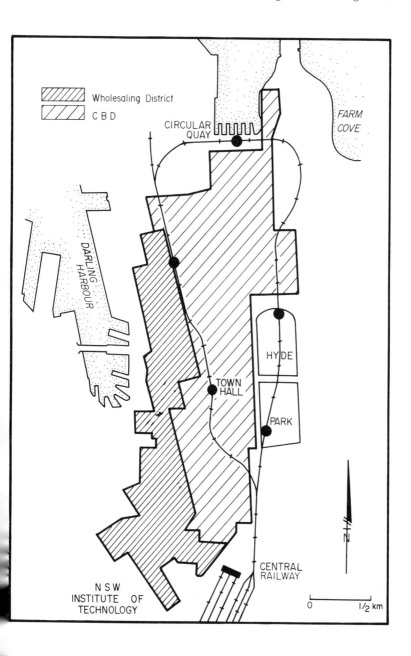

Figure 7.1   Sydney's CBD and wholesaling district in the mid 1960s

well located to serve the retail and business markets of the CBD; establishments away from the centre often found great difficulty in attracting buyers from the CBD to their showrooms (Simons 1966).

Less than twenty years ago, then, wholesaling remained clustered in the city centre and the traditional wholesaling district was still largely intact. But already great changes were beginning to occur in the distribution of wholesalers in response to changes in the organisation of the industry, the functions performed, the locational requirements of individual firms and the general pressures of urban development.

The nature and extent of locational change can be seen by comparing the 1957 and 1977 positions of the 2,382 consumer goods wholesalers identified in 1963 (Table 7.2). This procedure involves some obvious inaccuracies but it shows that more than half the firms surviving throughout the period changed their general location (while many others made local moves, not registered in Table 7.2). Overall, wholesalers were located further away from the inner city by 1977. This is indicated by the differences in the row and column totals in Table 7.2, the fact that 59 per cent of the new firms which survived were located outside of the City of Sydney, and the movement of 433 firms away from the city centre compared with only 64 relocations towards it.

There is also striking evidence of dispersal from the city centre by hardware wholesalers (Figure 7.2). Their mean distance from Sydney Town Hall increased by 3.6 km between 1965 and 1977. The biggest single component of change was the decline of the wholesaling district: 30 per cent of hardware wholesalers were located there in the mid

Table 7.2   Locations in 1957 and 1977 of consumer goods wholesalers identified in 1963[a]

| 1957 location | 1977 location | | | | | |
|---|---|---|---|---|---|---|
| | CBD | Wholesaling district | Rest of City of Sydney | Rest of metropolitan area | Out of business | Total (1957) |
| CBD | 142 | 32 | 71 | 97 | 273 | 615 |
| Wholesaling district | 21 | 92 | 58 | 92 | 217 | 480 |
| Rest of City of Sydney | 11 | 11 | 115 | 83 | 145 | 365 |
| Rest of metropolitan area | 5 | 5 | 11 | 135 | 173 | 329 |
| Not in business | 42 | 21 | 39 | 148 | 343 | 593 |
| Total (1977) | 221 | 161 | 294 | 555 | 1151 | 2382 |

Note: [a]The boundaries of the CBD and the wholesaling district are shown in Figure 7.1. Boundaries of the City of Sydney and the metropolitan area are as defined in 1963.
Source: Survey by Simons

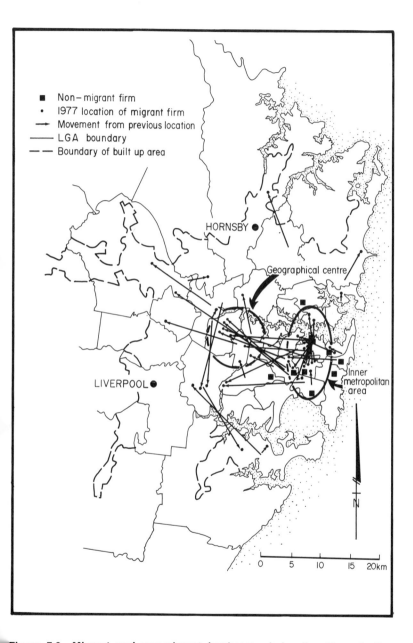

Figure 7.2   Migrant and non-migrant hardware wholesaling firms in the Sydney metropolitan area, 1965-1977

1960s, but only four per cent by 1977 (Table 7.3). The very high level of mobility is underrepresented in Table 7.3 because intrazonal moves are not registered. In fact, 80 per cent of all these firms relocated between 1965 and 1977, ten per cent of them twice. Consequently, by the latter date only eight per cent were left in the City of Sydney and 55 per cent were to be found outside the inner metropolitan area.

## 7.4   Locational requirements of hardware wholesaling

Decentralisation of wholesaling is one manifestation of a wider physical and economic restructuring of urban areas. Most cities have experienced a growing dispersal of people, production, retailing and to a lesser extent wholesaling (Kain 1975), and a change in the physical appearance and economic function of the CBD associated with the growth of office based activities (Daniels 1975). Sydney is no exception to these trends, although the dispersal of wholesaling has come later and perhaps been less marked than that of housing, production or retailing (Neutze 1977).

The processes of urban restructuring have been widely discussed (e.g. Johnson 1974; Kain 1975). These factors have been paralleled, but not always duplicated, in the processes influencing locational change in Sydney's wholesaling industry. Discussions with hardware wholesalers generally point to the growing unattractiveness of central locations, first because of the increasing difficulty of operating in an inner city environment and, second, because a range of economic, organisational

Table 7.3   The locations in 1965 and 1977 of 51 hardware wholesalers surviving in Sydney in 1977[a]

|  | 1977 location | | | | |
|---|---|---|---|---|---|
| 1965 Location | Wholesaling district | Rest of inner metropolitan area | Geographical centre | Rest of metropolitan area | Total (1965) |
| Wholesaling district | 2 | 11 | 2 | 0 | 15 |
| Rest of inner metropolitan area | 0 | 10 | 4 | 3 | 17 |
| Geographical centre | 0 | 0 | 0 | 3 | 3 |
| Rest of metropolitan area | 0 | 0 | 2 | 14 | 16 |
| Total (1977) | 2 | 21 | 8 | 20 | 51 |

*Note:* [a] Zonal boundaries are shown in Figure 7.2
*Source:* Nugent (1977)

and technological changes have weakened their ties with the CBD, so facilitating dispersal. The latter permissive factors are discussed later but collectively they mean that the wholesaling district is no longer necessary for the successful operation of wholesaling firms. The former 'push' factors and the growing unsuitability of an inner city location are reflected in the responses (in rank order of importance) of the 13 firms leaving the wholesale district between 1965 and 1977. When questioned (by Nugent 1977) about their reasons for departure, they referred to:

(i)   lack of premises of sufficient size;
(ii)  access for trucks difficult because of narrow streets and traffic congestion;
(iii) rates and rents too high;
(iv)  parking difficult and costly for staff and customers;
(v)   buildings unsuitable for modern materials handling and distribution; and
(vi)  problems of attracting staff from outer suburban areas.

With the exception of the final point, a problem faced by only a few firms, these responses reflect the costs of central locations associated with land, buildings, congestion and a generally outdated physical fabric increasingly unsuited to modern requirements.

Despite changing locational requirements, there is an important element of inertia reducing the rate of change in geographical patterns of economic activity. Firms often retain an old location long after the reasons for selecting it have ceased to be relevant. High disinvestment and movement costs added to disruptions to both supply and market linkages mean that relocation is often put off as long as possible, with firms tolerating poor locations for lengthy periods. The final stimulus to move is often lack of space for expansion; almost 60 per cent of relocating hardware firms cited this as the major factor in the decision to move. The growth of the firm is, then, the major catalyst of locational change in wholesaling in Sydney, as it is in other activities and other cities (Rimmer 1969; Daly and Webber 1973). However, lease termination and the imminent demolition of occupied property to make way for office blocks, car parks or distributor roads are important stimuli in some cases.

Once a decision to relocate has been made, what considerations influence the choice of destination? Discussion of these locational preferences is based on the answers of the 48 hardware wholesalers responding to requests to 'rank the factors ... most important for the location of a firm such as yours' (Nugent 1977).

*Availability of space*

The most important locational requirement appears to be the availability of suitable warehouse space at a reasonable price, a finding

which confirms the results of previous work on commerce and manufacturing (Neilson 1972; Daly and Webber 1973) and wholesaling
(Simons 1967:242). This is a corollary of the growth of the firm being
the major catalyst to movement: the concern is primarily to find
suitable premises at an acceptable price and only secondarily with
where they are located.

There is no indication that wholesalers are always able to obtain
cheaper warehouse space by dispersing from the inner area. One factor
here is competition with other wholesalers and light manufacturing for
sites away from the inner city; this is particularly important when taken
in conjunction with limitations on supply due to physical availability
and zoning of land (Cardew and Rich ch 6). A related consideration is
that because the CBD is off-centre, the geographical centre of the
metropolitan area may be particularly attractive, for example to firms
distributing to a metropolitan wide market. Perhaps the most
important determinant of both price and adequacy of premises is,
however, the age and nature of buildings and the physical structures
required as a result of the revolution in goods handling and transport
technology. Operating costs can be lowered more by using a modern
warehouse designed for efficient handling than by distributing from the
most accessible site (Vance 1970:134). Old premises in central areas
frequently have difficult access and are unsuited to modern handling
techniques, while land costs, congestion, small sites and building
regulations inhibit conversion or reconstruction to meet modern
requirements. Consequently, rents in Pyrmont and Ultimo are amongst
the lowest in the metropolitan area. Away from these areas and the old
wholesaling district, however, building design is generally suitable for
wholesaling and thus not a major influence on rents or on the locational
preferences of wholesalers.

*Market access*

Market linkages continue to be important considerations. Some
wholesalers in the inner city likewise see proximity to transport
terminals, such as Kingsford Smith airport, as advantageous in maintaining links with and distributing goods to non-metropolitan
customers. The locations providing market access and the nature of
links with customers have, however, changed significantly, so
encouraging the dispersal of wholesaling. First the spread of the
metropolitan area and decentralisation of retailing within it meant a
westward shift in the centre of gravity of the market, well away from the
wholesaling district. Some firms still in the inner metropolitan area feel
disadvantaged by their deteriorating market access, but insufficiently so
to justify immediate relocation. Second, locations to which customers
are easily attracted have declined in importance; a buyers' circuit

enabling comparison of goods before purchase is no longer required, so facilitating departure from the wholesaling district. Increasing use of branded goods and standardisation of many products means that merchandise can be ordered without inspection. Contact with distant customers has become easier with the improvement in telecommunications. Similarly, the specialisation of many wholesalers in a limited range of hardware goods helps develop a reputation, probably reduces the number of direct competitors and might well attract custom from more distant markets.

These changing spatial links with customers are reflected in the way in which goods are sold and distributed. The great majority of hardware wholesalers rely on travelling salesmen as their avenue of contact with customers. None of the firms sees customer visits to the warehouse as the main means of selling, while only one requires customers to collect their purchases. About half of the wholesalers have their own transport fleet, in some cases supplemented by the use of haulage contractors for exceptionally large, difficult or perimeter deliveries. For those with the turnover to justify it, this offers flexibility to adjust delivery schedules to suit the overall operation of the firm or meet the emergency needs of customers. Other firms, mainly the smaller ones, rely wholly on contract carriers for metropolitan deliveries. Within the built up area transport charges depend on the number, size and weight of packages but not on distance. For the haulier uniform rates are easier to administer. For the wholesaler the effect is to reduce the frictional effects of distance, so further reducing the need for a location highly accessible to the whole market.

## Proximity to manufacturers and suppliers

While forward linkages with customers remain an important consideration, backward linkages with manufacturers and other sources of supply are generally much less significant in wholesalers' order of locational priorities. Proximity to manufacturers in nearby industrial areas allows a few firms in the southern part of the inner metropolitan area to reduce inventory and warehouse costs by carrying smaller stocks; any savings may, however, be offset by the need for more trips between supplier and wholesaler and for more efficient operations to maintain services to customers (Gilmour 1974:321). For importers access to wharves is no longer important because goods are imported in containers which are transported to suburban depots, the main one being at Chullora near the geographical centre of the metropolitan area. From there rates for delivery of containers vary with distance, but few firms deal in quantities sufficient to fill a container; any advantages in proximity to container terminals are often lost because of long delays in breaking down container shipments and loading trucks.

*Labour*

Availability of labour has been cited as an influence on the location of manufacturing (Daly and Webber 1973) and offices (Alexander 1976b) in Sydney, but it seems to be of only minor importance to most hardware wholesalers. Certainly, labour is an important requirement for firms, but there are few problems of attracting adequate staff in most parts of the metropolitan area. Only firms in the geographical centre considered labour to be an important locational influence. One possible explanation is that those entrepreneurs particularly conscious of labour supply problems deliberately chose locations accessible to the large labour pool in the western suburbs. Alternatively, it could be that recent relocations made by most of them had demonstrated the desirability of choosing a new location acceptable to existing staff; disruptions to a firm's operations are minimised if staff turnover is small during relocation.

*CBD transactions*

Spatial links with other businesses have weakened: with the break up of the buyers' circuit, locations near competitors are no longer important, while external contacts have also declined because of the tendency of wholesalers to internalise more of the functions associated with the marketing process. The locational pull of the CBD has weakened too, but easy contact with certain centrally located activities, especially ancillary services, may still be significant when links can be maintained without too great a cost; this is particularly true of personal or informational contacts, but much less so of links involving the handling of goods. Wholesalers with significant importing activities may benefit particularly from proximity to the CBD, which allows easy access to the services provided by customs agents, shipping agents and banks handling international transactions; this is perhaps reflected in the presence of almost 60 per cent of Sydney's hardware wholesaler-importers in the inner metropolitan area.

As a consequence of these considerations, the biggest single concentration of firms is still in the inner metropolitan area, even though hardware wholesaling has almost disappeared from the wholesaling district. That this cannot be explained solely as an historical legacy is emphasised by the number of relocations *within* the inner metropolitan area (Figure 7.2): many firms seeking to avoid the costs and difficulties of operating in the wholesaling district have at the same time apparently tried to maintain locations within easy reach of the CBD. Others have sought to maintain CBD contacts in different ways. At least one firm built a large warehouse in the geographical centre but retained its head office in the CBD, so splitting its information and operational functions and giving each the kind of location required: face to face contacts can be maintained in the CBD while goods are handled efficiently and distributed from the centre of the metropolitan market.

*Non-economic criteria*

Non-economic factors, such as proximity to the owner-manager's house, can be important locational influences. Other personal factors can, on occasion, either stimulate or retard relocation by wholesalers. Generally, such issues arise only in the smallest firms, but in such cases they are often the dominant consideration. Many smaller firms do not approach the location decision with a great deal of rigour, often selecting the first site that seems acceptable (Townroe 1972:264; Lever 1974:316). Consequently, they may show less economic rationality in their locations than larger, more cost, revenue or profit conscious firms with greater ability and information at their disposal (White and Watts 1977:179). The implication is that the firm basing its decisions on economic criteria will show a greater propensity to survive, a conclusion supported by evidence on manufacturing firms in Brookvale (Logan 1968b:285). On the other hand, it is possible that some firms might survive financial returns unacceptable to more economically conscious enterprises by substituting greater non-monetary rewards.

## 7.5   Conclusion

Discussions of economic restructuring have most commonly focused upon changes in manufacturing. It is clear, though, that marketing in general and wholesaling in particular have undergone substantial and rapid organisational change over the last two decades. Equally significant have been the accompanying locational shifts. These changes and the processes involved have several implications for urban planning.

First, despite growth of direct trading and the declining role of specialist wholesalers, wholesaling functions, particularly warehousing, have not diminished in significance. Indeed, warehousing may even have become more important because of the rationalisation of manufacturing capacity during the 1970s (Cardew and Rich ch 6). In other words, restructuring of marketing and decline of specialist wholesalers has coincided with continued expansion of the warehousing function and associated demand for suitable premises.

Following from this, the high rate of locational change by wholesalers in the last two decades and the equally rapid changes among the warehousing activities of manufacturing and retailing concerns have been important contributors to the physical development of the Sydney metropolitan area. Organisational changes in marketing, new handling and storage technology, growing dependence on road transport and distributional advantages of suburban locations have stimulated relocation, so that urban change and industrial property development have continued, even during the slow national economic growth of the 1970s. The growth of leasehold occupation of industrial property (Cardew and Rich ch 6) is likely to reduce locational inertia, further encouraging mobility and sustaining urban change in the 1980s.

Third, vertical integration in marketing means that traditional land use classifications are increasingly out of step with the structure of firms and may become difficult to sustain. Firms manufacturing and storing goods or those performing warehousing and retailing functions, for example, may resist land use zoning which distinguishes between these functions.

Finally, if desertion of the inner area by wholesalers has been stimulated by inadequate space and inappropriate buildings, then inner city councils seeking to retain their economic and employment bases would do well to revise their planning and building regulations to facilitate amalgamation of adjacent premises and modernisation to meet current requirements. But dispersal is not simply the product of push factors. Positive incentives may be required to offset the distributional, labour market and other advantages of suburban locations if firms are to be encouraged to remain in the inner city.

# 8 Retailing in Sydney

RICHARD V. CARDEW AND PETER L. SIMONS

## 8.1 Introduction

Retailing has undergone considerable change since the abolition of the vice-regal parking space outside Farmers' department store in Market Street, Sydney. In the early postwar years supermarkets and planned shopping centres were yet to be introduced. The CBD dominated the provision of comparison goods shopping until the mid 1950s; the down-town shopping trip was frequently a major family outing, often combined with a visit to the 'pictures' or, in somewhat less agreeable circumstances, with a trip to a Macquarie Street medical specialist. In contrast, suburban centres and corner stores stocked convenience items. The structure of retailing was relatively simple. Since then it has undergone considerable change, which in some ways has intensified in recent years. This paper examines the principal changes in a bid to explain the current pattern of retailing in Sydney.

Whilst many of the changes in retailing in Sydney have been common to metropolitan centres in Australia (Alexander and Dawson 1979) and North America (Berry 1967; Simmons 1966), there have also been significant differences. The sheer size of Sydney, its pattern of growth by envelopment of communities on railway routes linked to the suburban network, and lack of sites for free standing planned shopping centres has meant that established centres are commercially stronger and more numerous than in other cities.

Retailing is now suburbanised with regional centres, such as Chatswood and Bankstown, performing the role once the preserve of the CBD. For a while the large suburban centres threatened to overwhelm the retailing structure, but recently small centres and corner stores have made a partial comeback; specialty trading of various forms is a strengthening trend, and pedestrian malls are rejuvenating selected centres. Competition, once predominantly between stores within centres, is now more evident between centres, as rival retail corporations in association with retail property developers battle for market shares (Poulsen ch 9).

In the transition to modern retailing patterns, the concept of the supermarket has spread upwards to department stores via discount houses and the focus of retailing within centres has migrated backwards and forwards with new developments. There has been a certain levelling of retailing: all major stores in some way cater for the masses, the department stores by moving down market, the variety stores by moving up market. As in most competitive fields, aggressive, innovative and expansionary firms survive; those clinging to older concepts and family business structures have largely disappeared (SMH 15 Aug 1981). Finally, not only has the metropolitan pattern of retailing changed, but so too has the structure of centres and the layout within stores.

To understand these changes it is necessary to consider consumer trends as well as changes in distribution, marketing and retail property development. Since the 1940s, consumers have become more numerous and dispersed (Spearritt 1978), more affluent, discriminating and mobile. Dispersal of income has accompanied the dispersal of population, and disposable income has been high even in the relatively disadvantaged western suburbs of Sydney. Though real income has grown substantially faster than population, there has been a marked change in expenditure patterns: automobiles, household durables and housing have claimed an increasing share of expenditure at the expense of food, clothing, alcoholic beverages and tobacco (Australia. IAC 1977). Nevertheless, per capita spending on these latter items has increased in real terms.

The rapid postwar spread of car ownership has had a major effect on retailing. The car has provided consumers with greater mobility, so that most people are within 20 minutes driving time of several major centres. Consumers are able to select centres using criteria other than distance; such factors as price, quality, variety and service are of increasing importance. Consumers are also able to shop less frequently by purchasing a wider range of merchandise in a single trip, and travel further to large centres to the detriment of smaller centres. Adequate parking and freedom from traffic congestion have become significant criteria for the success of shopping centres.

## 8.2    Changes in distribution and marketing

Throughout the postwar years, competitive processes have worked against the small, independent retailers in favour of large firms. Many of the changes have been associated with the practice of direct trading (the transfer of goods direct from manufacturer to retailer rather than through a wholesaler), so that to understand them some appreciation of the distribution sector is required (Nugent *et al.* ch 7). Independent retailers have had to adapt to these changes to survive and have been able to maintain a significant but more dependent place in the industry.

Direct trading expanded rapidly in the 1960s at about the same time as disposable income and consumer mobility accelerated. Use of direct channels of distribution enabled large retailers and chain stores to offer significantly lower prices as smaller retailers, especially in very low order centres, experienced the effects of increasing mobility, more discriminating purchasing, and other changes in shopping behaviour. Many smaller independent retailers were driven out of business while some smaller centres in older parts of the city suffered decline or eclipse.

Independent retailers responded to the changing circumstances in a number of ways. An approach adopted by small retailers handling a broad range of products was to become linked to a wholesaler also affected by direct trading. It was usual in these voluntary chains for the wholesaler to provide some combination of advice on store organisation and layout, accountancy, stock control, promotional material and advertising in return for an agreement by the retailer to buy all or most of his mechandise from the wholesaler. This new form of linkage allowed the self-service wholesalers and the independent retailers to counter the economies inherent in direct trading with economies of their own. The wholesaler could supply the retailer with goods at lower prices; hence the retailer could reduce investment in stock and pass on to customers the periodic 'specials' offered by the wholesaler. In Sydney, voluntary chains were first organised in grocery trading (e.g. Four Square stores) and spread to electrical goods (e.g. Retravision, with 38 Sydney stores in 1981), hardware (e.g. Mitre 10, with 38 stores) and other goods (e.g. Tyrepower).

A second strategy, usually of specialist retailers, was to locate in larger centres and offer a complete range of sizes and styles. The archetypal example is the boutique but other examples include gift shops, specialty food and import shops. These stores could compete effectively because they handled distinctive merchandise and/or very limited varieties of goods which were sold by staff who (presumably) had a better knowledge of the items they sold. Several of the more successful of these retailers — including Just Jeans, Katies, Best and Less, and Toyworld — later developed chains of stores.

The essence of both strategies lay in the ability of small, independent retailers to accept lower profit margins because their overheads were usually lower than those of larger stores. Further, despite direct trading, small retailers were able to compete with larger corporations as long as they emphasised either competition on the basis of convenience, where spatial monopoly (Chamberlin 1956:62-65) and longer trading hours were key factors, or market segmentation (Crane 1967; Frank 1967), where specialised goods, a better range and more knowledge of the product were important. In some cases, such as the string street centre along Military Road from Spit Junction to Neutral Bay, shops moved up market by supplying such goods as antiques, luxury cars and clothes for the high status surrounding suburbs. In other cases, lower rents attracted new functions (such as secondhand book stores and pet parlours) to replace those that were unable to survive in marginal locations on the fringe of oversized centres (e.g. Eastwood) or centres whose location for general purposes became obsolete (e.g. Concord West).

Important changes in the method of operation of large retail organisations affected the types of stores in Sydney and the form of competition between them. Many of these effects are directly attributable to the introduction of new technology which became possible as a result of scale economies in direct trading. However, higher consumer incomes and greater mobility also played a role. The most obvious and widespread example of a change in the method of store operation was the introduction of self service. In its supermarket format this was intended to recreate the old village market and improve employee productivity through increased capital investment. It incorporates a sophisticated presentation of goods based on analysis of consumer psychology. The success of the concept is indicated by its introduction to discount department stores, such as K mart, Target and Venture stores.

These particular stores are also probably the best examples of a change in the type of store resulting from direct trading. Not surprisingly, the first discount stores (the defunct Sydney-Wide chain is a good example) sold the electrical goods of only a few manufacturers; wholesalers' and retailers' margins were traditionally high for these goods. Retail prices were low, partly as a result of direct trading and partly because only minimal warranties and aftersales service were available. However, sales volumes were high and eventually proved irresistible to the remaining electrical manufacturers and, in time, to manufacturers of other household goods. As a reaction, large department stores, the traditional outlets for these goods, also began to buy direct, thereby lowering prices, but continued to offer service. Gradually the larger discount houses extended their services by improving showrooms, offering credit and making deliveries and other services available. The result has been that large discount stores selling electrical and household goods acquired modes of operation similar to those of department stores.

In the meantime, department stores were also facing a challenge from large supermarket chains, particularly Coles and Woolworths. The latter had expanded their businesses from a chain of variety stores into supermarkets and then discount department stores (Big W). Coles followed a similar pattern by introducing K mart stores, initially in a joint venture with the American chain of the same name. Myer and David Jones, two of the larger department store chains, reacted by opening Target and Venture stores respectively. In contrast, Grace

Bros. retained the department store format and, through a combination of early selection of prime sites in the suburbs and a merchandising policy which emphasised value for money more than simply quality, anticipated changing consumer locations and purchasing characteristics.

The success of discount store operations has put pressure on the department stores and has led to a rationalisation of their operations. Most department store groups have recorded drops in profits recently, while both David Jones and Waltons have succumbed to takeover bids. On the other hand, discount stores of one form or another have been highly profitable because they dominate sales of groceries, electrical goods and general household items, although for other goods, especially clothing, the highly specialised stores remain viable alternatives to supermarket based operations. Recently, however, increased competition in the discount area has severely reduced margins (by one third, on average, in the second half of the 1970s) and brought the failure of several companies, including National Investments (Sydney-Wide), Col Buchan Discounts, Costless Imports and Winns. There has also been

**Table 8.1   Numbers of selected types of retailing establishments in the Sydney metropolitan area, 1956/57 to 1973/74[a]**

| Type of business | 1956/57 | 1961/62 | 1968/69 | 1973/74 |
|---|---|---|---|---|
| Department stores | 30 | 40 | 61 | 61 |
| Supermarkets | b | b | 172 | 202 |
| Grocers, tobacconists | 5,301 | 5,042 | 4,938 | 3,799 |
| Butchers | 1,564 | 1,796 | 1,883 | 1,742 |
| Fruit, vegetables | 1,498 | 1,551 | 1,329 | 1,115 |
| Confectionery | 1,156 | 1,190 | 1,413 | 1,216 |
| Cakes, bread | 751 | 750 | 695 | 584 |
| Hotels, wine saloons | 742 | 709 | 736 | 732 |
| Furniture, floor coverings | 380 | 456 | 422 | 469 |
| Clothiers, drapers | 2,875 | 2,966 | 3,131 | 3,377 |
| Footwear | 357 | 425 | 436 | 450 |
| Appliances, music | 553 | 609 | 605 | 734 |
| Jewellers | 411 | 378 | 490 | 501 |
| Newsagents, books | 653 | 650 | 862 | 893 |
| Chemists | 952 | 1,197 | 1,459 | 1,386 |
| Sporting goods | 194 | 206 | 332 | 405 |
| Florists | 307 | 245 | 332 | 388 |
| Used motor vehicles | 227 | 301 | 491 | 509 |

*Note:* [a]Only selected types of retailing business are included because of changes in the classifications used at each Census, particularly between 1961/62 and 1968/69. Establishments included are those within the metropolitan area as defined at each Census; it is not possible to convert data to a consistent spatial basis.
[b]Not available
*Source:* Australia. Commonwealth Bureau of Census and Statistics, *Census of retail establishments* for years ending 30 June 1957,1962, 1969 and 1974

rationalisation and closure of small unprofitable stores by Coles, Woolworths and other groups (Australian Stock Exchange Journal 1979).

Other effects of direct trading and consumer trends on the composition and location of retailing are difficult to document though it is possible to obtain a general indication of the level of the changes. For example, the number of grocers, butchers, confectionery, fruit and vegetable and cake shops, has declined in the face of expansion of supermarkets (Table 8.1). The differing periods in which these declines have occurred for each commodity group reflects the sequence of expansion by supermarkets into new types of goods. The effects of expanding surplus income are identifiable in the increasing number of establishments (essentially discount and specialty goods stores) in all other categories (Table 8.1). There has been a substantial decline in the number of chemists between the last two censuses. Presumably, this is a result of supermarket competition (McDonald 1978), which has only partly been countered by the formation of chains, such as Chem-Mart, and diversification (by Soul Pattinson and others) from traditional pharmaceutical lines to include items such as toys, photographic equipment and jewellery.

## 8.3    Integrated shopping complexes and retail property development

One of the most visible postwar changes in retailing has been the development of planned shopping centres (Fiegel 1980). First introduced to Australia in Chadstone, Melbourne (Johnston and Rimmer 1967), they vary in size from neighbourhood to large regional centres. [There is some variation in terminology, as the industry sometimes refers to any planned developments within existing centres, regardless of size, as neighbourhood centres (Rydges 1979)]. Essentially, they are integrated shopping complexes in single ownership and management. Often, the initiative, location decision, size and store mix is undertaken by a property developer, such as Lend Lease or RDC Holdings, rather than a retailing firm. In other cases, retailers like Grace Bros. conceive, design and locate complexes, drawing in finance institutions and construction firms to complete the project.

The main characteristic of these centres is their integrated design. Store mix is carefully related to centre size and major tenants are normally located at both ends of the centre (Dawson 1979:290). The large pedestrian flows created by these stores are planned to maximise the trade of the smaller specialty shops and commercial offices (DJ's Properties 1972; Saddington 1974). These smaller occupants pay the highest rentals, a component of which is based on turnover. Considerable attention is paid to architecture and decor to make stores attractive and encourage movement throughout the complex. Entry is usually easily identified, but internal complexity, obscured exits and limited signposting of level and location, are deliberately intended to ensnare the shopper in a confusing world of tempting merchandise. Centre design has also to work under the constraint of major tenant requirements; for example, GJ Coles have store modules of approximately 6,000, 7,000 and 8,000 square metres with predesigned layouts to maximise returns.

The principal tenant of these complexes may be a department store, a discount department store or a grocery supermarket, depending on the size of the centre. Developers exhibit clear orders of preference for stores within the first two classifications. It is the task of the developer to attract the tenants and the first preferences may not always be realised, though a few developers manage to obtain the same principal tenant: for example, Leda Holdings built many centres with a Coles New World supermarket (Rydges 1979:163).

Subsidiary tenants are also important. Inappropriate tenant mix and poor relationship between management and tenants can result in poor trading by centres (Rydges 1981). Centre management regularly assess trading performance, appearance and operation of tenants. In well located centres there is no shortage of prospective tenants, though the onerous conditions of many leases has given rise to concern (Retail Traders Association Newsletters 1980, 1981). In general, the status and condition of subsidiary tenancies confirms the shift from competition between stores within a centre to competition between centres, in which the important criteria are location and type of principal tenant (Poulsen ch 9).

The owners of centres may not be the managers. In fact, there are three roles that non-retailers may perform: owner, head lessee and manager. The owner may be an institution (such as a superannuation fund), the head lessee a property developer who subleases to all tenants and pays the institution a net rent. In this way, the institution is freed from the outgoings and management traditionally associated with property investment and simply receives a regular return on investment. The appeal of this form of investment partly explains the massive flow of funds into various property sectors in the last two decades (Daly ch 2; Cardew and Rich ch 6). Management of the centre may be undertaken by contract without the property rights associated with a lease.

Since the early days of Benjamins at Top Ryde and Grace Bros. at Roselands, there has been a major change in the retail development industry. Firms whose initial purpose was primarily investment in retail real estate are divesting, and retailers are entering the property development field. During the 1960s and early 1970s, many companies entered the retailing field for investment and/or development purposes. Some, including Lend Lease and Stocks and Holdings, were major property corporations with diverse interests; others were more specialised, such as Westfield, which began as an investor solely in retail property. Now one of the largest in the retail field, with interests valued at $670 million in 1981, Westfield has undertaken a major reconstruction of the company in order to diversify. A heavy emphasis on freehold ownership has been replaced by head leases (valued at $274 million in 1981) and management agreements ($139 million in 1981), leaving only $187 million invested in freehold ownership (Westfield Holdings Ltd. 1981).

Among the retailers, David Jones entered the development field with DJ's Properties in 1972. Its objectives were to invest in strategically located regional shopping centres and city and inner city properties with above average growth or redevelopment potential (DJ's Properties 1972). These objectives covered options to purchase existing David Jones stores, presumably to free capital for expansion and modernisation of retailing operations and make David Jones less vulnerable to corporate raiders. However, the options were not exercised, and ultimately DJ's Properties was taken over by Adelaide Steamship Co. More recently, Myer has contemplated divestment of $120 million by sale and leaseback of some of its stores. The redeployment of this capital, possibly into other property, could generate an extra $15 to 20 million profit per annum (AFR 30 July 1981:52).

Property developers perform a major role in shaping the geography of retailing. In many instances sites for individual stores in established centres as well as planned shopping centres are first selected by developers who then search for tenants. With construction of the Warriewood centre in the Warringah peninsula, the large property development corporation Lend Lease completed its twenty-eighth regional centre. Another developer, Westfield Holdings Ltd, produced eight major complexes in Sydney, six of which included a department store.

Finding and consolidating suitable sites, obtaining approvals from various government authorities, and constructing complexes is a major undertaking. Bankstown Square involved the amalgamation of more than 100 properties, took a comparatively brief five years to plan and construct, and was valued at nearly $19 million in 1971 (Vandermark and Harrison 1972). These factors are important to the scale, location and viability of centres and are thus basic determinants of the spatial pattern of retailing. RDC Holdings took six years to reach agreement with Ku-ring-gai Council over major extensions to the St Ives shopping centre. The absence of vacancies within the centre and strong trading patterns indicated that expansion could have occurred earlier. Similarly, Stocks and Holdings was forced by Baulkham Hills Council to reduce the scale of its complex for Baulkham Hills, and the same fate befell GJ Coles proposal for Newtown (AFR 25 Sept 1981).

The problems of finding suitable sites for regional centres and ob-

taining local authority approvals is one of the main reasons why commercially strong string street centres are more common in Sydney than
in Melbourne or Brisbane. Established administrative and medical
services combined with good public transport connections have helped
to strengthen their position (Rydges 1978:118). They also appeal to
small owner occupant retailers. Pedestrianisation of parts of some of
these centres has also led to significant rejuvenation, for example at
Bankstown and Lane Cove (Hastings 1978; Royal Australian Institute of
Planners Journal 1981).

## 8.4 Trends in the distribution of retailing in Sydney

The early postwar pattern of retailing was dominated by the CBD with
large downtown department stores supplying comparison goods
(Wolfers 1980). Suburban centres were largely strip developments
supplying convenience goods and located along tram or bus routes or at
major rail-bus interchanges. It was not long before a ring of centres,
such as Burwood, Chatswood and Bondi Junction, emerged around the
city acting as interceptors to the CBD (Jones *et al.* 1979:8).

Centres were developed and expanded in the inner and middle
suburban zones to service the increasingly suburbanised population and
to provide parking facilities for car oriented shoppers. For example,
Grace Bros. expanded its Bondi Junction store in 1954, 1957 and 1962,
extending its floor area from 700 to 18,580 square metres. Woolworths
and Coles also expanded their stores nearby. These developments put
considerable pressure on smaller local retailers and created traffic
congestion problems between through traffic and shoppers seeking
parking space (Shiels 1979).

A somewhat similar situation has emerged in Chatswood, the location
of another Grace Bros. store. Chatswood grew very rapidly in the 1960s
and 1970s because of its function as a rail-bus interchange, access to the
North Shore market and the success of the Grace Bros. store. Rapid
development has brought growing traffic congestion, conflicts over the
siting of David Jones' proposed department store and questions about
whether excessive retail space has been provided (Poulsen ch 9).

There was progressive suburbanisation of new retail construction
until the mid 1970s. As the inner and middle zones became adequately
supplied, attention switched to the rapidly developing outer suburbs,
especially to the area beyond Parramatta. Faulkner (ch 14) outlines the
development and impact of the Macarthur business centre in Campbelltown. Most recently construction has entered a consolidation phase in
which additions have been made mostly to existing centres in the
established suburbs (such as Hurstville and Bondi Junction). Some of
these later developments are quite different from earlier centres in both

design and concept, partly as a result of location and site requirements, but mainly as a reaction to the increasing need to differentiate a centre from its competition. For example, the Macquarie Centre at North Ryde, opened in 1981, emphasises its function as a community facility, open seven days a week with ice skating and theatre facilities in addition to its shopping centre functions. Another example of this trend is Birkenhead Point: this is also open every day to cater for convenience plus low order comparison goods shopping and for tourists who are attracted to its various museums and other entertainments (Spicer 1980). It is able to do this because most of its stores are small enough to avoid employing unionised labour. However, it has not traded well and a recent purchaser has plans for further developments (Chong 1981).

As a result of these trends, retailing has suburbanised rapidly. The City of Sydney's share of metropolitan retail sales fell from 52.2 to 29.3 per cent between 1949 to 1962, and (within smaller LGA boundaries) from 18.8 to 13.6 per cent between 1969 and 1974. Virtually all suburban LGAs increased their share of sales with, for example, Warringah rising from 0.7 to 3.3 per cent between 1949 and 1974. Another indicator is the changing balance between proportions of retail sales and of resident population across the metropolitan area (Table 8.2). The resulting sales/population index for the City of Sydney fell throughout the 1949 to 1974 period. In middle distance suburbs largely developed before the Second World War, index values were maintained or increased up to 1969 but usually declined subsequently as their trade was increasingly intercepted by newer, larger shopping centres further out. The outer LGAs all moved consistently towards balance between sales and population throughout the period. Even after allowing for escape spending across LGA boundaries and for varying socioeconomic status, it is apparent that retailing activity was more evenly distributed across Sydney in the mid 1970s than it had been in the late 1940s: after being heavily concentrated in the centre, retailing had suburbanised more rapidly than but not as far as population.

Though there has been a dramatic decline in the percentage of Sydney's retail sales in the CBD, the rate of decline has been moderated by sales to office workers. Retail expenditure of city office workers accounts for between 40 and 50 per cent of the CBD's retail turnover (City of Sydney 1980). The relative decline of the CBD has also been arrested since the late 1970s by the success of prestige retail developments such as Centrepoint and the MLC Centre. Both these centres are in the heart of the main shopping section with large pedestrian flows and both have been designed to project an exciting image aimed at attracting affluent, quality conscious and modish shoppers.

The end result of all of these trends is the spatial pattern of retail centres depicted in Figure 8.1. By 1979 there was a reasonably regular hierarchy of centres throughout the metropolitan area but it was also possible to identify the stellar lobate pattern which has always been part of Sydney's urban development. The CBD still contained the largest single concentration of retail floorspace. Around it there was a ring of

**Table 8.2   Retail sales/population indices for local government areas in the Sydney metropolitan area, 1949 to 1974[a]**

| LGA[b] | 1949 | 1957 | 1962 | 1969 | 1974 |
|---|---|---|---|---|---|
| City of Sydney | 435 | 430 | 408 | 355[c] | 306[c] |
| Leichhardt | 62 | 78 | 87 | 109[c] | 109[c] |
| Marrickville | 62 | 79 | 84 | 102[c] | 99[c] |
| Botany | 50 | 60 | 71 | 100 | 92 |
| Woollahra | 60 | 75 | 84 | 126[c] | 141[c] |
| Waverley | 52 | 61 | 68 | 83 | 83 |
| Randwick | 42 | 54 | 59 | 59 | 61 |
| North Sydney | 68 | 97 | 114 | 120 | 111 |
| Drummoyne | 53 | 87 | 96 | 109 | 82 |
| Ashfield | 63 | 84 | 86 | 119 | 106 |
| Hunters Hill | 33 | 33 | 48 | 60 | 60 |
| Lane Cove | 33 | 46 | 56 | 60 | 60 |
| Mosman | 67 | 77 | 100 | 73 | 70 |
| Rockdale | 47 | 71 | 90 | 94 | 93 |
| Burwood | 90 | 120 | 129 | 150 | 173 |
| Canterbury | 44 | 56 | 69 | 89 | 94 |
| Willoughby | 48 | 67 | 109 | 140 | 189 |
| Concord | 41 | 64 | 69 | 80 | 56 |
| Strathfield | 43 | 54 | 91 | 140 | 100 |
| Manly | 85 | 94 | 100 | 93 | 79 |
| Kogarah | 46 | 53 | 59 | 72 | 81 |
| Hurstville | 100 | 97 | 116 | 96 | 96 |
| Ku-ring-gai | 40 | 47 | 53 | 60 | 63 |
| Ryde | 46 | 65 | 81 | 84 | 88 |
| Auburn | 64 | 88 | 111 | 139 | 175 |
| Bankstown | 41 | 48 | 67 | 80 | 95 |
| Parramatta | 97 | 112 | 122 | 129 | 115 |
| Baulkham Hills | 43 | 50 | 34 | 35 | 39 |
| Warringah | 32 | 45 | 62 | 77 | 81 |
| Hornsby | 47 | 45 | 50 | 59 | 72 |
| Holroyd | 44 | 50 | 65 | 70 | 79 |
| Fairfield | 38 | 50 | 60 | 61 | 73 |
| Sutherland | 38 | 47 | 64 | 68 | 78 |
| Liverpool | 50 | 69 | 91 | 83 | 114 |
| Blacktown | 33 | 40 | 41 | 50 | 65 |

*Notes:* [a] The index = [(percentage of metropolitan retail sales/percentage of metropolitan population) × 100]. The measure was first used by Beed (1964).
[b] LGAs are arranged in approximate order of increasing distance from the CBD. Only those LGAs lying within the metropolitan area throughout the period are included.
[c] On 1 August 1968 parts of the City of Sydney were transferred to Leichhardt, Marrickville and Woollahra, and the new Municipality of South Sydney was created. Approximate adjustments for the transfers have been made, while the new municipality remains combined with the City of Sydney in this table.
*Source:* As for Table 8.1, and Australia. Bureau of Census and Statistics, *Estimated population in local government areas,* 1949, 1957, 1962, 1969 and 1974

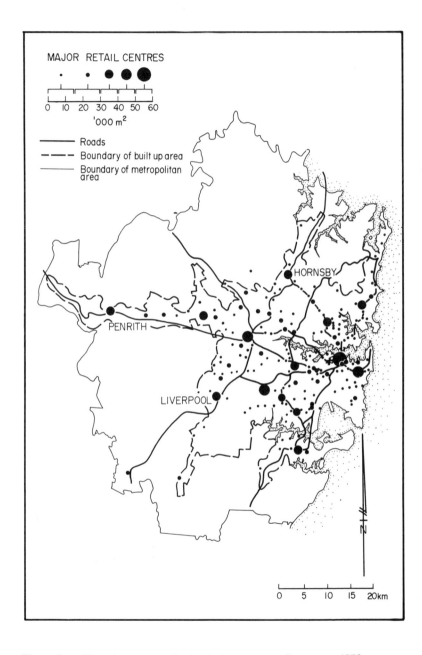

**Figure 8.1    Shopping centres in the Sydney metropolitan area, 1979**

large centres in LGAs with sales/population indices of over 100 (see Table 8.2), while smaller centres were arranged along the transport routes. Centres in the outer suburbs were either planned or had large planned components added to the originally unplanned centres located at transport junctions. In the older, inner suburbs, most centres were unplanned and tended to be strung along major roads or former tram routes so that they formed part of the radial pattern of ribbon development.

Retail development has not been confined to either established string street centres or planned shopping centres. The early discount department stores sought cheap locations either on the fringe of existing centres (for example, Sydney-Wide in the CBD and Eastwood) or by themselves on major transport routes (Keith Lord at Carlton and Ashfield). Discount furniture stores, some involved in direct trading, sought similar locations. Industrial zones mainly composed of small businesses, such as Brookvale, also attracted retail outlets. Permewan Half-Case warehouse secured an industrial site in Sutherland Shire, effected a change in zoning, and successfully operated a supermarket.

Important location changes have also occurred within shopping centres with successive increments of retail construction especially of the scale of integrated shopping complexes. In Burwood the main focus of retailing was taken from the south to the north side of the shopping area by Westfield's development. Subsequently, it has been counterbalanced by Burwood Plaza on the southern side of the railway line. Similar shifts have occurred in Parramatta, whilst the relocation of supermarkets have had similarly dramatic effects in smaller centres such as Beecroft.

## 8.5   Conclusions and future trends

The future may see a lessening of the pace of change. The major forces for change have brought rapid development to Sydney's retailing scene but their effects have almost worked through, as major businesses have gone into liquidation, rationalised their operations, or begun to scale down their investment in retail property development. The opportunity for major integrated shopping complex developments is limited, because of availability of sites and limited growth in consumer demand (Poulsen ch 9). It is unlikely that many new department stores will be opened in Sydney for some time (Jones *et al.* 1979). Most large developments will be discount department stores, supermarkets and a few hypermarkets.

Hypermarkets are one of the major innovations likely to emerge in retailing: the first is to be constructed at Mona Vale. Essential elements are the combining of grocery and variety supermarket functions under

one roof in a single level structure. It is in effect combining a Coles New
World supermarket with a K mart in a store of at least 12,000 square
metres. Until now variety and grocery functions have been kept separate
even in the training of staff. Hypermarkets are one stop shopping
facilities and capitalise on the trend for customers to move down market
in their purchase of clothing and small household items. At the same
time, there is a movement up market in the merchandise to be carried
by these stores and existing discount department stores. This is partly a
response to the reduced opportunities for continued expansion in the
number of stores (AFR 12 March 1981).

The down market trend in consumer demand is expected to favour no
frills merchandising, currently found in food lines. Minimal servicing,
low cost, and limited range of packaging and brand names are features
of this trend. Already present in supermarkets within existing centres, it
is also associated with retailing from warehouses in industrial zones.
Planning attitudes and practice in Sydney may restrict the latter type of
development more than in other cities.

Novelty, tourist and recreation based retailing centres such as Birkenhead and the Argyle Centre in The Rocks may become more significant.
These rely on the trend toward longer shopping hours and the
commercial strength of small specialist retailers. However, they are very
risky developments as Birkenhead has shown, so that much depends on
the trading pattern exhibited by these centres in the next few years.

Shopping from home, the promise of rapidly evolving communications technology, is still a distant prospect (Langdale ch 4). Cashless
shopping, the computerised transfer of charges to the customer's bank
account, is likely to precede the widespread use of videotex for ordering
and purchase of goods. However, purchasing from home may prove to
be just as tedious as the shopping trip for convenience items. And the
impact on level of expenditure freed from the enticements created by
store and strategically located non-essentials and 'specials', may cause
retailers to think harder about inducements to come to the store. These
changes though unlikely to be quickly implemented promise to be as
revolutionary as those during the past three decades.

# 9 Retail development
## Competition versus government control
MICHAEL POULSEN

## 9.1 Introduction

Retailing has undergone dramatic change in Sydney since the 1950s. The merchandising revolution has been accompanied by rapid suburbanisation of shopping facilities (Cardew and Simons ch 8). A most important change has been the development of large integrated shopping complexes, either as additions to established retail centres (such as the Westfield development at Burwood) or on new sites away from existing developments (for example, Roselands). These developments have led to the emergence of regional centres as a major feature of Sydney's retail pattern.

Proliferation of such centres was expected to slow in the 1970s, but instead the trend has continued almost unabated with new projects in both the growing fringe suburbs and older communities. The expansion was the product of a number of forces. One was expanding demand brought by increasing population, rising disposable income and the growing proportion of that income devoted to shopping (Simons ch 8). Increased sales were also generated by marketing strategies that on the one hand promoted rapid obsolescence of household goods and fashion changes in clothing while stimulating consumer desire for ever widening ranges of products, and on the other enabled the resulting demand to be satisfied. Another factor was intensified competition between large retailers attempting to capture a larger market share. This strategy placed great pressure on the viability of small businesses.

A third reason was that expansion programs created a treadmill effect: firms needed to continue growing to service borrowings made to finance earlier expansion. Perhaps more importantly, firms needed to maintain growth in order to sustain high profit/fixed asset ratios and adequate share prices; the alternative was to risk takeover and asset stripping.

The fourth factor was that some developers attempted to exploit the suboptimal location of certain shopping centres. For example, a large retailer might attack the market area of a suboptimally located or poorly designed competitor by building an attractive centre in a more accessible location. Conversely, the threat of a competitor adopting this strategy might result in defensive actions by the threatened firm, for example, by building an additional store on a more optimal site to protect its previous investment.

Fifth was the emergence of new concepts of retail centre design brought about by architectural developments and the resulting obsolescence of existing centres. Bigger, brighter and better remain key elements of shopping centre attractiveness, the single most important factor in marketing. In Sydney in the 1980s the 'mini city' and the 'hypermarket' are new concepts, their appeal resulting from advanced architectural designs and new building materials.

Finally, retail development provided an outlet for large scale investment by major non-retailing companies and institutions, principally insurance companies, superannuation funds and overseas investors. With the collapse of the office and residential sectors of the property market in 1973 and 1974, domestic and overseas investors turned with renewed vigour to retailing and later to the industrial sector, so encouraging continued expansion of major retail centres (Daly ch 2).

Rapid growth of major regional centres has raised important questions about the nature and role of the planning system. For example, to what extent can and should planners intervene to regulate large retail developments? How can the planning system be structured and what techniques can be used to ensure that the public, and not just powerful firms, benefit from new retail development? These are the primary issues addressed in this chapter. The next section outlines some of the problems raised for planners, while the appropriate role for planning and a desirable structure for the planning system are discussed in section 9.3. This is followed by an outline of one technique that could be used to guide planning decisions about retail development (section 9.4) and a brief review of the results of applying it (section 9.5).

## 9.2    The planner's dilemma

Rapid expansion of major retailing centres has led to considerable opposition from several groups. For some, expansion has been excessive and represents a waste of resources (Blake 1976; Gruen 1978). In many cases, the public has benefited from improved retail provision with lower prices and increased choice, but in others it has suffered from additional traffic congestion and noise, as well as from the decline of lower order shopping centres whose viability has been undermined. Traditionally, most opposition has come from small entrepreneurs whose livelihood was threatened by large scale development. Opposition has also come from other major retailers whose existing stores may be less profitable because of new developments. However, opposition has escalated with retailing becoming an issue of growing concern to local councils, chambers of commerce and the public, often with planners caught in the middle. Yet, a large modern retailing complex often has great appeal to customers. It provides a more pleasant and exciting place to shop. When combined with community facilities, such as cinemas, bars or ice rink, it can no longer be seen simply as a shopping centre. Proposals to develop new retail centres thus put local governments in a difficult position.

Planners have been posed a dilemma: what should be the extent of their control over retail development, both in total and with respect to the location of individual projects? The dilemma strikes at the roots of the philosophy of planning inherited from Britain, that it is government which should determine how much and where retailing occurs. In Australia retailing is conducted in a mixed economy, an imperfect market regulated by government whose regulatory activity itself may contribute to the degree of imperfection. However, many planners following British tradition adopt the attitude that it is government that should determine the quantity and location of retail development. They have, in a number of cases, protected existing shopowners and refused to accept the view that the market might drive out the less efficient stores and centres and produce better retail facilities in terms of goods, prices and environments. They have consistently refused to face up to the issue of retailing obsolescence.

There are reasons for supporting greater control by planners: investment in new development is often on a very large scale and the impact on existing retailers can be catastrophic. Developers are unlikely to take account of the effect of their decisions on secondary retailers; thus the fortunes of these firms are not so much governed by direct competition for particular lines or retail sectors, but by competition from the leading retailers.

Moreover, land use zoning and the planning process offer a form of protection to retail developers who succeed in obtaining rezoning or development approval, since the odds are that the planning authority will resist granting further approvals for potential competitors within their immediate environs. The initial firm thus secures a dominant position in the retail trade area before it builds the centre, a far cheaper and less risky approach than in freer market conditions.

Thus the planner's dilemma has an ironic twist. Not only are many planners unclear about the appropriate degree of control, but the very system they operate exacerbates the problems they face. Moreover, the solution does not lie simply in a choice between a command and a market economy. The retail sector cannot be divorced from other sectors of the economy. The task is to find the balance where the imperfections and monopolistic elements of the market are minimised, a basic reason for government involvement in the marketplace (Neutze 1978). Because of the lumpiness of the investment, the indiscriminate impact of new developments on secondary retailers, and the investment driven demand, there is a case for government involvement.

## 9.3   The planning role in retail development

Planners then are faced with the problem of establishing some means of assessing the impact of new retail developments as well as determining the policies and criteria that will govern their regulatory activity. The problems are complex and formidable, sufficient to lead to some very ambitious proposals such as the recent one by Golledge (1979) for the Victorian Town and Country Planning Board. Though hardly feasible, it illustrates the nature of the problems and provides a means of identifying some of the difficulties in implementing consistent policies and procedures.

Golledge proposed that planning be split into land use sectors of which one would focus exclusively on retailing. A tight, hierarchically structured chain of decision making would link the levels of planning in each state. In essence, a state retailing policy would be passed down to regional planning authorities who would implement the relevant regional objectives and in turn pass on to local government the responsibility for local details. Decision making would be governed by a set of clearly established procedures and technical manuals prepared and monitored by committees and a research program. To be effective the system would require complete implementation.

It is doubtful if Golledge's system could be adopted in other than a command economy. However, recently amended planning legislation in NSW has a number of similarities with Golledge's approach. A three tiered structure of plans has been introduced. whereas previously there was only one statutory form — the planning scheme devised individually for each LGA and amended from time to time by Interim Development Order and, rarely, a Varying Scheme. A few regional plans, for example the Sydney Region Outline Plan, existed but had no statutory force.

The Environmental Planning and Assessment Act 1979 provides for state, regional and local environmental plans, as well as Section 117 directives which may be similar in form to state or regional plans (NSW 1979). In addition, various new provisions widen the scope of planning instruments: state and regional environmental plans may take the form of policy statements instead of or as well as cartographic forms; the aims and objectives of environmental plans must be made explicit; social and economic factors must be taken into account in determining development applications and, by implication, in preparing environmental plans; and land uses deemed designated developments require an environmental impact statement. In sum, the new Act removes planning from the confines of the local authority land use zoning scheme, which was often devised without consistent, explicit objectives or with little cognisance of urban development processes.

Nevertheless, whilst the legislation introduced two new tiers of plans with statutory force, its purpose was also to encourage devolution of authority to local government and to turn the Department of Environment and Planning's emphasis to matters of state and regional significance. It had tended to ignore the latter under the weight of local matters referred to it by local authorities either on request, through lack of planning staff, or simply through unwillingness to make locally controversial decisions. Ironically, this intention of the legislation has been regarded by some with scepticism, mainly because of the powers given to the Minister for Planning and Environment. Nevertheless, the Act gives more power to local authorities than envisaged in Golledge's scheme.

In the absence of regional or state environmental plans incorporating specific objectives relating to retailing, this land use sector is presently subject to a series of local environmental plans, mostly prepared by local authorities. All the current statutory planning schemes prepared under the previous legislation have been deemed statutory environmental planning instruments. Hence there are numerous plans, more than there are local councils. In addition, the new legislation makes it easier to amend existing schemes.

Apart from loose alliances of some councils, the impact of retail development proposed in one LGA on shopping centres in another LGA is usually not given much attention by the determining local authority, unless of course it is to that authority's advantage. The level of cooperation between councils is increasing, but it is usually conducted in the absence of comprehensive, metropolitan wide policies. Similarly there is a lack of techniques for assessing impacts, relevant expertise and even facilities for employing the techniques.

A starting point in the planning process is the development of assessment techniques to examine the impact of new centres as well as the efficiency and level of retailing service offered by the existing system. In effect, this is part of the technical manual and procedures of Golledge's system. A further reason for the establishment of procedures (including means of technical analysis) is the problems currently faced in litigation. Lack of a set of acceptable procedures facilitates the practice of countering one expert with another. The problem is worsened by the tendency of the courts to favour the rights and freedom of individual developers. They work from the legitimate basis that retailing is a competitive business and are careful not to establish an unworkable precedent.

The remainder of this paper outlines a modelling procedure for assessing the level of service in present regional retail centres and the impact of new and proposed developments. It demonstrates that analytical procedures with even fairly simple assumptions and incomplete data sets can provide a useful basis for assessing the retail system.

## 9.4   A basis for assessment

A model for assessing the impact of new retail developments is just one of a range of technical procedures that could be established. Similarly, there is a range of models to choose from; the sequential allocation approach adopted allocates centres in an incremental manner, taking into account the existing distribution of centres. Such an approach facilitates comparisons between optimal and actual retail distributions.

Use of mathematical models in planning has generated considerable debate and disenchantment (Chait 1978; Mackett 1977). They have been used extensively in planning retail facilities, particularly by developers in providing a basis for shopping centre location decisions. The models provide a means of interpreting large and complex data sets and of formalising assessment procedures of planners. However, their value is governed by their sensitivity to changes in assumptions and parameters as well as by the quality of data used.

A complete modelling approach to the allocation of retail space would consider all levels in the retailing hierarchy simultaneously. The model described here is incomplete in that it examines one level of the hierarchy, namely, regional centres. Clearly, there are important interdependencies between the various levels; however, this approach represents a first step in the development of a more general model.

Data needed as input for the model include a demand surface of consumers by residential location, a threshold for the viability of a regional shopping centre and a range or distance from the centre within which a proportion of the consumers will shop at the centre if it is established. The model begins by identifying the most likely supply point for the initial centre, assessing its viability given the threshold, removing the satisfied demand from the demand surface and giving the centre the retailing characteristics appropriate to satisfaction of that demand. It repeats this procedure until it is no longer possible to establish an additional centre. The remaining demand is then distributed to the established centres using a retail interaction model and the size and retailing characteristics of each centre adjusted, where necessary, to match the demand (Figure 9.1).

The model locates centres in a sequential manner. It does not assume, as does the more conventional location-allocation model, that there is an instant supply of centres for the whole region (Scott 1970). The sequential allocation model described here is preferable since it more accurately reflects the sequential nature of development decisions. While firms such as Grace Bros. may have an overall plan for building stores, the general approach is to build one at a time and adjust the overall plan to variations in consumer demand and competitors' strategies.

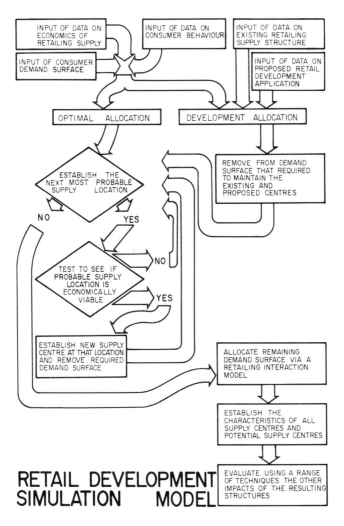

**Figure 9.1  Structure of the sequential allocation simulation model of retail development**

The model can also be used to simulate the existing retail structure by entering the details of established centres. The demand necessary to satisfy their thresholds can be calculated and removed to identify locations of potential new centres; the steps are the same as those used to establish the first set. For example, if the model were used in assessing the impact of a new retailing centre of 50,000 square metres, it would first be used to simulate the existing pattern. Introduction of the new centre could then be assessed in terms of its impact on existing centres and the extent to which it took the pattern toward or away from the desired pattern which would have been derived from the regional environmental plan.

To demonstrate the uses of the model a limited version is applied to the following issues: identification of suboptimal sites that might be exploited by large scale retail development; identification of acceptable locations for new developments; and assessment of recently constructed projects to determine whether their development was for the purpose of competition with existing centres, rather than the provision of a facility in areas of relative consumer disadvantage.

The demand surface for the Sydney metropolitan area used for this model is a grid of 3,054 cells and the supply surface a grid of 458 cells, each of which is a potential location for a retail centre (Figure 9.2).

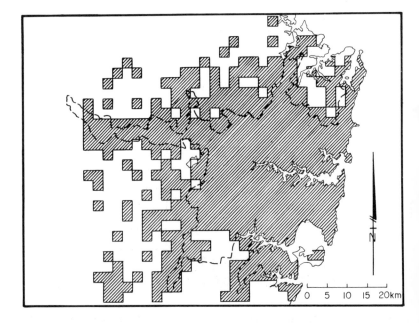

**Figure 9.2    Areas used in the simulation model of retail development**

Consumer travel is not directionally constrained and straight line distances are used. Both decisions are acceptable for this preliminary exercise, but would have to be modified if the model were to be used for planning purposes. The model is applied to the location of regional centres rather than to the entire retailing hierarchy.

## 9.5    Results of the model

The model optimally allocated 19 major retailing centres to satisfy consumer demand and meet the thresholds necessary for viability of the centres. This is two more than the 17 existing in January 1980 and suggests that there was some scope for new development. Of more interest is a comparison of the optimal versus actual locations (Figure 9.3), as it reveals the problem of site obsolescence and competitive strategies of retailers. In comparing these locations three features stand out.

First, and perhaps most strikingly, is that no centre close to the CBD was computed in the optimal set of 19. Consumers around the CBD would be served by centres on the Lower North Shore and in the Kingsford area. While this finding is partly a product of the crude

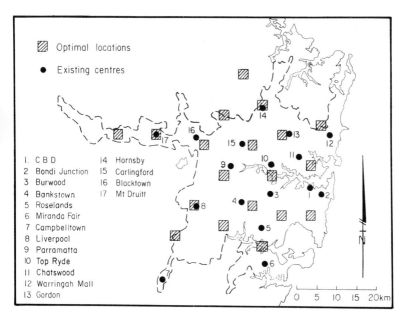

**Figure 9.3    Simulation 1: comparison of the optimal and existing locations of major retail centres**

assumptions relating to travel behaviour and neglect of the purchasing power of the CBD workforce, it nevertheless shows that the CBD is vulnerable to competitive development strategies in these two areas. Similarly, no optimally located centre was computed for Bondi Junction, the better site being Kingsford, so that Bondi Junction is also vulnerable to competition from the Kingsford area.

With the exception of these two major differences and Campbelltown, which was a state government sponsored development (Faulkner ch 14), the second feature of the simulation is the close proximity between many of the optimal locations and existing centres. Yet at a more detailed scale there are sufficiently large differences to see where developers might find possibilities for alternative sites which could capture trade from existing centres and undermine their viability. Chatswood on the North Shore could be challenged by a new complex at St Leonards or Crows Nest; Warringah Mall at Brookvale appears to be located too far south and east for an optimal location and could be affected by a large centre at Frenchs Forest. Similarly, Parramatta could be challenged from a site in the Granville area, Roselands from Hurstville, and Miranda from Jannali. The existence of two major centres, Top Ryde and Burwood, with only one optimal location midway between them, suggests their viability could also be threatened by a new development. Overall then, this simulation suggests that there are many opportunities for developers and retailers to exploit the suboptimality of existing locations by building major complexes in new locations.

A third feature of this simulation is the computation of centres having no direct association with existing major centres. Besides two outside the metropolitan area, these locations are Castle Hill and Penrith both toward the fringe of the metropolitan area, and Kingsford to the south east of the CBD. It will probably only be a matter of time before major department stores locate at these centres in new complexes, whilst the Kingsford location is being approximated by Grace Bros.' development at Maroubra.

This sequentially optimal distribution of 19 centres is not ideal for all consumers. If more than 15 minutes travel time to a major retailing centre is used as a criterion of relative disadvantage, then partly because of the shape of the metropolis, there are several areas that may be so described (Figure 9.4), in particular the inner city, northern areas of the eastern suburbs and the northern beaches. Two of these are peninsulas where the population is not sufficient to create the threshold of viability for additional developments.

*Opportunities for net retail expansion*

As the first simulation of 19 sequentially optimal locations showed,

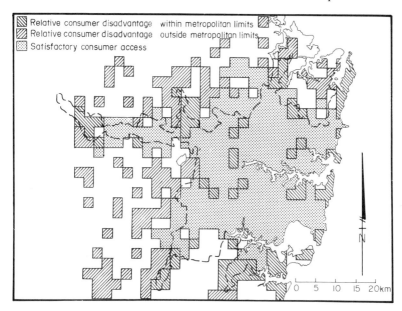

**Figure 9.4   Simulation 1: areas of relative consumer disadvantage**

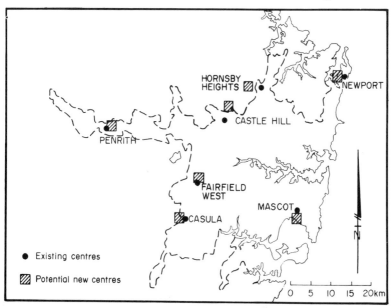

**Figure 9.5   Simulation 2: potential sites for major retail developments**

there is room for retail expansion. If the model is used to simulate the 17
centres existing in January 1980 and allocate consumer demand to them
on the same criteria as used in the first run, the results suggest that seven
further centres could be added without significantly affecting the
viability of the existing 17 (Figure 9.5).

The location of the seven additional centres approximates the
location of existing smaller centres at Hornsby Heights, Newport, Castle
Hill, Penrith, Fairfield West, Casula and Mascot. With the exception of
Newport and Mascot, the seven are peripheral sites which emerged as a
result of residential expansion on the urban fringe. In respect of
Newport, the nature of urban expansion in the Manly-Warringah area
limits the ability of any one centre to dominate the entire peninsula;
with Warringah Mall serving the southern part of the peninsula,
Newport would be able to dominate the northern section, although the
Warriewood development would provide competition. For Mascot, the
suboptimal location of Bondi Junction appears to be the explanation.

As in the first simulation of 19 centres, these 24 do not allow all
consumers to be within 15 minutes travel time of a centre. The main
areas of relative disadvantage extend in a band across the north western
sector of the metropolitan area, the southern fringe of the Municipality
of Bankstown, and the Engadine-Heathcote-Menai area of Sutherland
(Figure 9.6).

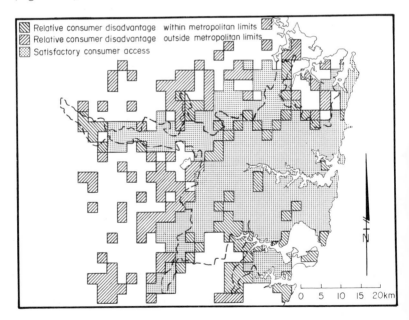

**Figure 9.6    Simulation 2: areas of relative consumer disadvantage**

*Recent development proposals*

There have been several new developments and proposals in recent years. This section assesses these developments (as at January 1980) in light of the simulations outlined above and demonstrates the value of these simulations in uncovering the motivations behind the developments. The proposals and developments selected are: Grace Bros.' program including the Macquarie Centre at North Ryde; new centres at Hornsby and Castle Hill; upgrading of Roselands; David Jones' development in association with the state government at Ambervale, Campbelltown; the Birkenhead Point complex; and Lend Lease's proposal for Warriewood in Warringah LGA. Finally, extension to the existing centres of Bondi Junction, Chatswood, Parramatta and the CBD are considered (Figure 9.7).

By comparing these developments with the second simulation of the existing 17 centres, only two appear warranted: the projects at Castle Hill and Hornsby. However, a further centre at Mt Druitt could be justified. Macquarie shopping centre at North Ryde has been built to compete with Myer stores at Gordon and Carlingford and to defend Grace Bros. stores at Chatswood and Top Ryde. Also, the development of Birkenhead Point is not warranted on the basis of relative consumer disadvantage. Apart from its unique character involving the recycling

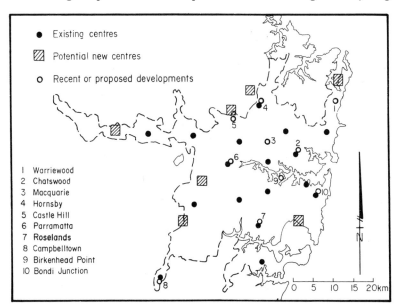

**Figure 9.7 Recent and proposed major retail developments in Sydney**

of industrial buildings, it appears to be an attempt to exploit the locational disadvantage of Top Ryde and Burwood in relation to the CBD. Grace Bros. appear the shrewdest in the competition for existing consumer demand. Their expansion at Maroubra, near the Kingsford site identified in both simulations, had by 1981 already become a major contributor to their profits (Grace Bros. 1981).

Expansion of Chatswood, Bondi Junction and probably Parramatta would appear to be a partly defensive strategy. The expansion is not supported by the model results, and so is most likely intended to maintain the strength of these centres by expanding and drawing some custom away from competing centres. The proposal for Warriewood also appears questionable. Although it is intended to be smaller than some of the other major centres, its location will have an important impact on the opportunities for future retail development. Even given further residential development in the Warriewood Valley, a site five kilometres further north, near Newport, would appear from the second simulation to be better for the majority of consumers. This interpretation has been subsequently reinforced by the initial profitability of Warriewood and by proposals for a major development at Frenchs Forest and the construction of Sydney's first hypermarket at Mona Vale.

## 9.5   Conclusion

The results of the model must be treated with some caution. As mentioned earlier, the travel behaviour assumptions are restrictive. More importantly, the model has examined only one level of the retail hierarchy. Expansion of regional shopping centres has an impact not only on other regional centres, but also on the viability of community and neighbourhood centres. Ideally, a more complete model would incorporate all levels of the retailing hierarchy: expansion in the number and size of regional centres would have an impact on the location and viability of other regional centres as well as on lower order centres.

However, the model has achieved its objectives. First it provides empirical evidence of the nature of competitive strategies of retailers and developers. Gruen's (1978) views, that retail development is no longer primarily oriented toward satisfying growth in consumer demand, but to fierce competition for existing demand in established areas with a possible consequence of over investment in retailing facilities, are shown to be applicable to Sydney.

Second, the model shows that a set of technical procedures can be developed to formalise assessment of retail development and provide a substantial aid to the planning system. The model can be used to develop regional environmental plans as well as assess the impact of particular developments. There are, of course, other factors that enter into planning decisions, including local environmental impacts, opportunities to recycle old buildings and create exciting urban environments, and linkages between retail developments and other land uses. However, any examination of large quantities of data such as is required to assess retail development, involves the use of a model of some kind. This paper has demonstrated the type of model offering most promise.

The establishment of assessment procedures, most likely using the type of model described here, is an essential step in planning, irrespective of one's stance in the debate over the degree of government control. It can serve as a basis for regional planning strategies, to be modified by other factors considered in dealing with specific applications. In identifying potential impacts of new developments, it can contribute to the form of government regulation, or at least identify the areas where planners might have to cope with commercial decline and the problems thereby generated.

## 10 Unemployment in metropolitan Sydney
## Spatial, social and temporal dimensions

IAN H. BURNLEY AND SUSANNE R. WALKER

### 10.1 Introduction

Unemployment has become a long term problem in Australia. The persistently high rate of unemployment since 1974 has evoked much discussion and has become a politically sensitive issue. Nevertheless, public concern has been dampened by national figures suggesting that, unlike the situation in the Great Depression of the 1930s, there has been only a low incidence of unemployment among heads of households. Instead, the burden has been borne by school leavers and inexperienced young adults. Concern for such groups has been reduced by the widespread view that individuals can be supported by their parents, a view which ignores the psychologically damaging effects of prolonged unemployment and the fact that many young unemployed do not live at home. In any case, arguing from national figures misses some vital features of the present situation. There are considerable spatial variations in characteristics of the unemployed and in the nature and severity of the unemployment problem. In some areas there are concentrations of unemployed adult breadwinners, while in others there are large numbers of school leavers with little prospect of finding jobs. This chapter first identifies the geographical patterns of unemployment in Sydney and changes in that pattern from boom (1971) to recession (1976). Secondly, it investigates the nature of unemployment in inner areas and explores its interrelation with other social problems.

Increasing unemployment has been largely a product of an expanding workforce, recession and structural change in manufacturing, and the inability of the tertiary sector to absorb all available labour (Rich ch 5). Manufacturing decline has been most severe in inner areas, often in labour intensive under capitalised industries which exploit a pool of low wage migrant labour, such as clothing production. In addition, inner areas have continued to lose manufacturing and warehousing as many surviving firms seek larger or more suitable premises in middle and outer suburbs (Cardew and Rich ch 6; Linge 1979b).

Some of the groups most vulnerable to changing demand for labour,

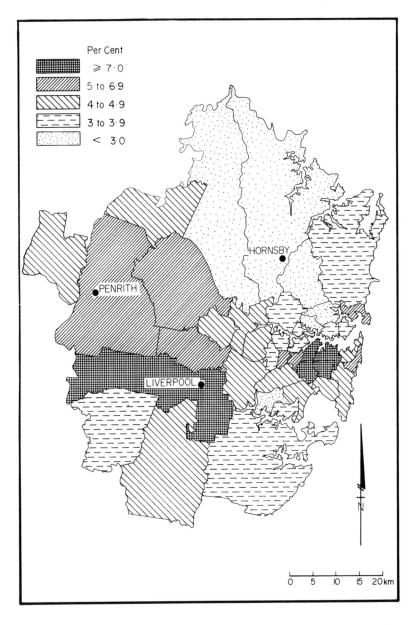

Figure 10.1   **Percentage of the male workforce unemployed by LGA in the Sydney metropolitan area, 1976**

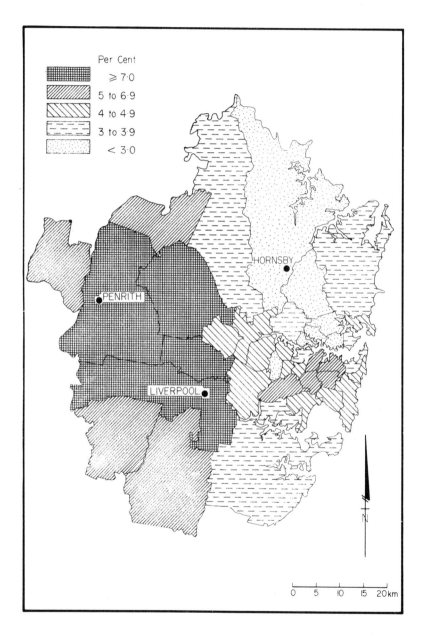

**Figure 10.2   Percentage of the female workforce unemployed by LGA in the Sydney metropolitan area, 1976**

especially the foreign born and less skilled, are heavily concentrated in the inner areas of Sydney. Rapid contraction of employment opportunities for such people has produced a marked increase in unemployment. The recession, coupled with economic restructuring and urban dispersal, has severely affected non-English speaking migrants, because of their concentration in the most affected industries and their disadvantages in respect of language, education and level of skill on arrival in Australia. Aside from unemployment, inner city people face higher incidences of mortality, suicide, depression, stress and some physical illnesses than people elsewhere in Sydney (Burnley 1977, 1978; Gibson 1979). To what extent are these problems related to unemployment? In a provocative discussion of unemployment in Australia, Windschuttle (1979) has established the familial, ideological, economic and political context of the recession and has argued that the various economic problems have led to marked increases in illness and stress. The second part of this chapter provides further evidence of these associations, but first the pattern is examined at metropolitan scale.

The chapter relies mainly on two sources of data. First the 1971 and 1976 Censuses are used to explore metropolitan patterns and associated population characteristics. Then a sample survey of mostly inner suburban areas is used to examine the nature of unemployment among population groups in these areas. It is also used to supplement Census data in the analysis of metropolitan patterns. The sample survey involved interviews of 2,590 immigrant and Australian born people in seven neighbourhoods of high migrant density: Leichhardt, Newtown, Redfern, Marrickville, Lakemba, Bossley Park and Bellevue Hill. The first five of these are low socioeconomic status inner areas and are the focus of discussion here. These neighbourhoods were chosen on the basis of dominant ·minority groups, using census collectors districts as sampling areas. Leichhardt was sampled to include Italians, Redfern to include Greeks and Lebanese, Newtown for Greeks and Yugoslavs, Marrickville for Greeks, and Lakemba for Lebanese. In each area, other persons from major immigrant source countries and Australian born were also present and appear in the analysis. Random sampling, with a sampling ratio of approximately one to four, was used to select interviewees. The response rate, after up to three visits, was over 90 per cent in all areas.

## 10.2    Patterns of unemployment in Sydney

The 1976 Census revealed marked variations in unemployment levels between Sydney's LGAs. Male unemployment rates varied from 1.8 and 2.1 per cent in the higher socioeconomic status LGAs of Ku-ring-gai and Baulkham Hills respectively, up to 8.0, 8.5 and 10.2 per cent in lower status inner LGAs of Marrickville, South Sydney and Sydney (Figure 10.1). Female unemployment rates were similarly very low across much of the northern part of Sydney, but in contrast to the pattern of male unemployment, highest rates were found in the outer western LGAs, particularly Blacktown, Fairfield, Liverpool and Penrith (Figure 10.2).

At the finer collectors district scale, male unemployment reached 12-15 per cent in Redfern (within South Sydney LGA), Newtown (in Marrickville), and Woolloomooloo (in Sydney) (Table 10.1). Given the occupational distribution of unemployment at the national level, it is almost certain that unemployment amongst manual workers reached 20 per cent in these areas. This is confirmed by sample survey data.

Census data indicate a close association between the percentage of the male labour force unemployed and the proportion of residents born overseas. Furthermore, male unemployment is higher in areas of Balkan or Levantine (Lebanese and Turkish) settlement than in areas of Italian immigration. The sample survey confirmed these relationships, both at the ecological level (Table 10.1) and amongst individuals (Table 10.2). On the other hand, the highest incidence of female unemployment is in areas where school leavers comprise a large proportion of the workforce and where jobs appropriate to them are in shortest supply.

*Relative change in unemployment, 1971-1976*

All areas of Sydney experienced marked increases in unemployment between 1971 and the recession year of 1976. The same broad pattern existed in both years: for example, in each case male unemployment rates were highest in Sydney and second in South Sydney. Nevertheless, there were some important changes in the relative standings of LGAs. Such changes can be measured by comparing each LGA's standardised unemployment score for 1971 and 1976. Standardising scores involves converting raw variables to a common form, with a mean of zero and a standard deviation of one (Norcliffe 1977:61-62); use of such scores permits direct comparison of the unemployment performance of each LGA relative to other LGAs in the metropolitan area in the two census years. To take one example, Marrickville increased its score from 0.83 to 1.83, or from seventh in 1971 to third highest level of male unemployment in 1976.

Three basic patterns of relative change in male unemployment stand out (Figure 10.3). First, there were marked increases in Blacktown, Liverpool and Holroyd in the outer western suburbs. Second, Marrickville, Ashfield and contiguous areas of the inner city also suffered substantial increases. Finally, increases were well below the metropolitan average in north shore suburbs, City of Sydney and a wide belt of central western suburbs. The relatively small increase in the City of

**Table 10.1   Unemployment in selected areas of Sydney**

| Locality LGA | Sample survey district | 1976 Census | | 1977/78 sample survey | | |
|---|---|---|---|---|---|---|
| | | Male unemployment in LGA (%) | Male unemployment in sample (%) | No. of unemployed household heads | No. of employed household heads | Unemployment rate among household heads (%) |
| South Sydney | Redfern | 8.5 | 12.4 | 26 | 185 | 12.3 |
| Leichhardt | Leichhardt | 7.2 | 8.0 | 16 | 159 | 9.1 |
| Marrickville | Newtown | 8.0 | 12.5 | 11 | 79 | 12.2 |
| | Marrickville | 8.0 | 6.0 | 19 | 95 | 16.7 |
| Canterbury | Lakemba | 4.9 | 5.4 | 23 | 102 | 18.4 |

*Source:* 1976 Census, unpublished tabulations
1977/78 sample survey

**Table 10.2  Birthplace of employed and unemployed people in sample survey areas**

| Birthplace | Household heads | | | Males | | Females | |
|---|---|---|---|---|---|---|---|
| | Unemployed | Employed | % unemployed | Unemployed | % unemployed | Unemployed | % unemployed |
| Italy | 7 | 75 | 8.5 | 7 | 8.2 | 3 | 6.8 |
| Greece | 15 | 121 | 11.0 | 20 | 14.1 | 8 | 9.9 |
| Yugoslavia | 9 | 34 | 20.9 | 7 | 15.9 | 8 | 34.8 |
| Lebanon | 28 | 99 | 22.0 | 30 | 22.7 | 9 | 25.0 |
| Britain | 2 | 28 | 6.7 | 2 | 7.7 | 2 | 10.0 |
| Other overseas | 19 | 114 | 14.3 | 16 | 13.4 | 10 | 15.3 |
| Australia | 15 | 149 | 9.1 | 19 | 10.0 | 11 | 7.8 |
| | $x^2 = 16.54$ | | | $x^2 = 13.99$ | | $x^2 = 20.54$ | |
| | df = 6 | | | df = 6 | | df = 6 | |
| | p = <.05 | | | p = <.05 | | p = <.01 | |

*Source*: 1977/78 sample survey

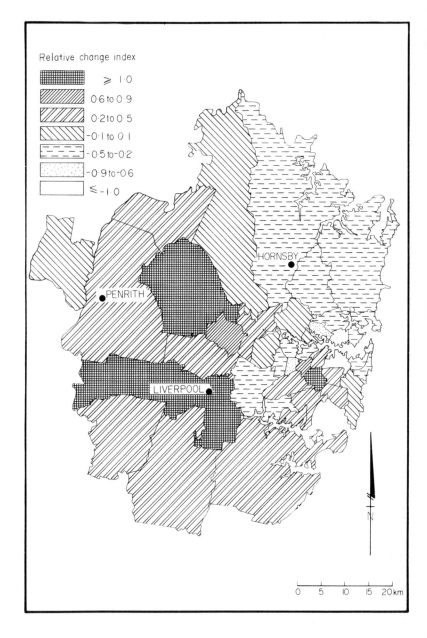

Figure 10.3   **Relative change in the percentage of the male workforce unemployed by LGA in the Sydney metropolitan area, 1971-1976**

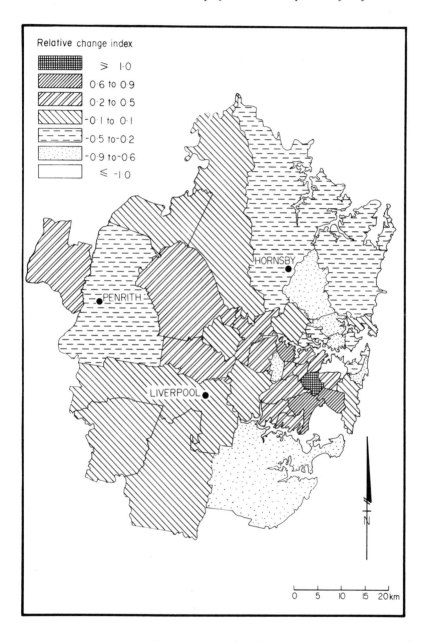

**Figure 10.4   Relative change in the percentage of the female workforce un-
employed by LGA in the Sydney metropolitan area, 1971-1976**

Sydney was more a product of especially high unemployment levels in 1971 than an enviable performance in 1976. The City has long had a high proportion of people living outside the normal social ties, including the homeless, particularly men, and those divorced or separated; many have few skills and so have been amongst the first to suffer as the job market tightened.

The largest relative increases in female unemployment between 1971 and 1976 were in the inner suburbs, centred on Marrickville, but extending into Botany and Rockdale (Figure 10.4). There were lesser but still substantial increases in adjacent areas and also in Blacktown, Fairfield and Blue Mountains.

### Socioeconomic associations and unemployment change

In the case of male unemployment the largest relative increases are associated with low socioeconomic status, coupled in the west with a high proportion of school leavers and, to a lesser extent, in the inner city with southern European and Levantine populations. More generally areas with high proportions of less skilled people became more vulnerable than hitherto during the first half of the 1970s.

To explore in more detail the relationship between unemployment and other socioeconomic characteristics, principal components analysis was performed using 1976 Census variables and statistics on unemployment and unemployment change. Principal components analysis groups

**Table 10.3    Variables used in principal components analysis**

| | |
|---|---|
| *Unemployment* | - percentage change in male unemployment |
| | - percentage change in the percentage unemployed |
| | - percentage unemployed in 1976 |
| *Socioeconomic status* | - percentage of males in managerial and professional occupations |
| | - percentage home owners or owner buyers |
| | - percentage of male residential workforce in production process and labouring occupations |
| | - percentage of male population aged 25 or more with university degree |
| *Industrial structure* | - ratio of manufacturing employees working in the area to those residing there |
| | - ratio of manufacturing establishments to the number of manufacturing employees |
| | - percentage of employees working in the clothing and textile industries |
| *Life cycle stage* | - child-woman ratio |
| | - percentage population increase, 1971-1976 |
| | - males aged 15-24 as a percentage of total male population |
| | - divorced or separated as a percentage of males over 15 |
| *Ethnicity* | - percentages of the male population in 1976 born in Australia, Greece, Italy and Yugoslavia |

variables most closely related to one another into major dimensions or factors (Smith 1977); in this case, it is used to show the major interrelations between unemployment and the other indicators selected. The latter included measures of both societal structure (socioeconomic status, familism and life cycle stage, and ethnicity) and of economic change (Table 10.3).

Unemployment indicators figure strongly in the two main factors derived (Table 10.4). Measures of change in unemployment were closely related (in factor 1) to concentrations of manual workers and young

**Table 10.4  Factors derived by principal components analysis**

| Factor | Major loadings[a] | % of variance accounted for[b] | Cumulative % of variance accounted for |
|---|---|---|---|
| 1 | Percentage change in male unemployment<br>Child-woman ratio<br>Percentage population increase, 1971–1976<br>Males aged 15-24 as percentage of all males<br>Percentage of male population born in Australia<br>Percentage of male residential workforce in production process and labouring occupations | 31.9 | 31.9 |
| 2 | Percentage of employees in clothing and textiles<br>Percentage of male population born in Greece<br>Percentage of male population born in Yugoslavia<br>Percentage of male residential workforce in production process and labouring occupations<br>Percentage of male workforce unemployed | 30.8 | 62.7 |
| 3 | Mean size of manufacturing establishments<br>Percentage of male residential workforce in production process and labouring occupations<br>Percentage of male population born in Italy<br>Ratio of manufacturing employees working in the area to those living there | 8.7 | 71.4 |

[a] Loadings represent the correlation coefficient between an initial variable and a derived factor; major loadings thus represent those variables most closely associated with a particular factor.
[b] The proportion of variance accounted for by a factor is a measure of the 'strength' of the factor, that is its ability to represent the variance underlying the original variables.

adults and to population growth. High scores on this factor were found in outer suburban LGAs (Figure 10.5), the areas of substantial unemployment increase and rapid population growth, with large numbers in the school leaving age group. Areas with large proportions of manual workers also experienced above average increases in unemployment, although this association was weaker than that between unemployment change and concentrations of young adults.

The second factor can be interpreted as indicating structural change in the economy and labour market in relation to ethnicity (Table 10.4). The percentage of male unemployment in 1976 was strongly associated with the percentages of Greek and Yugoslav born, the percentage of employees in textiles and clothing industries, and the concentration of manual workers. High absolute levels of unemployment were found in the inner city linked with certain immigrant concentrations and the presence of the economically marginal clothing and textile industries (Figure 10.6).

Three critical factors stand out in the geography of unemployment in Sydney. First, there were high relative increases in low status western suburbs with rapid population growth and high proportions of young children and young adults. The significance of this pattern in terms of the known high level of unemployment amongst school leavers is clear.

Second, higher absolute levels of unemployment in the inner city were associated with large proportions of Greeks, Yugoslav and Levantine settlers. These were areas with high proportions of manual workers, especially the unskilled. They also contained concentrations of heavy manufacturing industry, as well as clothing, footwear and textile production, some of which have experienced rapid decline.

Third, there has been a geographical polarisation of unemployment in Sydney. Relative increases in unemployment have been geneially small in the higher status northern suburbs and Woollahra, containing more highly skilled and educated persons. Relative increases have been much higher in the inner southern suburbs of working class migrants and Australian born. On the other hand, the unemployment differential between the inner city and outer areas was reduced (Vipond 1981).

## 10.3   Unemployment and social wellbeing in inner areas

The sample survey was intended to explore the associations suggested by the second of the factors derived by the principal components analysis. The survey was thus designed to measure the level of unemployment in inner areas, especially among immigrant groups, and identify the characteristics, such as age, education, language, length of residence, health and stress, closely associated with unemployment.

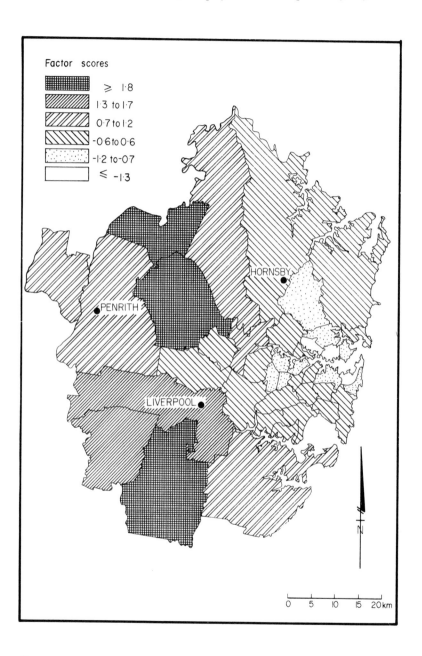

**Figure 10.5   LGA scores on factor 1**

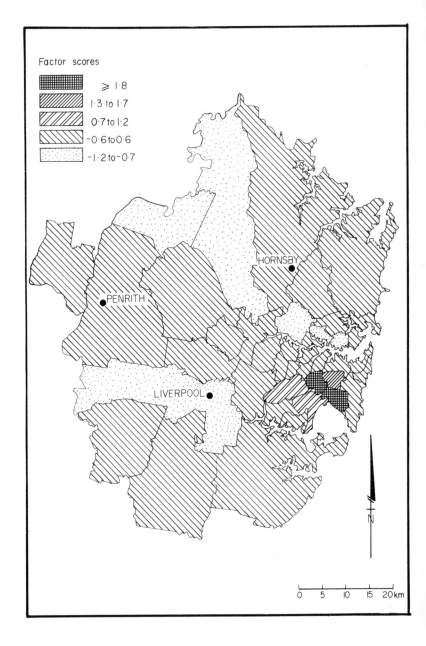

**Figure 10.6    LGA scores on factor 2**

The survey was conducted in 1977/78, during the depths of the recession. In some areas, including South Sydney, Leichhardt and Newtown, unemployment rates measured in the survey conformed closely with those registered for census tracts in the 1976 Census, even though national unemployment levels had risen considerably in the interim. In other areas, the survey showed a marked worsening of unemployment. For example, in Marrickville the much higher rates seem to be partly a product of the departure of employed people, while in Lakemba a substantial rise resulted from a large influx of Lebanese refugees.

Unemployment in these inner areas was well above the national average. This was true of almost all groups (Table 10.2), but unemployment was most severe amongst the Lebanese and was also high among the Greek and Yugoslav communities. As at the national level, there appears to be a strong ethnic dimension underlying unemployment in Sydney's inner areas. This is particularly true of household heads, with Greeks, Yugoslavs and Lebanese suffering very high levels of unemployment. Australian born heads of households also experienced twice the incidence of unemployment as the equivalent group in Australia as a whole.

## Occupation and education of the inner city unemployed

Occupational status was a significant element in inner city unemployment, as it was at the national level (Table 10.5). Amongst household heads, there was a marked difference between groups of differing degrees of skill. Unemployment was much higher among manual workers than white collar employees, while within the manual category it was highest among the semi-skilled and unskilled. Unemployment levels in the latter two groups were considerably above both the corresponding state levels and the state unemployment level in manufacturing. Thus, the high levels of unemployment in the inner city were not simply the result of the concentration there of semi-skilled and unskilled people nor the disproportionate concentration of some foreign born groups (particularly Lebanese, Yugoslavs and Greeks) in those occupations. After controlling for low occupational status, unemployment was still higher among Greek, Yugoslav and Lebanese born communities as well as the other foreign born (excluding British and Italians).

Level of education (measured by years of schooling) adds another dimension to inner city unemployment (Table 10.6). Male unemployment varied significantly with years of schooling; unemployment was much higher for men with only a few years at school. In contrast, no such variation was evident in female unemployment. Indeed, unemployment among women with seven to ten years schooling was higher

**Table 10.5   Occupation of employed and unemployed people in sample survey areas**

| Occupation | Household heads | | | Males | | Females | |
|---|---|---|---|---|---|---|---|
| | Unemployed | Employed | % unemployed | Unemployed | % unemployed | Unemployed | % unemployed |
| Professional and clerical | 7 | 129 | 5.1 | 6 | 4.8 | 3 | 2.3 |
| Skilled manual | 28 | 195 | 12.6 | 30 | 12.9 | 5 | 8.5 |
| Semi-skilled and unskilled manual | 55 | 295 | 15.7 | 61 | 16.7 | 27 | 13.6 |
| | $x^2 = 9.87$ df $= 2$ p $= <.01$ | | | $x^2 = 11.36$ df $= 2$ p $= <.01$ | | $x^2 = 12.05$ df $= 2$ p $= <.01$ | |

*Source:* 1977/78 sample survey

**Table 10.6 Education levels of employed and unemployed people in sample survey areas**

| Years of education | Males | | | Females | | |
|---|---|---|---|---|---|---|
| | Unemployed | Employed | % unemployed | Unemployed | Employed | % unemployed |
| 0 — 3.9 | 15 | 114 | 11.6 | 10 | 78 | 11.4 |
| 4 — 6.9 | 43 | 168 | 20.4 | 18 | 102 | 15.0 |
| 7 — 9.9 | 20 | 130 | 13.3 | 11 | 61 | 15.3 |
| 10 + | 23 | 218 | 9.5 | 12 | 113 | 9.6 |
| | $x^2 = 11.8$ | | | $x^2 = 2.24$ | | |
| | $df = 3$ | | | $df = 3$ | | |
| | $p = <.01$ | | | $p = >.05$ | | |

*Source:* 1977/78 sample survey

than among either males with equivalent education levels or women with fewer years at school. Far from women in the inner city contributing to general unemployment through high workforce participation rates and the taking of jobs formerly held by men, many moderately well educated women seeking jobs could not find them.

## Unemployment and length of residence

Among foreign born males, there was a weak inverse relationship between length of residence in Australia and level of unemployment, but even long term residents continued to experience substantial unemployment rates (Table 10.7). Amongst women, the inverse relationship was much stronger. A large number of young recently arrived females had considerable difficulty finding work, and their level of unemployment was much higher than among males. Almost one fifth of women resident from six to ten years in Australia were out of work. Many of these women were starting families in a situation of low family income where a second wage was necessary.

## Unemployment, health and anxiety

There was also a clear relationship between unemployment and chronic illness among males. For example, 39 per cent of unemployed men were experiencing continuing illness, compared with 16 per cent of employed men. Ill health was thus a factor in inner city male unemployment, almost certainly as a cause and possibly as a consequence. Amongst women there was little difference in the incidence of chronic illness between those employed and those unemployed. Nevertheless, the proportion of breadwinners who were unemployed and suffering chronic ill health was serious in terms of the wellbeing of the whole family.

Unemployed people experienced considerably more stress than the employed. Unemployment itself was an important source of this anxiety. By implication unemployment, especially if it becomes prolonged, may have a considerble impact upon mental well being and on stress-related physical illness.

## Language knowledge and unemployment

Level of spoken English was a crucial factor underlying unemployment among immigrants in the inner city. It ranged from 10 per cent among those speaking English fluently, through 18 per cent of those speaking correctly but difficult to understand, to 20 per cent of those whose English was scarcely comprehensible. The differences between the sexes in this respect were revealing. Whereas 10 per cent of foreign born men

**Table 10.7 Duration of residence in Australia and unemployment amongst the foreign born in sample survey areas**

| Years in Australia | Males | | | Females | | |
|---|---|---|---|---|---|---|
| | Unemployed | Employed | % unemployed | Unemployed | Employed | % unemployed |
| 0 — 5 | 19 | 81 | 19.0 | 15 | 50 | 23.2 |
| 6 — 10 | 35 | 174 | 16.7 | 16 | 67 | 19.3 |
| 11 — 15 | 12 | 89 | 11.9 | 6 | 47 | 11.3 |
| 16 + | 19 | 141 | 11.9 | 4 | 71 | 5.3 |
| | $x^2 = 3.77$ | | | $x^2 = 10.65$ | | |
| | $df = 3$ | | | $df = 3$ | | |
| | $p = > .05$ | | | $p = < .05$ | | |

*Source:* 1977/78 sample survey

speaking English fluently and 16.5 per cent of those whose English was poor were unemployed, the corresponding figures for women were 9 and 24 per cent. This situation runs counter to that identified with level of education: whereas length of schooling was closely associated with unemployment rates for men but not for women, English language ability was very important for women but rather less so for men.

These results suggest that women of non-English speaking backgrounds have more difficulty in getting work if they have poor English knowledge than their menfolk with comparable English language skills. This is the case even when educational skills are comparable. However, a relationship between education in the home country and language acquisition was apparent, and this may have affected the employment possibilities for the immigrant women. More women than men from Greece, Yugoslavia and Lebanon did not go beyond the village school or even failed to complete village school: this possibly made the acquisition of English more difficult in Australia as no adequate foundation in their own language had been laid. It also affected the range of occupations they could consider: most were semi-skilled factory operatives, especially in the garment, footwear, textiles and food processing industries. At the same time, many of the immigrant women from south eastern Europe and the Levant have resided in protective ethnic neighbourhoods, often subordinate to husbands in their family launching phase of settlement, prior to entering the workforce in increasingly large numbers (despite family commitments) to make ends meet (Australian Population and Immigration Council 1976). Other questions in the survey also indicate that immigrant women from these countries, and men to a lesser extent, had experienced discrimination in the search for employment, while men had also experienced this in the quest for housing.

### Age and unemployment

In contrast to statewide and national trends, age did not emerge as a major factor in immigrant or Australian born unemployment in the inner city areas sampled in this survey. Among foreign born, 14 per cent of males and 16 per cent of females under 25 were out of work, but these proportions were only slightly above levels for older immigrants and resulted largely from recency of arrival. Long term settlers, older people and household heads with families were experiencing serious unemployment, much more so than the Australian born.

One reason for the relatively low proportion of young adults unemployed was the demographic structure of the localities sampled. Most Greeks, Italians and Yugoslavs were aged over 25, while the second generation Greeks, Yugoslavs and Lebanese had not reached the young adult age group. In contrast to the outer suburbs, comparatively few Australian born were in this age group.

Age structure and household composition have other important implications. A high proportion of older unemployed household heads from Greece, Yugoslavia and Lebanon not only had large numbers of dependent children but were also committed to mortgage repayments which were high relative to the housing costs of the Australian born. This was in part because the Greeks, Yugoslavs and Italians in particular, despite lower incomes and occupational status, had striven towards home ownership before the onset of the recession and higher unemployment. As it was, 55 per cent of the unemployed were renting compared to 39 per cent of the employed household heads. Among the foreign born, 70 per cent of the unemployed were owner-purchasers, two thirds of whom were paying mortgages. Many buying old homes had been forced to pay high rates of interest on short term loans, forcing a considerable proportion of the immigrant population from south eastern Europe and some from the Levant well below the poverty line after housing costs. Even in normal times of fuller employment the inner city has experienced relatively high levels of poverty after adjusting for housing costs: the high cost of housing relative to income has accentuated levels of poverty (Australia. Commission of Inquiry into Poverty 1975). With the marked increase in unemployment since the Poverty Inquiry and the diminution of the cheap rental housing market in the inner suburbs of Sydney, the proportion of inner city population below the poverty line must have increased greatly beyond the 14 per cent recorded in that survey, more especially for the non-English speaking immigrant population.

## 10.4 Implications and conclusions

Unemployment has not been spread evenly throughout the community: it is concentrated in particular parts of the metropolitan area, such as the old working class suburbs near the city centre and the new working class suburbs on the outskirts. The most severe adult unemployment has been in the inner suburbs where adult males, many of them household heads, comprise the great majority. Youth unemployment is a problem mainly in the outer western and certain beach suburbs.

Census tract and survey data indicate unemployment rates exceeding 20 per cent among some groups, more than half the levels experienced in the Great Depression. In 1933, over 25 per cent of the male workforce in Balmain, Leichhardt and Marrickville was unemployed, although amongst the industrial population in the inner suburbs it sometimes exceeded 50 per cent.

Several factors contribute to high inner city unemployment, most notably the socioeconomic status of the population, ethnic characteristics of the population, and the English language knowledge of immigrant communities. Another aspect of this regionalisation of unemployment has been the rapid contraction of employment opportunities in heavy industry and textile, clothing and footwear production in the inner city. In such circumstances, many recent immigrants with inadequate English have found the search for employment very difficult. With an inadequate grasp of the wider city environment and the opportunities it offers, they are even more handicapped in the search for jobs than the less skilled Australian born in these areas.

While young adult unemployment was serious in the inner suburbs, that of the immigrant and Australian born population in the 25-49 age group was much more severe than that of equivalent age groups among the general population. Unemployment was almost as severe in the over 50 age group. Household heads with dependent children still at home were particularly affected, especially those from Greece, Yugoslavia, Lebanon and other southern European and middle eastern countries except Italy. The easier situation with Italians reflects in part their greater concentration in skilled crafts rather than in unskilled manufacturing jobs as well as the establishment of linkages within the building and construction industry, which, while recessed, could still provide avenues for diligent and experienced tradesmen.

Language emerges as a crucial problem, more important perhaps than ethnicity. Lack of facility in English makes the search for employment and housing doubly difficult, especially in times which are economically depressed. This has policy implications at a time when multiculturalism and the teaching of ethnic languages is being emphasised in the wider society and in inner city communities. Immigrants were asked what aid they would most like to have had but did not get on arrival and what would be most important to them at the present time. Over 30 per cent showed a preference for English language instruction for themselves and their children; this was far more than for any other option and much more than instruction in their native language (Burnley and Walker 1978).

Linked in part to an increased incidence of poverty is stress associated with unemployment, which may contribute to a higher incidence of anxiety among the unemployed as well as to physical ill health; this occurs with both foreign and Australian born unemployed. Local community medical, social health and counselling facilities are required in inner city communities, especially since less than one quarter of the Greeks, Yugoslavs, Lebanese or Italians interviewed in this survey belonged to or had any real contact with ethnic voluntary associations. There are implications here for government welfare funding, for the Galbally Report recommended that funding or subsidies for immigrant welfare should be channelled through these institutions (Australia. Migrant Services and Programs 1978). Certainly they should be supported, but given that the great majority of the immigrant communities in areas of high migrant density have no contact with them, other aid is necessary. The immigrant communities themselves all favoured aid through the federal government on the one hand or from relatives on the other. The majority, however, preferred self help as far as possible.

There are serious human consequences of urban and economic change. Unemployment is one of the most important, but also there is a clear relationship between unemployment and physical illness as well as mental conditions such as anxiety and stress. Occupational skill is a key factor in unemployment levels and in vulnerability to unemployment. Knowledge of English is also very important. At a time when multi-cultural ideas are being expressed, the need for immigrants to have a working knowledge of written and spoken English should not be forgotten.

# 11 Coping with change
## New directions for the Sydney Water Board?

PETER CRABB

## 11.1 Introduction

Perhaps more than anything else change and turbulence characterise our modern world and our metropolitan areas in particular (AIUS 1980). It is thus rather ironic that the institutions and organisation of all levels of government are so fixed and unchanging. Such a general observation can be applied to all forms of administrative structure, despite their great variety. The most common are departments and statutory authorities, two extremes separated by a very large indeterminate area (Spann and Curnow 1975:87-107). As a general rule, departments can be set up by the government of the day without any parliamentary sanction and so can be changed or abolished at will (Spann 1979:43-112; Australia. Royal Commission on Australian Government Administration 1976:67-81). A department is directly responsible to a minister and hence to the government and parliament. For statutory authorities, the main focus of interest in this chapter, the situation is generally rather different (Spann 1979:113-145; Wilenski 1977:53-60). Established by Act of Parliament, their powers and functions are clearly defined. This gives them a certain prestige or status and, though it is variable, an autonomy not enjoyed by departments with direct ministerial responsibility. Yet, because of their legally defined nature, it is easy to regard their objectives as unchanging. It is also difficult to reorganise or abolish them. Of all forms of government administration, they can be particularly unresponsive to changing needs and situations. The words of Wilenski (1977:4) are particularly apposite:

> Like generals using the strategies that would have been effective in a previous war, many such government organisations, bound by the Acts which created them, are geared to deal best with the problems that were most relevant to a previous generation. Furthermore, as each pursues the objectives laid down in its legislation — and often pursues these very successfully — problems of coordination arise,

sometimes resulting in considerable conflict, duplication and waste, while new problems, which cut across (or fall between) organisational boundaries, are often overlooked.

Further,

The specialised public works authorities are often very long on technical competence, but short on adaptability (Paterson 1978).

Statutory authorities exist in large numbers and many forms in Australia at both state and federal levels (Wettenhall 1976). Over 200 have been identified in NSW alone (Spann 1979:116-117). The Sydney Water Board, or to give it its full title, the Metropolitan Water Sewerage and Drainage Board (MWSDB), is a particularly interesting example.

## 11.2   The Metropolitan Water Sewerage and Drainage Board and the Sydney area water supply system

Provision of water supply and sewerage services in Sydney can be traced to the foundations of the city in the late eighteenth century (Aird 1961). As presently constituted, however, the MWSDB dates from the Metropolitan Water, Sewerage, and Drainage Act of 1924 and its amendment in 1935 (as well as numerous other amendments to 1979). The Board is responsible for the provision of water, sewerage and certain stormwater drainage services in an area extending from the Hawkesbury River in the north to Gerroa in the south and west to the Blue Mountains, an area of 12,900 km$^2$ (Figure 11.1). The area includes both Sydney and the industrial region of Wollongong-Port Kembla. One of the largest undertakings of its kind in the world, it supplies water to an estimated 3.2 million people. (Unless otherwise stated, all information in this chapter refers to the situation as at 30 June 1980. On the following day, the MWSDB assumed responsibility for water supply and sewerage services in the Blue Mountains City Council area, considerably extending its area of operations.) The area's water needs are mainly supplied from reservoirs on three major catchments — Upper Nepean, Woronora and Warragamba (Table 11.1). The total available storage capacity of the major storage reservoirs is 2,375,790 megalitres (Ml). Linking the storage reservoirs to the consumers are some 16,968 km of watermains, 212 service reservoirs (with a total capacity of 4,655 Ml) and 130 pumping stations; water has to be pumped to 80 per cent of the population served by the Board, some of it more than once. The Upper Nepean and Warragamba Reservoirs supply water to the Prospect Reservoir, the main service reservoir, from where it is fed to most parts of the Sydney metropolitan area. The South Coast areas, including

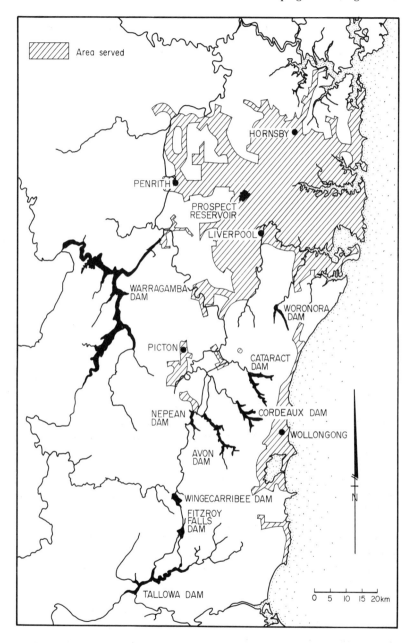

**Figure 11.1 Area served with reticulated water supply by the MWSDB, together with major reservoirs, as at 30 June 1980**

**Table 11.1    Catchments and reservoirs supplying the MWSDB system, 1980**

| Reservoir and completion date | Catchment area (km²) | Available storage capacity (MI) |
|---|---|---|
| Cataract (1907) | 130 | 94,300 |
| Cordeaux (1926) | 90 | 45,500 |
| Avon (1927) | 140 | 146,700 |
| Nepean (1935) | 320 | 52,000 |
| Unregulated | 220 | |
| Total Upper Nepean Catchment | 900 | |
| Woronora (1941) | 85 | 71,790 |
| Warragamba (1960) | 9,000 | 1,886,000 |
| Wingecarribee (1974) | 40 | 33,500 |
| Fitzroy Falls (1975) | 31 | 10,000 |
| Lake Yarrunga (1977) | 5,750 | 36,000 |
| Devines Weir (Lower Nepean) | 375 | |
| Hyams Creek Dam | 1 | |
| Fountaindale Creek Dam | 3 | |
| Richmond-Windsor | 140 | |
| Penrith | 451 | |
| Total Catchment Area | 16,780 | |

*Source:* MWSDB (1980) *Ninety-second annual report, year ended 30 June 1980*, MWSDB, Sydney, pp. 17 and 19

Wollongong, are supplied from the Avon, Cordeaux and Cataract Reservoirs.

With the completion of the Warragamba Dam in 1960, the MWSDB considered it had sufficient water to meet its needs until the early 1980s. However, the early 1960s provided indications that further supply sources could be needed. Following the examination of a number of catchments (Table 11.2), it was decided to develop the 7,250 km² Shoalhaven River catchment (Sydney Water Board Journal 1976; MWSDB 1978). The $128 million Phase I (of Stage I) of the Scheme became operational in 1977. It involves three reservoirs and three pumping stations and incorporates pumped storage hydroelectric power generation, with two of the three pumping stations also serving as generating stations (Figure 11.2). Phase II will entail doubling the pumping and generating capacities at Bendeela and Kangaroo Valley Power and Pumping Stations and of the pressure conduit system between Kangaroo Valley and the Fitzroy Falls Reservoir. In addition, the capacity of the Burrawang Pumping Station will be increased by two thirds to 3,450 Ml per day. Stage II will provide a major addition to water supplies as the planned Welcome Reef Reservoir on the Upper Shoalhaven River will cover an area of 150 km² and have a capacity of 2.68 million Ml. Phase II and Stage II are complementary in that the

**Table 11.2    Relative merits of potential sources of water for the Sydney area**

| Catchment | Additional available storage (Ml per day) | Relative capitalised cost per Ml per day additional storage ($000) |
|---|---|---|
| Shoalhaven | 2,137 | 460 |
| Colo | 614 | 940 |
| Lower Nepean | 136 | 1,260 |
| Wollondilly (Warragamba) | 205 | 1,070 |

*Source:* Snowy Mountains Authority (1968) *Report on proposals to augment the water supply to Sydney and the South Coast*, MWSDB, Sydney, p. 12

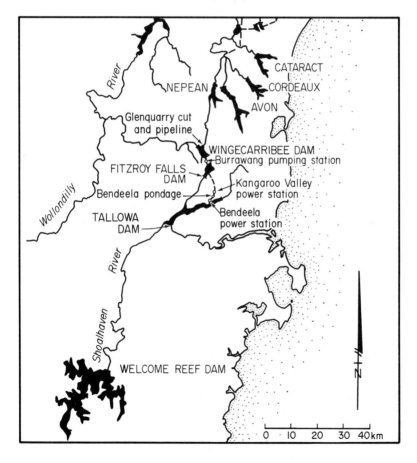

**Figure 11.2    The Shoalhaven Scheme**

additional water supplies from Welcome Reef are necessary to justify the additional pumping capacity. However, demand for electricity could result in construction of Phase II before the current scheduled date of the early 1990s.

## 11.3 Water supply: the pursuit of the Board's prime function

Though the MWSDB has several responsibilities, there can be no doubt that water supply is its prime function. This is clear from its enabling legislation and from the interpretation of the legislation by both the Board and successive state governments. Further, though a statutory authority, the MWSDB has been subject to considerable influence by successive state governments. Thus it is perhaps not surprising that, like most of Australia's water supply authorities, it has responded to rising demands by increasing available supplies, seemingly almost regardless of need or cost. The Board was careful to point out in 1976 that the Shoalhaven Scheme had been built 'to secure present and future adequacy of water supply for its millions of users — happily, not to meet a crisis situation but to avoid one' (Sydney Water Board Journal 1976). In view of the fact that the Shoalhaven Scheme did not contribute significantly to the Board's water supplies until early 1981, it is fortunate that demand has not risen as predicted and that Shoalhaven water will not be needed in the immediate future. Such a situation clearly raises a number of questions about the Board's philosophy, planning and decision making, not least in terms of its single-mindedness in satisfying the demand for water.

As the Board's annual reports and other publications have made clear, there are many difficulties and unknowns in forecasting future demands for water. Two factors, however, are of critical importance — namely the total population and per capita water consumption. The wide variations and the changes that have been made in the projections of future population used by the Board present it with a major problem. When completed in 1960, Warragamba Dam was expected to meet the Board's additional needs until the 1980s, but with predictions by the early 1960s that the Board's area would have a population of around 5 million by the end of the century, this was soon in question (MWSDB 1968). Such figures confirmed earlier expectations that the growth of Sydney and the South Coast would necessitate a new source of supply by the mid 1970s (Walder 1969). But the rapid growth of the area was not to continue, and important changes in its population became evident by the late 1960s and early 1970s. By the mid 1970s, maximum predictions for the Board's area were around 4.8 million by the end of the century (NSW. PEC 1976a). Continued decline in the birth rate and in net immigration have resulted in even lower projections than those made in the earlier study.

Sydney's population is now projected to grow from its current 3.1 million to reach between 3.5 and 3.9 million by 2001 which is significantly lower than the 3.9-4.8 million range of the last projections. A reduction of 600,000 in the projection implies that some reassessment of future development in Sydney's rapidly growing outer areas may be necessary (NSW. PEC 1979:7-8).

To this projection has to be added a figure of between 250,000 and 300,000 for the Wollongong-Port Kembla area. Thus on the basis of population alone, future requirements for water are expected to be lower than predicted only a few years ago.

The second area of difficulty is the prediction of future per capita consumption. It would appear that the Board essentially uses linear extrapolations of past data to predict future consumption. This is a procedure fraught with errors. To begin with, the figures will vary with the particular base period used. Further, the method assumes 'that the demand determinants will continue to operate in the same way as they have done in the past, and misleading projections will result if this assumption is invalid' (Rees 1976a). Many factors influence demand, as a whole and within each of the main water use sectors. For example, in the domestic sector, which (excluding garden use) accounts for about 36 per cent of total consumption, there is unlikely to be much future increase in demand from new (as opposed to replacement) washing machine sales (more efficient machines could reduce demand), but a significant increase in dishwashers would result in increased water consumption (Gallagher and Robinson 1977; Heeps 1977a). Watering domestic gardens and public parks and lawns accounts for about one quarter of total consumption, but this demand is both seasonal and dependent on the weather. Industry accounts for about 20 per cent of consumption. Its demand increased at about 4 per cent per annum through the 1960s and was the main reason for rising total per capita consumption, but recycling and more efficient use have since greatly reduced the rate of increase (Bell 1972). Of the remaining consumption, commercial activities account for 5 per cent, miscellaneous (including public institutions and buildings) 5 per cent, and leakages 10 per cent. Clearly, simply using past data raises questions about the Board's projections of future per capita consumption. Past projections appear to have been generally higher than the actual figures, and it is difficult to see future projections being realised (Tables 11.3 and 11.4).

The Board derives its figures of future total demand from the projections of population and per capita consumption. However, it uses more than 'total demand' to determine the capacity of its supply system. It is quite clear that periods of drought and consequent water restrictions have been and continue to be major factors. As Munro (1974) observed, 'every time a drought occurred, the development of Sydney's

**Table 11.3   Water consumption in the area served by the Sydney Water Board, 1964/65 to 1979/80**

| Year | Total consumption (Ml) | Mean daily consumption (Ml) | Maximum daily consumption (Ml) | Minimum daily consumption (Ml) | Per capita consumption (L) |
|---|---|---|---|---|---|
| 1964/65 | 481,385 | 1,318 | 2,196 | 832 | 496 |
| 1965/66 | 380,968 | 1,046 | 1,396 | 750 | 382 |
| 1966/67 | 388,151 | 1,064 | 1,809 | 782 | 386 |
| 1967/68 | 449,968 | 1,227 | 2,018 | 796 | 441 |
| 1968/69 | 501,637 | 1,373 | 2,355 | 932 | 482 |
| 1969/70 | 472,861 | 1,296 | 2,091 | 941 | 441 |
| 1970/71 | 485,786 | 1,332 | 1,832 | 959 | 441 |
| 1971/72 | 490,241 | 1,341 | 2,132 | 964 | 446 |
| 1972/73 | 518,062 | 1,418 | 2,391 | 986 | 464 |
| 1973/74 | 504,575 | 1,380 | 1,930 | 1,025 | 447 |
| 1974/75 | 545,180 | 1,494 | 2,537 | 930 | 476 |
| 1975/76 | 538,465 | 1,471 | 2,595 | 1,133 | 470 |
| 1976/77 | 570,623 | 1,563 | 2,652 | 1,019 | 512 |
| 1977/78 | 593,479 | 1,626 | 2,686 | 1,108 | 515 |
| 1978/79 | 568,816 | 1,558 | 2,665 | 1,094 | 488 |
| 1979/80 | 627,629 | 1,715 | 2,863 | 1,186 | 532 |

*Source:* MWSDB annual reports

**Table 11.4   Predicted demand on the Sydney water supply system, 1980-2000**

| Year | Population served (millions) | Mean daily per capita consumption | |
|---|---|---|---|
| | | Annual average (L) | Drought periods (L) |
| 1980 | 3.18 | 552 | 583 |
| 1985 | 3.37 | 578 | 609 |
| 1990 | 3.56 | 605 | 636 |
| 1995 | 3.75 | 631 | 662 |
| 2000 | 3.94 | 658 | 689 |

*Source:* Submission to the Board of the MWSDB, January, 1978

headworks storage made another spurt forward'. The eight year drought that ended in 1942 was a major factor in the construction of the Woronora and Warragamba Reservoirs and very largely continues to determine the Board's total water storage; such a drought has been estimated to recur only once every 300 to 3,000 years (Bell 1972), although there is now evidence of much more severe droughts in the first half of the nineteenth century (McAfee 1980). The drought and restrictions of 1965-67 (Table 11.5), as well as demand projections, were major factors in the decision to construct the Shoalhaven Scheme. The explanation lies in the fact that the Board's objective is a reserve supply capacity

> sufficient ... to serve peak needs (which are two to three times greater than normal daily usage) in the event of nine consecutive drought years. These nine years are made up of the eight worst drought years ever recorded, plus a further year comprising the twelve worst drought months (Rees 1976b).

The result is that Sydney stores over 845,000 litres per capita, more than any other major city in the world, giving its supply system an extremely high degree of reliability. Nonetheless, the 1978-81 drought may well lead to a further increase in the reserve capacity.

Of all the factors that contribute to the demand for water, none is more significant than garden watering (Baumann and Dworkin 1978). This is not a new situation nor is it unique to Sydney. Over twenty years ago 48 per cent of water supplied to the Adelaide metropolitan area was used on domestic gardens (Dridan 1964). In the early 1970s garden watering accounted for 30 to 50 per cent of total water usage in parts of Melbourne, Geelong and Yallourn (McMahon and Weeks 1973), while in Sydney 'approximately 24 per cent of the total annual consumption is attributed to the watering of domestic lawns and gardens, market

**Table 11.5   Restrictions on water use imposed by the MWSDB, 1940-1980[a]**

| Date | Duration | Reason for restriction |
|---|---|---|
| 1 May 1940-16 Oct 1942 | 2 years, 5 months | Last phase of record eight year drought |
| 27 Oct 1948-27 May 1949 | 7 months | Inadequacy of the distribution system |
| 14 Nov 1951-16 May 1952 | 6 months | Dry spell and inadequacies in supply system |
| 17 Nov 1953-24 Feb 1954 | 3 months | Dry and hot weather conditions |
| 20 Nov 1956-20 Feb 1957 | 3 months | Weather conditions |
| 11 Oct 1957-10 Feb 1958 | 4 months | Weather conditions |
| 2 Nov 1958-28 Jan 1959 | 3 months | Weather conditions |
| 27 Jan 1960-1 Feb 1960 | 6 days | Heat wave |
| 27 Aug 1965-6 Sept 1967 | 2 years, 10 days | Severe drought and initial inadequacies in supply system |
| 20 Dec 1979-2 Jan.1980 | 13 days | Bushfire emergency; northern suburbs only |

*Note:* [a] There is a year round ban on the use of fixed hoses and sprinklers between the hours of 9 pm and 6 am.
*Source:* MWSDB annual reports

gardens and parks' (Bell 1972). More recent studies have confirmed a continued high level of garden watering in Hobart (Water Resources Newsletter 1979), Wollongong where it accounts for 45 per cent of total domestic use (Gallagher 1976), and Melbourne where it is approximately 30 per cent of domestic demand (Heeps 1977a, 1977b). Even higher figures have been recorded in Townsville and Perth (Power 1980; Winkler 1979). Not only does garden watering add significantly to total use, it is a major factor in the periods of peak demand: in Melbourne, for example, on a hot summer day, garden watering can account for 65 per cent of total demand (Living City 1980). Further, maximum daily consumption is usually more than double the minimum and well above the average (Table 11.3). The supply system is such that it is capable of coping with this very high summer demand, which reaches extreme levels at certain times of the week and of the day, even though such demands last for only between 20 and 30 hours per year. Such demands can be attributed almost entirely to garden watering and in particular to the use of fixed sprinkler systems. If any confirmation of this latter point is needed, it is readily provided by the impact of bans imposed on their use in Perth during 1977-79 as a result of severe drought conditions (MWSSDB 1979a). In 1977/78, total annual water consumption was some 62 per cent of that in 1976/77, but the maximum daily consumption figure was cut to 47 per cent.

The response of the MWSDB to rising demand and to predictions of future increases has been to expand the supply system. This can be regarded as the typical 'engineering solution' to an actual or potential shortage. The Board 'appears to disregard the possibility of inducing regular constraints on water consumption and to accept the largely unchecked water consumption trends as the determinant of supply needs' (Butlin 1976b:138). Thus, for example, very limited use is made of water charges to control demand, particularly the peak summer demands for garden watering. The only exception would be the large industrial consumers, but this is a self imposed control in the interest of containing costs rather than one imposed by the Water Board to control consumption. Even though virtually all properties are fitted with a meter, which is read regularly, water rates are based essentially on property values rather than the quantity consumed (Table 11.6). The rates paid permit the consumer to use a given quantity of water (a quantity that has been declining as the unit charge has increased); consumption above this figure incurs an 'excess' water charge. Many writers have argued that such a system tends to encourage consumption rather than conservation, though it clearly provides the utility with an assured income (Gallagher 1977; Hanke 1972). The Board maintains that its present rating system is the most satisfactory and that a usage charge has no effect on consumption (NSW 1967:74,81) (although it is likely that the Board will gradually raise usage charges so that they become a larger part of total charges to the consumer). Such views are not shared by the Perth Metropolitan Water Board: basing water charges on property valuations is regarded as neither efficient nor equitable, and it is seen as resulting in waste of resources and premature construction of costly supply schemes (MWSSDB 1979b:52-54). The current situation in Perth is still clouded by the 1977-79 drought and the responses to it, with water consumption in 1979/80 below that of 1970/71. However, it will be interesting to see the long term effect of the new pricing system introduced in mid 1978 based primarily on actual consumption.

The MWSDB has given very little consideration to reducing water consumption through such means as advertising campaigns and the education of its consumers. The use of periodic water supply restrictions (say once in twenty years) as a strategy for coping with increased demand — one of a number of options put to the Adelaide public by the South Australian Engineering and Water Supply Department — appear to be abhorrent to the Board.

Given the situation that has been outlined in this section, it is perhaps doubly fortunate that the Shoalhaven Scheme is a flexible one. Granted the observation is made from hindsight, but there can be little doubt about the premature construction of the Scheme. The 1977 completion of Phase I of Stage I was behind schedule, while it was 1981 before it was making any significant contribution to Sydney's water supplies. The construction of Stage II, originally due for completion in 1984 (MWSDB n.d.a), has been put off on a number of occasions and no clear statement is now available as to when it will be built. The

**Table 11.6    MWSDB water rates and charges, 1979/80**

| | |
|---|---:|
| *Residential properties* | |
| On that part of the unimproved value not exceeding $20,000 | .332¢ in $ |
| On that part of the unimproved value exceeding $20,000 but not exceeding $40,000 | .166¢ in $ |
| On that part of the unimproved value exceeding $40,000 | .083¢ in $ |
| Minimum charge | $45.50 |
| *Non-residential properties* | |
| On the assessed annual value | 4.640¢ in $ |
| Minimum charge (unoccupied land) | $26.00 |
| Minimum charge (occupied land) | $45.50 |
| *For all properties* | |
| Each 18.5¢ of water rates allows the use of one kilolitre of water without further charge. All usage above this allowance is charged for at 18.5¢ per kilolitre. | |

*Source:* MWSDB (1980) *Ninety-second annual report, year ended 30 June 1980*, MWSDB, Sydney, p.26

deterioration of general economic conditions gives some point to the fact that had the Scheme not been built when it was, it might well not have been started. Yet some questions remain. Is Stage I justified without Stage II, and will the existence of Stage I be used as justification for the construction of Stage II? Regardless of the 'flexibility' of the Scheme, this is a particularly valid question given the small storage capacity of Stage I. What will be the final cost of water supplied from Stage I, and how does this compare with that predicted for the total project (Stages I and II)? And what will be the impact of the 1978–81 drought on the project and the Board's planning?

## 11.4  Some consequences of the Board's single-mindedness

The response of the MWSDB to the rising demand for water has simply been to increase supply. Such a single-minded response is becoming increasingly costly and more difficult to justify. Some of the reasons for this are not uncommon, such as the financial cost of storage structures, their environmental costs and implications and the wasteful or uneconomic uses of water that frequently flow from unlimited supply (Rees 1976b). On top of this, the wasteful use of water imposes an added cost on the sewerage disposal system, which has to be unnecessarily large. Where there is a very large safety margin in the water supply system, additional costs are imposed. Facilities are built well ahead of need; the costs are never compared with the benefits of the additional water, it being assumed that the latter must exceed the added supply costs; and rarely, if ever, is any attempt made to calculate the costs and benefits of providing for very low probability drought occurrences. Costs seem to be only considered when simply comparing various schemes for supplying a given quantity of 'needed' water.

The consequences extend much further, however, certainly in the case of Sydney. Major resource misallocation and some serious current problems have resulted from the Board keeping strictly to the terms of its legislation and satisfying political pressures for an assured water supply (Butlin 1976b:139). This is a situation that is not fully reflected in the Board's capital expenditures (Table 11.7). A number of topics are worthy of some consideration: namely water quality, sewerage services, stormwater drainage, and environmental quality improvement work. In many statements on water quality by the Board, the justification for increased treatment has been presented solely in terms of reduced control over catchment areas, particularly those in the Shoalhaven Scheme (MWSDB 1977). However, there is more to the problem than this. The greater part of the Warragamba catchment is outside the Board's control, while some years ago the Board's president acknowledged that the treatment was not up to the standard accepted in many overseas cities (Walder 1969). Full treatment is given to water supplied to small parts of the system and there are plans for the full treatment of all water supplied by the Board. However, one cannot help wondering if the Shoalhaven Scheme has not provided the Board with an opportunity for the introduction of a greatly increased and long overdue program of water treatment facilities.

By mid 1980, 94 per cent of the population supplied with water by the Board also had sewerage services. The figure was only 75 per cent ten years earlier, when some 750,000 people were without such services (Cleaver 1979). The large backlog in the provision of sewerage facilities can be attributed, at least in part, to the previous emphasis on providing water supplies. Lack of coordination with other authorities concerned with the growth of Sydney and the absence of an effective overall planning strategy for the metropolitan area before the 1970s were other factors. There was much improvement during the 1970s, aided by federal assistance from the 1973-75 National Sewerage Program (Australia. Senate Standing Committee on National Resources 1978:7-8, 56). Despite the improvement, major problems remain in a number of outer suburban shires, such as Hornsby, Warringah, Camden and Penrith, where large districts are still dependent on septic systems. The northern suburbs present particularly difficult and costly problems because of terrain and geology: in some areas, the cost of sewerage provision was put at up to $2,000 per capita (NSW. SPCC 1977:14). Residential development in such areas clearly raises some questions.

**Table 11.7  Expenditure on construction work by the MWSDB, 1966/67-1979/80**

| Year | Water $m | Water % of total | Sewerage $m | Sewerage % of total | Drainage $m | Drainage % of total | Total expenditure $m |
|---|---|---|---|---|---|---|---|
| 1966/67 | 19.5 | 42.4 | 24.4 | 53.2 | 2.0 | 4.4 | 45.9 |
| 1967/68 | 18.5 | 40.2 | 24.8 | 54.0 | 2.7 | 5.8 | 46.0 |
| 1968/69 | 17.9 | 37.4 | 26.5 | 55.3 | 3.5 | 7.3 | 47.9 |
| 1969/70 | 20.1 | 38.8 | 29.5 | 56.8 | 2.3 | 4.5 | 51.9 |
| 1970/71 | 22.9 | 30.6 | 50.4 | 67.3 | 1.6 | 2.1 | 74.9 |
| 1971/72 | 32.5 | 33.0 | 65.0 | 65.8 | 1.2 | 1.2 | 98.7 |
| 1972/73 | 42.9 | 35.8 | 76.1 | 63.4 | 1.0 | 0.8 | 120.0 |
| 1973/74 | 50.0 | 37.0 | 83.3 | 61.7 | 1.8 | 1.3 | 135.1 |
| 1974/75 | 63.8 | 37.4 | 105.2 | 61.7 | 1.6 | 0.9 | 170.6 |
| 1975/76 | 60.3 | 33.0 | 120.5 | 65.9 | 2.0 | 1.1 | 182.8 |
| 1976/77 | 45.9 | 24.8 | 138.3 | 74.6 | 1.1 | 0.6 | 185.3 |
| 1977/78 | 32.7 | 18.9 | 137.6 | 79.7 | 2.4 | 1.4 | 172.7 |
| 1978/79 | 36.7 | 21.3 | 131.2 | 76.2 | 4.3 | 2.5 | 172.2 |
| 1979/80 | 38.9 | 23.0 | 127.0 | 75.4 | 2.6 | 1.5 | 168.5 |

*Source:* MWSDB annual reports

Though the backlog of sewerage provision has been largely removed, the Board's task was not helped by the termination of federal funding in 1975. But limited services are not the only difficulty. Some 85 per cent of the sewered population is served by ocean outfalls, the main plants being at North Head, Malabar and Bondi. These facilities are unsatisfactory on a number of counts: the capacity of the plants particularly during and after heavy rain, the inadequate level of treatment and the near shore discharge points (resulting in pollution of Sydney's beaches). Improvements will come with the deep water submarine outfalls, over three kilometres offshore, but at a cost (in 1979) of over $100 million (MWSDB 1979). Though the quantity of sewerage involved is much smaller, disposal inland poses equally serious problems because of inadequate treatment and the fact that much of the effluent ends up in the Lower Hawkesbury, which also receives the runoff (including faecal matter) from large unsewered areas in northern Sydney (NSW. SPCC 1977).

Stormwater drainage has received particularly low priority and funding (Table 11.7). This is despite the fact that its inadequacies continue to contribute to the problems of the sewerage system, especially during periods of high rainfall and runoff.

Improvement of sewerage treatment facilities is the major task facing the Board today, namely improving the *quality* of its services rather than their *quantity*. A ten year works program compiled in 1978, costing over $1,550 million, was largely made up of environmental and pollution control projects. Such projects would not generate extra revenue for the Board, yet they would require substantial, some would say prohibitive, rate increases to finance them. For such reasons and the Board's existing substantial loan liabilities, a study of the MWSDB stated that its plans were 'unrealistic' and that expenditure on new works should be cut to $100 million per year (McKinsey and Co. 1978; Butlin 1976b:79-83). However, though these projects may not contribute dollars and cents to the Board's revenue, their cost prevention role for the whole community is considerable, as has been suggested for such areas as the Georges River, the Lower Hawkesbury, the offshore areas, and some of Sydney's beaches. The NSW government is clearly faced with a dilemma:

The social consequences of escaping the rate increases which the report foreshadows would be severe, especially if they involved halting remaining sewerage extensions, such as those in the Warringah and Hornsby-Berowra areas. Moreover, a $100 million plan to discharge sewerage three kilometres out to sea would have to be abandoned. The Government is in a quandary. It has pursued a policy of keeping rate increases down. It has looked to the Water Board as a job-creating source to relieve unemployment. It has projected itself as a champion of environmental protection and improvement (SMH, 28 December 1978).

The Board's single-mindedness has given Sydney a water supply system with a very high degree of reliability. However, this has only been achieved at considerable cost. It is a cost that is only partly reflected in the expenditures of the MWSDB. Further, it is a cost that in one way or another will continue to be borne by the whole community for many years to come.

## 11.5 Why has quantitative water supply been so preeminent in MWSDB operations?

The vast reserve capacity, the reliability of the supply system, and the very small use of water restrictions over the past three decades, including the severe 1978-81 drought, are indications of the success of the MWSDB in providing water for its customers. It was suggested earlier that the preeminence of quantitative water supply owes much to the 1934-42 drought. However, this is only part of the explanation. The water rationing imposed towards the end of that drought resulted in much criticism of the MWSDB, the press calling it the 'No Water Board'. As a result, the Board 'adopted a policy stating, in effect, that Sydney would never again be rationed for water' (Munro 1974:167-168). Justification for such a policy came from a number of quarters. The Board's enabling legislation certainly gives pride of place to water supply, while interpretation of the legislation, by both the Board and successive state governments, has given it added point. Not only are the Board and the government liable to severe criticism for any inadequacy in the supply system, additions to it can bring benefits in both professional and political terms. Both Board and government can point to very visible, worthwhile and beneficial structures and their contribution to the growth of the metropolitan area. One cannot ignore the dominance of the engineering professions throughout the structure of the Board and in its decision making machinery. It is hardly surprising that their views have generally prevailed and that 'engineering solutions' to problems should predominate (Davis 1980; Spann 1979:140). Further, in addition to the professional and political satisfaction found in such structures, they have also generally brought widespread public approval for both Board and government, in marked contrast to the reactions to supply restrictions.

If these factors go part of the way to account for the emphasis on water supply, they do not explain why comparable attention was not given to the Board's other functions, namely sewerage and stormwater drainage. Here, one can only make some suggestions. The Board has never had the financial resources to do everything. While everyone needs a water supply, septic systems do provide an alternative to a mains sewer system. Also, pollution flowing from septic systems has only become a matter of widespread concern over recent years. Finally, one might speculate that until quite recently, water supply structures have been seen as far more prestigious than sewerage treatment works for both professionals and politicians.

If it is possible to provide some explanation for the emphasis on quantitative water supply, it is much more difficult to provide justification. The Board provides little more than the factors of drought and urban expansion (MWSDB n.d.b). In terms of its water supply function, the MWSDB has to contend with major problems relating to both its supply sources and the demands of its customers. However, it is difficult to believe that Sydney needs to store more water per head of population than any other city in the world.

## 11.6   The question of responsibility and the wider issue of single-minded authorities

It has been argued that, while the population served by the MWSDB has one of the most reliable water supplies in Australia, it has paid a high price for the privilege and will continue to do so. It has been shown that the emphasis on quantitative water supply has been to the detriment of other functions for which the Board is responsible and that the consequent deficiencies now contribute significantly to Sydney's environmental and pollution problems.

With considerable justification the MWSDB can argue that it has capably and efficiently carried out its major functions as set down in its legislation. Also it has been subject to considerable political pressures, being little more than a branch of the state government despite its statutory authority status. Nonetheless, the Board must accept its share of responsibility for the current problems. Only the Board can account for the fact that 'much of its philosophy and planning is still in the "development phase"' (Winkler 1979). Further, there is little evidence to suggest that it has identified and sought to remedy the inadequacies of its legislation and functions, at least not until very recently (Cameron and Klaassen 1977). For example, nothing appears to have been done to give Warragamba Dam a flood mitigation role to ease the problem of flooding in the Lower Hawkesbury, while the Board must have played a part in the development of residential areas that are now proving so difficult and costly to sewer. On the other hand, there are signs that it is beginning to appreciate and tackle the changing environment in which it is now operating. In spite of continuing financial pressures, qualitative works are going ahead, such as new sewerage treatment works for effluent discharged into the Georges and Lower Hawkesbury Rivers and extension of ocean outfalls. Also controlled recreational use is being made of Lake Yarrunga and Fitzroy Falls Reservoir on the Shoalhaven Scheme.

Ultimately, however, the state government of the day must be held primarily responsible for the Water Board's priorities, resource allocation and decision making. It is the government that has the legislative responsibility and which also imposes the political constraints, as with the current limitations on the size of annual rate increases. The government is also responsible for other areas that have contributed to the Board's problems, particularly the lack of coordination between varies state and local government authorities and the absence of proper land use planning in the metropolitan area (NSW. SPCC 1977: foreword and 15-16; Gibbons 1976). It is only recently that there has been improvement in these areas (Wilenski 1978). Clearly, current issues are raising major social trade offs, such as holding down rate increases, constructing qualitative works, and providing a source of employment. As Wilenski has done (1977:58-59), it must be questioned whether or not the Board, as presently constituted, is the right place for making such decisions. Also, given the dominance of the engineering professions, it is questionable if the Board has the necessary skills to make the right decisions in areas that now have large environmental, social and income redistribution components. It is more than evident that the Board needs adequate funding to remedy the deficiencies of the past. Equally evident and important is the fact that it needs new priorities and legislation, which can only come from the state government.

It was suggested earlier that of all forms of government administration, statutory authorities are lacking in adaptability and are unresponsive to changing needs and situations. As a result, the necessary changes require legislative action. The Sydney Water Board has largely met its quantitative objectives and now requires a new role. It is not alone in this, and giving a statutory authority a new role is not without precedent. For example, once it had completed its task, the Snowy Mountains Authority was largely disbanded in 1970, but out of it came the Snowy Mountains Engineering Corporation, which is now providing a wide range of engineering and construction services in Australia and overseas. In Tasmania major changes have been proposed for the Hydro-Electric Commission (one of the most powerful statutory authorities in Australia) now that the construction of new hydro schemes is almost at an end (Townsley 1976:124-127; Wilderness News 1981). In making any changes to such instrumentalities, one cannot overlook their considerable skills and expertise in specialised areas while recognising their inherent vested interests. Thus, the MWSDB, as well as becoming much more concerned with environmental and social issues within the area it now serves, could put its expertise to use in other parts of NSW. One means of achieving this would be to create one authority with responsibility for all water resource matters in the State. This has been done in South Australia with the expanded role given to the Engineering and Water Supply Department (South Australia. Engineering and Water Supply Department 1980). In many cases, however, more than reorganisation, a new name, or even new specified functions are required. This has been indicated in the case of the Water Resources Commission of NSW (Wilenski 1977:57). A prime requirement is a change of attitude, one that is flexible to changing circumstances; this is an aspect of change that cannot be created simply by new legislation. Whatever is done, just as responsbility for much of the past rests largely with successive state governments, so do future matters relating to the Water Board, its various activities, and Sydney's water supply.

## 12  Land use-transport changes and global restructuring in Sydney since the 1970s
### The container issue

PETER J. RIMMER AND JOHN A. BLACK

... the development of techniques of transport and communication has created the possibility, in many cases, of the complete or partial production of goods at any site in the world — a possibility no longer ruled out by technical, organisational and cost factors ... This technology includes modern transport technology, which allows the rapid and relatively cheap transport of products between sites of intermediate or final production and consumption, of both large bulk cargoes and fragile items by specialised ocean carriers: containerisation ... (Fröbel *et al.* 1980:13,36).

### 12.1  Introduction

The arrival of the overseas container ship *Encounter Bay* during April 1969 heralded a new phase in Sydney's economic geography. Since then the long postwar boom has ended, and during the world recession of 1974 and 1975 Sydney experienced a period of economic crisis which accelerated restructuring of economic activities (Stilwell 1980). The resultant employment reduction and capital disinvestment are responses to a series of global changes: the new international division of labour geared to using highly productive labour per unit cost in Third World countries; the selective international fragmentation of production inherent, for example, in the world car concept; and the increasing stranglehold of international capital over production, enabling it to flit from one activity to another to take advantage of differential rates of return through rapid investment and disinvestment (Fröbel *et al.* 1980).

Global restructuring has brought many important changes in the economic organisation and physical structure of urban areas, not least in the volume, nature and pattern of goods movement. These latter changes are complex and the details difficult to disentangle. A useful starting point is the pattern of generation of commercial vehicle trips in 1971, the latest year for which figures are available (Figure 12.1). The CBD, inner city suburbs, North Sydney and Chatswood were by far the largest originators of commercial vehicle traffic, whereas the outer suburbs were relatively insignificant.

This basic pattern has been altered in many ways but not destroyed over the last decade by global economic, technological and organisational changes and their intrametropolitan ramifications. Clearly, the massive inflow of foreign capital into construction in Sydney (Daly ch 2)

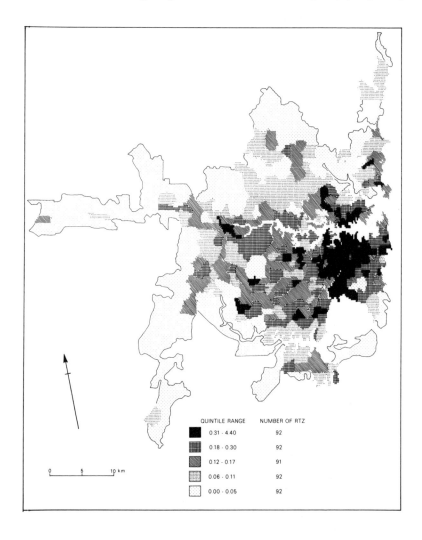

**Figure 12.1    Number of daily commercial vehicle trips generated per hectare, by road traffic zones (RTZ), 1971**

produced an upsurge in the transport of building materials to city sites and, on a longer term basis, changed the pattern of freight movements and commuter flows. Perhaps more important, though, has been the rapid dispersal of industrial (Cardew and Rich ch 6), commercial (Alexander ch 3), residential (Faulkner ch 14) and other development in response to a complex amalgam of global and local forces. This has had a major impact on personal movement (Aplin ch 13) as well as goods transport, with suburban areas undoubtedly responsible for a growing proportion of commercial vehicle traffic.

Recession and rising imports meant that industrial production fell by ten per cent in 1974/75. This not only reduced the volume of local goods movement but also changed its pattern because of the widely differing impact of economic conditions on firms. Reorganisation of branch plants of foreign companies to dovetail with global production strategies has also affected goods movement (Alford 1979). Cessation of manufacturing through increased purchasing of semi-finished materials and assemblies from overseas and reduction in import competing production have shifted the origins of some goods flows from manufacturing zones within Sydney to the port. Disinvestment and consolidation, as well as the movement of some productive capacity offshore, have thus reduced internal linkages. In addition, the growing importance of servicing, design and marketing of goods, as well as diversification into other activities, particularly mining and service industries, have changed the type of goods being transported.

Global forces have been highly significant in moulding Sydney's development. In the transport field, changing requirements for goods movement have altered traffic patterns and so brought severe new pressures to bear on the city and its inhabitants. Revolutionary changes in international transport and communications — for example, containerisation and jet travel — are external factors which have imposed internal pressures. Indeed, the need to accommodate changes associated with the introduction of containers has been an important force moulding urban development in the last decade. Container truck movements provide striking examples of the conflicts arising in urban areas from global pressures and the difficulties of coping with them.

In this chapter, we first outline the structure of the metropolitan land use-transport system and the various types of conflict that can arise in it (section 12.2). Then, the introduction of containers into Sydney is briefly described (section 12.3) as a background to an elaboration of the conflicts that have arisen (sections 12.4, 12.5 and 12.6). The use of policy instruments to resolve these conflicts is also discussed. The analysis bolsters Scott's (1980:3) contention that underlying each type of conflict is the same structural dynamic triggering fresh conflicts and constraining the ability of planners to deal with specific symptoms or to readjust the mechanisms which create them.

## 12.2    The land use-transport system

Stripped to its bare essentials, Sydney is a giant machine for the production, circulation and consumption of commodities, where the transport subsystem ties together production and consumption into a functional geographical whole. The key to understanding the circulation of urban goods is an appreciation of the logistical chain between producer and consumer (and any final disposal of waste). Sydney can be thought of as a spatial pattern of economic units (land use activities), such as terminals, manufacturers, wholesalers, retailers, households, institutions and waste depots, all connected by a transport network (Figure 12.2). Functional linkages between complementary economic units constitute the demand for the movement of goods within the metropolitan area. In addition, Sydney is an open system with strong regional, national and international links, and the freight flows resulting from such external influences are vital features when considering Sydney's transport requirements.

Three types of conflict can be identified within the system. First, activity conflicts (such as traffic generation or parking) occur at the interface between each economic unit and the transport network. Such conflicts originate from changes in industrial production or in the nature of socioeconomic organisations within an economic unit. Second, vehicle conflicts involve vehicles or vehicles and pedestrians on

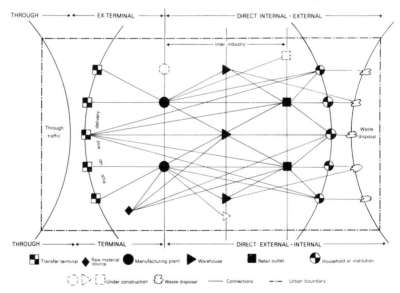

**Figure 12.2    External and internal transport linkages of economic units within an urban area**

the transport network (e.g. traffic delays, traffic accidents) and any spillover environmental effects (e.g. noise, pollution) of traffic on adjacent land uses. These conflicts are often heightened by the use of new technology, such as big trucks carrying 40 foot containers. Finally, locational restructuring conflicts stem from the addition of nodes (e.g. a new port) and transport links (e.g. a new freeway), which may be incompatible with existing land uses or socially or environmentally disruptive (Rimmer and Hicks 1979; Rimmer and Tsipouras 1977).

These conflicts have to be related to the actors playing distinctive though sometimes overlapping roles in the land use-transport system. Within civil society, six major roles can be recognised – shipper-receiver, shipowner, commercial vehicle owner, transport terminal operator, traveller-driver, and impactee (often the community). Within the state sector the main actors are the port authority, highway authority and transport planner (Table 12.1). Each actor may pursue different goals and objectives and might therefore perceive urban goods movement conflicts in different ways. Table 12.1 identifies some typical problems, which are the basis of inter-group conflict, and indicates possible solutions (though not mechanisms for conflict resolution). The transport planner aims to ensure the free flow of commodities (and workers), an objective necessitating the maintenance of high levels of accessibility in relation to the ever changing location of economic units. The state intervenes because uncoordinated decisions by individual firms and households may impose additional costs of inputs in commodity production, retard the circulation of commodities and boost wage demands to offset commuting costs (Scott 1980).

This conceptual model represents a static picture of a dynamic system. At any time a mutation of past land uses, transport technologies and transport organisations survives. New activities, technologies and organisations are prime agents of change in the spatial pattern of economic units. These agents may have been designed to resolve previous conflicts, but they are more likely to result from growth pressures which themselves often intensify conflicts. In fact, contemporary conflicts are largely results of the superimposition of organisational, locational and technological changes on the land use-transport system. Their resolution generally lags behind the emergence of further changes, so that new conflicts appear before any disequilibrating situation has worked itself out.

The means of regulating system growth, mechanisms of resolving conflicts and the power of different groups to influence decisions are vital topics in studies of change in the land use-transport system. In accommodating changes to the system, conflict may intensify, or it may be resolved in one place only to reappear elsewhere, or it may be resolved to the satisfaction of most or all groups. The containerisation of goods movement since the late 1960s has been one of the most

**Table 12.1   Actors in the Sydney land use-transport system and their perceived conflicts and solutions**

| Actor | Objective | Symptoms | Solutions | | |
| --- | --- | --- | --- | --- | --- |
| | | | Education | Enforcement | Engineering |
| *Civil Society*<br>Shipowner | Maximise ship earnings, reduce demurrage charges and delays in ports | Port congestion | – | – | Revamp facilities, new port |
| Truck operator | Maximise vehicle earnings | Terminal congestion | Improve spatial or temporal access | More loading zones, enforcement of parking regulations on private motorists | Revamp facilities, new terminals |
| | | Traffic congestion | | Exclusive truck lanes, designated truck routes | Freeways, truckways |
| Importer/ exporter | Minimise perceived costs | Delay and uncertainty | Improve vehicle scheduling | – | Improve port and highways |
| Traveller | Minimise perceived costs | Delays from truck-induced traffic congestion | – | Banish trucks during peak hours, pedestrian crossings | Grade separated rail crossings |
| Resident | Minimise disruption, maximise benefits | Noise, air pollution, property severance, community disruption (overnight truck parking), safety (trucks source of danger) | Lobbying, appeals, publicity | Vehicle bans, designated truck parks, insulation | Relocate offending terminals |

| *State* | | | | |
|---|---|---|---|---|
| Port operator | Maximise throughput | Port congestion | Improve labour relations | – | Resiting facilities, build new ports |
| Highway authority | Maximise net social benefits | Traffic congestion | Promote staggered working hours | Traffic management — change control signals | Widen roads, construct new roads |
| Transport planner | Maintain efficient multimodal transport system, protect environmental quality and safety | – | Recommend reduction in transport demand through non-transport solutions | Recommend regulation of vehicles and land use | Recommend investment, new transport facilities and urban structure |

*Source:* Based on Rimmer and Hicks 1979; Rimmer and Hooper 1977

important system changes because of its impact, conflicts engendered and government responses evoked.

## 12.3    The development of container facilities

Sydney was a port before it became a city. Its evolution reflects the multiple ripple effect caused by disequilibrating external influences, induced largely by the changing nature of world capitalism, and internal responses which have only partially resolved resulting conflicts. Its port system, and indeed the city itself, has developed since the nineteenth century in response to a continuing sequence of external stimuli and Australia's changing role in the world economy. Port development, though, has generally been poorly coordinated with other aspects of Sydney's growth and serious conflicts have arisen.

A key external influence, and one that has given rise to major conflicts and adjustment problems in Sydney, was the rapid introduction of container ships by major international shipping companies in the 1960s. This significantly reduced labour requirements and forced massive structural change on world ports (and, indeed, profoundly affected the companies themselves since they were later forced into consortia to operate vessels and terminal facilities). In Australia, the Commonwealth government held a Conference on Containerisation in 1966 to seek assistance from state port authorities in providing facilities for containerised cargo, mitigating the effects of consequent reductions in waterside employment and minimising inter-union disputes (already evident in arguments over who should handle containers and stuff and unstuff them). As a consequence Sydney's port authority, the MSB, like others around the world, 'became committed to the redevelopment of port facilities to cater to the new order' (Brotherson 1975:34).

Initially, Port Jackson was partially redeveloped with the first container terminal (leased to a British consortium and an Australian partner operating as Seatainer Terminals Pty. Ltd.) being constructed at White Bay in 1969. This involved 10.9 hectares of reclaimed land and expensive excavation of rock cliffs on the landward side. Glebe Island terminal. opened by the MSB in 1973 and operated by Glebe Island Terminals Pty Ltd since 1974, required the demolition of general cargo wharfage, reclamation and excavation to produce a facility with 10.1 hectares. It was suggested that these terminals would be adequate for 'known needs in the immediate and foreseeable future' (Australia. 1970 Part II:717-736). It was later conceded that the terminals were about half the required size, necessitating decentralised depots at Villawood and Chullora for container handling. (This aggravated strife between the Waterside Workers Federation of Australia and the Federated Storemen and Packers Union over who should handle containers in off-wharf depots; a decision was finally made in favour of the latter.) At the third terminal, Mort Bay, the depth of water at 9.5 metres was inadequate for the second generation of container vessels introduced in 1975. These site constraints were resolved to the satisfaction of the MSB by the planning and construction of a new supplementary port at Botany. Notwithstanding the involvement of other state government instrumentalities represented on an interdepartmental committee and the advice that transport connections to the new port would be adequate, Port Botany has produced a series of conflicts.

Within a decade (1969–1979) containers came to dominate cargo handling, with improved ship turnaround, more efficient use of ship's space, reduced pilferage and increased throughput per length of wharf. Substitution of capital for labour permitted a reduction in registered waterside workers by one third even though tonnage doubled (Table 12.2). By 1978/79, 69 per cent of all general cargo was containerised (149,000 containers passing through White Bay, 100,000 through Glebe Island, 47,000 through Mort Bay and 91,000 through other wharves).

## 12.4   Activity conflicts

Examination of the pattern of container movements draws attention to the traffic generating characteristics of terminals and the activity

Table 12.2   **Annual general cargo, container movements and waterside workers employed, Port Jackson, Sydney 1969–1979**

| Year | General cargo (000 tonnes) | Container movements (TEU[a]) | Registered waterside workers (number) |
|---|---|---|---|
| 1968/69 | 5,430 | 11,290 | 4,323 |
| 1969/70 | 6,469 | 85,018 | 4,560 |
| 1970/71 | 7,136 | 117,985 | 4,273 |
| 1971/72 | 7,065 | 150,148 | 3,700 |
| 1972/73 | 7,177 | 165,980 | 3,332 |
| 1973/74 | 7,823 | 243,745 | 3,493 |
| 1974/75 | 8,702 | 262,166 | 3,626 |
| 1975/76 | 7,675 | 267,882 | 3,095 |
| 1976/77 | 9,024 | 311,308 | 2,514 |
| 1977/78 | 8,123 | 298,232 | 2,453 |
| 1978/79 | 8,854 | 349,337 | 2,336 |

*Note:* [a] The TEU (twenty foot equivalent) is universally used to equate different sized containers to a common unit. One 20 foot container is one TEU while a 40 foot container is equivalent to two TEUs and a 10 foot container to 0.5 TEU.
*Source:* NSW (1980a Vol.I:7)

conflicts that arise at the interface between the transport network and economic units. In Sydney, container movements are concentrated in the central peninsula, the area between Port Jackson-Parramatta River in the north and Georges River in the south, which contains the major freight generating land uses of the metropolitan area. The peninsula has three main subregions (Figure 12.3). Within the eastern subregion there are three main foci: (a) Port Jackson, with container terminals at Glebe Island, Mort Bay (now closed) and White Bay, and conventional wharves handling containers at Darling Harbour and Woolloomooloo, container depots at Alexandria and Rozelle, and the main intrastate rail freight terminal at Darling Harbour; (b) the central industrial area (South Sydney, Botany, parts of Randwick, Marrickville, Sydenham and Sydney Airport); and (c) Port Botany (under construction). The mid peninsula subregion comprises the Milperra road haulage terminal, railway marshalling yards and workshops at Enfield, the container depot at Chullora, and the industrial areas of Auburn, Silverwater, Clyde, Homebush-Flemington (the location of the new city markets and a site earmarked for future transport terminals) and Bankstown. Com-

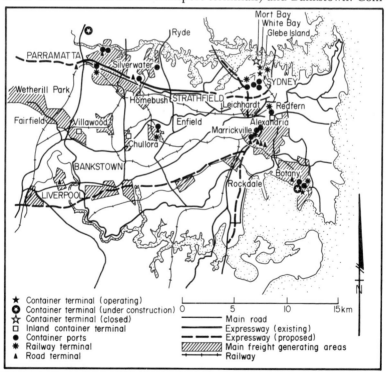

**Figure 12.3   Major freight generating areas and main transport links in the central peninsula of Sydney**

mercial vehicle movements in the western subregion are focused on expanding industrial areas at Blacktown, Wetherill Park, Smithfield-Fairfield and Liverpool, all of which attracted road and rail terminals (including the container terminal at Villawood) and outliers at St Marys and Campbelltown.

Most container movements are concentrated in the central industrial area (although dispersal of manufacturing and other business might change this pattern). In 1978, the mid and western subregions attracted only 32 per cent of FCL import container movements and produced 11 per cent of FCL export container movements. [Where a container is loaded with cargo for only one consignee it is referred to as FCL (full container load) and under normal circumstances would be transported by road to its ultimate destination. If the container is loaded with cargo for a number of consignees it is referred to as LCL (Less-than-container load). Because of different ultimate destinations of the cargo in any one container, LCLs are normally transported to a depot where they are unloaded and the cargo for each consignee separated and independently despatched.]

*Port Jackson*

Air, rail and road terminals have all been reorganised to accommodate containers, but sea terminals illustrate the activity conflicts arising at the interface between economic units and the transport network. For example, a survey in June 1978 at Sydney's then four major wharves — Darling Harbour, Glebe Island, White Bay and Mort Bay — over ten working days recorded almost 10,000 truck movements involving 6,500 containers (Edgerton *et al.* 1979). Another 4,500 containers were moved by rail, so that overall 61 per cent of containers were transported by road and 39 per cent by rail, but with significant differences in modal split between depots (Table 12.3).

**Table 12.3   Road-rail breakdown by wharf at Port Jackson, 1978**

| Wharf | Average daily throughput | | Average daily truck movements | |
|---|---|---|---|---|
| | Road and rail number (TEU)[a] | Road (%) | no. | % |
| Darling Harbour | 363 | 85 | 458 | 46 |
| Mort Bay | 126 | 100 | 205 | 21 |
| Glebe Island | 214 | 59 | 223 | 22 |
| White Bay | 350 | 24 | 111 | 11 |
| | 1,053 | 61 | 997 | 100 |

*Note:* [a] See note on Table 12.2
*Source:* Edgerton *et al.* 1979:66

Almost half of the trucks surveyed were moving to or from Darling Harbour where access was most difficult and truck queueing commonplace (Table 12.3). Glebe Island generated 22 per cent of all road movements, predominantly metropolitan FCL and LCL movements to and from the Liner Services Pty. Ltd. depot in Alexandria. Mort Bay movements were entirely by road, and they almost matched Glebe Island flows. White Bay, however, only accounted for 11 per cent of truck movements. Following congestion in 1973 and 1974 (after the reduction of tariffs had boosted imports), FCL containers from White Bay have been railed to Seatainers depot at Chullora. (In 1978/79 the Chullora depot handled 35,700 FCL containers and 11,750 LCL containers and employed 171 persons; comparable figures for Villawood depot are 4,000 FCL, 11,000 LCL and 161 workers.) Nevertheless, complaints have been made about noise from operations in residential areas adjacent to White Bay and inadequate access for heavy vehicles (even queueing into Victoria Road, a major arterial road, during peak periods in 1973 and 1974). Glebe Island, however, avoided similar complaints as operations were away from residential areas and trucks gained access via an underpass below Victoria Road.

More than two thirds of all trucks leaving the wharves were semitrailers, one quarter rigid trucks and the remainder semitrailers pulling dog trailers. (Trucks used for the distribution and delivery of LCL cargo were smaller, almost four fifths being rigid trucks and only one tenth being semitrailers.) Semitrailers, capable of carrying one 40 foot container or two 20 foot containers, were most prominent at Mort Bay. Most rigid trucks moved from Glebe Island and most semitrailers pulling dog trailers from Darling Harbour. There were, then, marked differences in the character of individual wharves, reflecting their propensity to serve specific trades. Vehicles leaving White Bay, for example, carried special cargoes such as refrigerated containers ('reefers'), chemicals, dangerous cargoes, and units with unusual dimensions unsuited to rail carriage.

Darling Harbour produced and attracted an average of over 65 truck movements an hour during the survey period, Glebe Island 32, Mort Bay 29, and White Bay less than 16. Traffic generation figures are not available on an hourly basis for individual depots. However, aggregate statistics (Figure 12.4) suggest a fairly even flow from 7.30 am to 2.30 pm, apart from the lull in movements from 11.30 am to 12.30 pm (coinciding with the lunch break on the wharves). Inward movements predominate between 7.30 am and 8.30 am as empty trucks arrive to pick up FCL for delivery; the inward stream continues at a lower level for the rest of the working day. Laden trucks leave from 8.30 am onwards, although more movements are recorded after 10.30 am. Container trucks are less of a problem during the afternoon commuter peak because few deliveries are made after 2.30 pm, as two hours are required for unstuffing. This temporal pattern emphasises the significance of the container truck in the traffic mix during the morning commuter peak but not the afternoon peak. Thus, it is important to examine the resultant vehicle conflicts because the 'container vehicle, even in a sea of cars, stands out as an elephant would stand out amidst a flock of pigeons' (NSW 1980a Vol.I:89).

## 12.5 Vehicle conflicts

Conflicts occur between vehicles carrying containers and other vehicles (or pedestrians) on the road network. They also occur because of the impact of heavy commercial vehicles on the adjacent physical and social environment. As trucks have become larger and more numerous, there has been increasing public nervousness, especially about road safety.

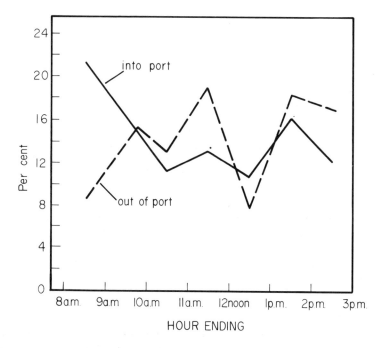

**Figure 12.4  Time profile of container truck movements to and from Port Jackson, 1978. (*source:* Edgerton *et al.* 1979:78)**

Traffic accidents between trucks and other vehicles are unevenly distributed across the Sydney metropolitan area. The highest incidence (on a *per capita* basis) is in the central peninsula, first in a triangular area lying between the City of Sydney, Botany and Drummoyne, and second in middle western and south western LGAs from Parramatta to Liverpool. In contrast, northern suburbs have relatively few truck accidents. Unfortunately, there are no figures on whether the trucks were carrying containers.

However, evidence from the Commission of Enquiry into the NSW Road Freight Industry highlights that trucks, especially articulated vehicles carrying containers, make a disproportionate contribution to fatal accidents. Although articulated trucks form only 0.6 per cent of registered vehicles in NSW, in 1977 they accounted for 1.4 per cent of all vehicles involved in tow-away crashes, 1.5 per cent of accidents where injury was reported and 5.3 per cent of all fatal crashes (NSW 1980b Vol.IV:5-18). Even when the incidence of crashes is related to kilometres travelled, articulated vehicles are involved in twice as many fatal crashes as other vehicles. The Enquiry attributed this accident proneness to design features, particularly inferior braking capability, weight and rigidity on impact. These statistics do little to assuage public fear of trucks carrying containers, particularly as the safety aspect is compounded by other environmental problems.

Noise emission from a container truck, like any other heavy vehicle, is higher than from a motor car and thus has a disproportionately larger effect on the noise level of the general traffic stream. The PEC estimated that the cost of additional noise from Port Botany is $8,270,000, of which $1,350,000 is attributable to container trucks (NSW 1980a Vol.I:173-174). Not only do trucks operate at high noise levels, they restrict visibility for overtaking and restrain the speed of other vehicles especially at traffic signals and on grades. There is, however, no evidence that container trucks significantly add to local or regional air pollution problems or ground or air borne vibration. Nevertheless, the 'passage of a container vehicle, especially under load is accompanied by fumes, noise and vibration' (NSW 1980a Vol.I:27). The way in which the combination of all three elements accentuates each ingredient is most spectacularly illustrated by the environmental problems at Mort Bay, Balmain.

## Mort Bay, Balmain

Roll-on roll-off facilities for interstate general cargo and passengers were initially developed by the Australian National Line in 1965 on the site of Mort's Dock Engineering Co. Ltd.; an additional wharf was constructed by the Line in 1969 to accommodate the Eastern Searoad Service operating between Australia and Japan. Container movements generated by these facilities had to negotiate narrow roads through residential areas. Not surprisingly, this led to hostility from residents in Balmain and Rozelle. A frequent complaint was that the MSB' has perhaps quite properly approached the question of the introduction of containers purely from a maritime point of view. It has not concerned itself with the overall economics envisaged let alone paid any attention to social costs' (Australia 1970:79-80). The situation led to the preparation of a report by Balmain residents arguing for the earliest possible elimination of cargo trucking through Balmain (Balmain Residents 1975).

Australian National Line figures indicated that approximately 1,000 trucks moved in and out of Mort Bay during the 66 hour week. They were concentrated on Ballast Point Road, Rowntree Street and Mort Street. In November 1974, Mort Street residents counted 79 trucks per hour at peak periods. All-day counts in April 1975 indicated average volumes of between 15 and 25 trucks per hour between 7 am and 5 pm. An assessment of the impact of container trucks on residential amenity found that the 140 households interviewed in three areas were frightened of the danger of container trucks, damage to parked cars and fatal accidents involving pedestrians. Complaints of irritability and nervous tension arising from noise, vibration and fear were noted by probe groups taking noise measurements in April 1975. Consultants taking vibration measurements found that it was the most frequently cited impact of container trucking, but its magnitude was not sufficient to cause structural damage to buildings. Nevertheless, penalties were encountered by the residents: estate agents perceived that there was a drop of between five and ten per cent in house prices and that a longer period than normal elapsed before a sale was effected.

There was no doubt that the Mort Bay terminals were an environmental mistake. The backlash was so severe that the Australian National Line quit the congested site in Balmain in April 1980 for Port Botany, which offered improved 'operational environmental conditions'. Forewarned by the confrontation between the Australian National Line and residents at Balmain, the host community in Botany feared that similar adverse environmental impacts would occur there once the port was fully operational. This raises the question whether any analogy can be drawn between Mort Bay and Port Botany, itself a classic example of locational restructuring conflicts.

## 12.6   Locational restructuring conflicts

The inadequacy of Port Jackson and adjacent transport facilities has been highlighted by recent economic and technological changes. Despite substantial port redevelopment to receive container vessels, sites have proved too small to handle revolutionary changes in bulk and general cargoes. Major transport network deficiencies have been identified (Rimmer 1978; Scott 1975: Urban Transport Study Group of NSW 1978): there were general shortcomings in north-south and east-west links in the central peninsula and more specific locations requiring traffic engineering works to facilitate container movements. Sydney's arterial road system has been progressively improved but traffic regulations and signs, signals and markings provide, at best, temporary relief in the face of rising private vehicle ownership. However, the freeways envisaged as part of the County of Cumberland Plan and later included in the plan recommended by the Sydney Area Transportation Study (NSW. SATS 1974a) were stillborn, especially in the inner city where new transport linkages have lagged behind changing requirements. As new engineering works involving the addition of major new terminals or transport linkages are capital intensive, indivisible and long lasting, there is a special need to examine any conflicts. Port Botany and associated road works provide an instructive case study of uncoordinated urban development (NSW 1980a, 1981).

*Port Botany*

As the state government wanted to maintain Sydney as Australia's premier port, a decision was made in 1969 to establish a port at Port Botany. It involved the physical transformation of Botany Bay, at a reported cost of $150 million (1980 prices), through dredging, construction of a breakwater and reclamation of a large area. A V-shaped port entrance channel 19.2 metres deep was dredged in the mouth of Botany Bay to accommodate 200,000 dwt tankers and to absorb much of the wave force when strong east-southeasterly winds blow. Ostensibly designed for petroleum imports and bulk cargoes, Port Botany's construction started in June 1971, the year before environmental impact statements and subsequent public inquiry became NSW government policy.

Rapid growth of container traffic through Sydney forced a review of plans for Port Botany in 1974 and the incorporation of terminals in the overall design. Hence, the development on the northern foreshore of the bay involved the reclamation of about 225 hectares of land and a re-entrant basin dredged to 15.3 metres with 1,936 metres of wharfage to accommodate two container terminals, each with three berths. In a largely industrial area, with the old Bunnerong Power Station, the Australian Paper Mills and the Caltex terminal, the development was thought likely to cause little conflict with existing land use. Nevertheless, the location decision was criticised by the Botany Bay Project because it disregarded 'the land-use impact on the hinterland, the effects on city design, the social disturbances to city residents, the efficiency and economic rationality of the investment project and the social implications for the land environment' (Butlin 1976a:94). In particular, the Project drew attention to the area's poor landward connections to the expanding industrial areas in the west, limited rail facilities, constraints imposed by Sydney Airport, and perhaps the most limited resource of all, community tolerance (King 1977:10).

The revised rationale for the new port was that the container facilities at Port Jackson would be hard pressed to handle 285,000 TEU (20 foot container equivalent units) let alone the rather conservative forecast of 418,000 TEUs for 1984/85. It is estimated that in 1984/85 65 per cent of containers (273,000 TEU) will move through Port Botany and 35 per cent (145,000 TEU) through Port Jackson (capacity 300,000 TEU). The opening of Port Botany's northern terminal operated by the Australian National Line in December 1979 (an industrial dispute delayed the commencement of operations until March 1980) and the southern terminal by Container Terminals Australia Ltd. (nearing completion in mid 1981) should relieve these problems. The difficulty, however, is that the shift to the Port Botany location has altered the modal split by moving containers from rail to road.

As the Botany Bay terminals have been designed for a road delivery system, fewer containers will travel by rail than was the case when trade was confined to Port Jackson: 53 per cent of the containers previously carried from Port Jackson will be transferred to road when Port Botany is fully operational. On the assumption that only 20 per cent of the 145,000 containers will be railed from Port Jackson in 1984/85, both the depots at Chullora and Villawood will be doubtful economic propositions. There will also be an increase in heavy vehicles movements (estimated at 1,600 per day at Port Botany). These will travel through hitherto relatively unexposed suburbs such as Rockdale, Bexley and Campsie, because the opening of Port Botany will reorient travel patterns.

An extra 512 container trucks per day will be funnelled through Rockdale, Bexley and Campsie alone. As they will be travelling on inadequate roads, it is not surprising that an analogy is drawn with Mort Bay, Balmain. Although the Rockdale roads are wider than those in Balmain, their greater width is insufficient for a marked attenuation of noise. Both areas are hilly but Rockdale will have to accommodate more trucks — 89 instead of 60 per hour at the peak in Balmain. Routes through Rockdale are most unsuitable for container trucks and there is little doubt that environmental degradation would ensue. The container companies, however, are adamant that there should be no interference in the exporter/importer's choice of transport mode in moving their units within Sydney. Their argument is that either containers do not cause any environmental problems or, if they do, operational, practical and financial considerations would make alternatives less desirable, if not impracticable. If the free market case prevailed, rail would, according to the NSW government (NSW 1980a Vol.I:71), account for 70,400 TEU (26 per cent) and road 273,000 TEU (74 per cent) in 1984/85, figures that would mean between 786 and 808 full containers and between 235 and 242 empty containers moving by road each day. In turn, these figures have to be inflated to reflect the number of trips generated, as each loaded FCL container involves on average 3.5 truck movements.

Local councils in the Botany Bay subregion strongly opposed this anticipated flow of container trucks. Clamour grew for the increased use of rail and the state government (NSW 1980a) considered two options other than road construction. One was the State Rail Authority's proposition offering environmental benefits by having 70 per cent of all containers carried by rail, through the establishment of depots at Cooks River goodsyard, Rozelle goodsyard, Chullora and Villawood. Import containers would be carried to the depot nearest their destination and export containers to the depot nearest their origin. The other was the western suburbs scheme, which would force all import or export containers originating within a defined western zone (including Campbelltown, Liverpool, Bankstown, Strathfield, Concord, Ryde and Hornsby) to be handled at decentralised depots at Villawood and Chullora rather than Port Jackson or Port Botany, a scheme mooted by the Botany Port and Environment Inquiry [The Simblist Report] (NSW 1976) and advocated also by the PEC. It would result in approximately 47 per cent of the containers handled by Port Botany moving by rail.

Unlike these two options, a new road does not offer an immediate solution to the container problem as it would take at least ten years to build. After rejecting both the environmentally damaging free market and the cumbersome State Rail Authority proposals the Commission of Inquiry into the Kyeemagh-Chullora Road (NSW 1980a) recommended that the western suburbs scheme be adopted. It had the advantage of not cutting across shipping line affiliations with particular depots and offered relief to Rockdale, Bexley and Campsie because it reduced the number of trucks per day from 512 to 67. The extra cost of railing all containers destined for or originating in the defined western zone was estimated by the Commissioner at $20 per unit (though no attempt seems to have been made to estimate the value of time). The Inquiry then went on to examine a series of road options as a possible long term 'solution' to the problems caused by containers generated by Port Botany.

### The Kyeemagh-Chullora Road Inquiry

Container truck traffic, specifically that from Port Botany, and growth of commuter traffic demand led to the commissioning of the

Kyeemagh-Chullora Road Inquiry in 1978. It commenced in June 1979 to look into major road deficiencies in the linking of the new port with the industrial areas in the west and south west of Sydney. Three options were examined: (a) the Cooks River route along the Cooks River valley, which was a road reservation in the County of Cumberland Plan in 1951; (b) the south west route along the Wolli Creek valley, also a protected corridor in the County of Cumberland Plan; and (c) the Bexley Road route where there were two possibilities, the Bestic Street/Villiers Street (Rockdale) alternative, and the Bay Road/Harrow Road (Rockdale) route, both of which are linked to Bexley Road and the Campsie bypass (Figure 12.5).

The land use-transport implications, economic criteria, social effects and environmental consequences considered by the government (NSW 1981) in assessing the three options are summarised in Table 12.4. (Equity criteria could not be adequately incorporated into the Inquiry.) The Bexley Road route was unacceptable because it achieved little in transport terms and the attendant human costs were disproportionately

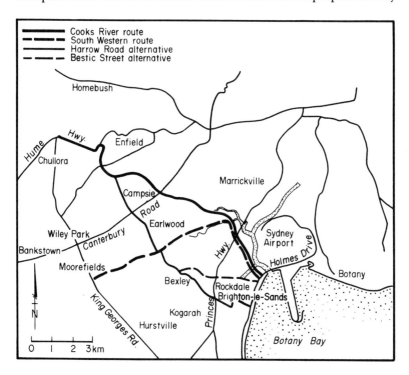

**Figure 12.5    Principal options studied by NSW Commission of Inquiry into the Kyeemagh-Chullora road**

high: the circuitous Harrow Road route adversely affected Brighton and Bexley shopping centres and, although the Bestic Street route avoided these difficulties, even worse social problems were created. The radial south west route was not recommended because it accentuated the attraction of the city centre and the central industrial area, encouraged longer journeys, generated further traffic, competed with rail, had a benefit-cost ratio of less than one and had the worst environmental consequences. The Cooks River route, at $88 million (1978 prices) the most expensive of the three options, was also rejected because of lack of enthusiasm for a northern route alignment that circumnavigated the airport and the southern alignment which would have created additional congestion problems in Marrickville and destroyed 'regional self-containment'. Other alternatives considered feasible by the Inquiry, in addition to the zonal regulation of containers, were establishment of a road hierarchy, establishment of truck routes, spot improvements at critical intersections, and restructuring shopping centres away from main roads. All of these options had been canvassed previously (Rimmer 1978), emphasising the limited number of strategies available. Indeed, the state government's reliance on inquiries may suggest a weak-handed approach to conflict resolution. As the choice between

**Table 12.4    Analysis of the options and major sub-options considered by the Kyeemagh-Chullora Road Inquiry**

| Criteria | Bexley Road | | South West | Cooks River |
| | Harrow Road | Bestic Street | | |
| --- | --- | --- | --- | --- |
| 1 Transport implications | | | | |
| Length (km) | 14.6 | 13.3 | 16.7 | 13.0 |
| Cost ($million 1978 prices) | 15.2 | 17.8 | 56.6 | 88.0 |
| 2 Economic effects | | | | |
| Benefit/cost ratio | 1.51 | 1.54 | 0.95 | 1.16 |
| 3 Social impact | | | | |
| Buildings displaced | 49 | 91 | 158 | 212 |
| Partial acquisitions | 80 | 86 | 51 | 115 |
| Properties injuriously affected | 520 | 620 | 115 | 480 |
| Accidents | increased | increased | safest | increased |
| Severance | insubstantial | severe | reduced | increased |
| 4 Environmental consequences | | | | |
| Noise immediate | less severe | substantial | reduced | severe |
| Noise regional | less severe | substantial | worst | improved |
| Air pollution | no change | severe | unfavourable | severe |
| Open space | 2.0 ha loss | 0.9 ha loss | 36 ha loss | 6.6 ha loss |
| Visual effects | slight | slight | worst | minimal |

*Source:* Based on NSW (1981 Vol.4); see also NSW. DMR and PEC (1979)

approaches is essentially a philosophical one, we follow King (1977) and venture into the realm of political economy to examine different perspectives on conflict and conflict resolution.

## 12.7 Conclusion

In essence, government is a standardised arrangement for taking common decisions (or resolving conflicts) affecting different 'actors' in the community. When rival groups propose exclusive policies that resolve conflicts to their own satisfaction, the government must replace sectional self-interest with some common binding policy of unanimity. Theoretically, such a policy is implemented by the exercise of political power ranging from coercion to persuasion. At different times, as a study of the mechanisms of conflict resolution concerning goods movements in Sydney would demonstrate, different styles of government will be apparent. One cogent way of distinguishing these governmental styles is to ask the question: how far is the public involved or excluded from the governing process? In a democracy the extent to which the public shares in the process of government is marginal: their principal role is to control the activities of government by their ability to elect (or reject) representatives.

For much of Sydney's history, urban affairs have remained outside the mainstream of policy issues and any social objectives of urban development have been submerged by the overriding acceptance of the market as the arbiter in determining the pattern of development. Where the government has been responsible for providing and maintaining essential services, such as roads, railways and port facilities, the responsible authorities have, according to Healey (1977), subscribed to a market oriented consensus model of society. These conservative organisations are 'hierarchical and inegalitarian, with a decision process which is elite oriented, and planning procedures based upon the concept of the expert' (Healey 1977:205).

The principal acts administered by the MSB, for instance, include the control and administration of wharves and other harbour facilities, together with the provision and maintenance of adequate wharfage, channels and port facilities. Under its statutory borrowing powers, the Board can raise loans to finance major capital works (in addition to loan money made available by the state government). Planning procedures and decisions (including the 1913 Master Plan, the decision by the Labor government in 1961 to place Botany Bay under the jurisdiction of the MSB, the redevelopment of Port Jackson to accommodate container ships in 1969, and the eventual commencement of construction of Port Botany in 1971) have been based on objective technical expertise; the community has been excluded from any participation.

In the early 1970s the diversity of interests and values which characterised society was exacerbating tensions between planners and the community. The social system (and its members and groups) was perceived to be in 'differential disequilibrium' with its environment and was adjusting to its changing moods with differing degrees of effectiveness depending on its command of resources of wealth, education and political power (King 1977). The more affluent, better educated and politically powerful were able to further their own interests by advocating freeways and ports to serve their activities or firms. All investments, therefore, were seen as being generated by social conflict and competition. This was reflected in the clamour for popular participation to incorporate 'quality of life' and environmental issues previously excluded by the market dominated planning process.

When the MSB began its investigation into the feasibility of developing Botany Bay, environmentalists, ecologists and local residents began drawing up their battle line to suspend development. The Botany Bay Management and Coordination Committee identified 25 environmental studies dating back to the 1950s, although the Coalition government remained convinced that development could proceed without destroying the unique features of Botany Bay. As protests over the likely effects of container truck movements grew with the rapid adoption of this new method of handling overseas cargo, lack of coordination between ministers and departments responsible for metropolitan public works and services became increasingly evident. Hence, the urban planning authority, acting as a coordinating body of reference, acquired a powerful consultative role. Nevertheless, this power has at times been insufficient against ministers and their departments unwilling to forego freedoms to respond to exigencies by deferring to some other organisation. In the hope that they will engender the necessary organisational changes to resolve conflicts, the state's way out of the impasse has been to appoint committees and inquiries.

The operations at Botany Bay have spawned a series of organisational changes and inquiries to cope with conflicts related to port traffic. In 1976, the Botany Bay Port and Environmental Inquiry [The Simblist Report] (NSW 1976) was established. Then, in 1977, the PEC established the Botany Bay Subregion Planning Team 'to act as a focal point for public participation'. Between September 1977 and September 1978 the DMR and the PEC (NSW. DMR and PEC 1979) were preparing a joint study of the Cooks River route to link Port Botany with the western suburbs (public comment was invited), but the Labor government intervened and established a Commission of Inquiry. Public awareness about the Inquiry was heightened by extensive publicity. The Commissioner received 1,436 written petitions and submissions, about 60 of which were substantial contributions, and some 200 appearances were invited whereby, in an open court-style procedure, submissions could be elaborated and their credibility examined.

The Kirby Report represents a masterly synthesis of wide ranging evidence and provides a set of recommendations (NSW 1980a, 1981). It also encapsulates a liberal perspective as questions of equity are kept absolutely external to the policy or investment. 'Decisions are to be made on efficiency grounds alone, and then compensation or specific welfare policies are to be urged to remedy any non-preferred equity effects resulting from real income distribution or other impacts' (King 1977:1). As a corollary to this approach, the Commissioner has been adamant that projects should not be used to achieve social welfare objectives. Thus, Kirby implies that the planner's role should be to make all differential effects explicit so that they could be tackled by other aspects of public policy.

Social conflicts and competition underlie the generation of projects but they are themselves the result of historical processes. Activity, vehicle and locational restructuring conflicts in Sydney associated with the onset of global restructuring have threatened the collective conditions for facilitating production and reproducing labour. We have seen that the planner's response to dislocations in urban form, produced by the anarchical decision making by private firms and individuals, in relation to containers, has been to provide a series of stopgap measures to overcome the symptoms of what Scott (1980) has described as 'urban pathogenesis'. As the new set of spatial arrangements trigger another round of decision making by private firms and individuals, fresh dislocations and dissonances are created. These, in turn, prompt more state intervention and a new set of palliative and piecemeal public decisions. So the process goes on, with the state cast in a reactive role in a bid to avoid the 'self-paralysis' endemic in the myriad of decisions made by private firms and individuals (Scott 1980:189-191).

# 13 Planning and the journey to work

## Sydney's North Shore and Northern Beaches region

GRAEME J. APLIN

## 13.1 Introduction

Cities remain vital because of the interaction and movement within them. The wide range of talents, functions and activities available attract people and organisations to them. But variety and choice mean little if the activities and resources involved are not readily accessible. One important aim of urban planning must be to promote access and facilitate interaction.

There are two ways of promoting accessibility. One is to improve transport and communications to facilitate flows of people, goods and information. The other is to allocate facilities and land uses so that the need for movement is reduced. In the past, planners have tended to concentrate on land use zoning and leave transport planning to other authorities, or have been forced to solve transport problems after land use decisions have been made. Only recently have the two approaches become more effectively integrated at both metropolitan and local planning scales. However, both have also to be done in the political context of state and local government, where sectional community interests may be in conflict with planning objectives or with strategies that would be most equitable for the wider community.

This chapter examines the conflicts between planning objectives, transport proposals and community interests relating to the pattern of movement within and from the North Shore and Northern Beaches region (Figure 13.1). An extensive but fragmented, mostly high status, residential area, it houses a large number of people who cross the Sydney Harbour Bridge daily to work. Employment generating land use and high density residential subdivisions are discouraged in much of the area; both would help to reduce the length of work journeys. It is an area where community interests have been effective in controlling land use. Thus, it is a useful case study of the effectiveness of land use and transport planning practices where conflicts exist with an informed, influential electorate.

The chapter considers the relationship between urban form and

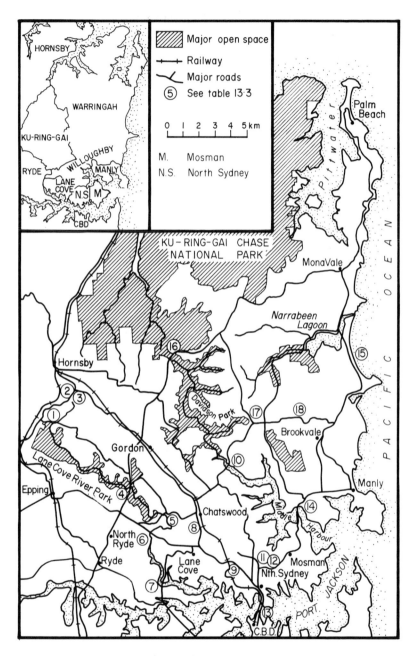

**Figure 13.1    The North Shore and Northern Beaches region**

movement patterns, pointing to the influence of planning approaches (section 13.2). It then outlines the major planning schemes and transport proposals for the area (section 13.3) and describes its present transport links (section 13.4). Contemporary journey to work patterns are evaluated using criteria employed in planning (sections 13.5 and 13.6), providing the basis for a consideration of future developments and the implications for planning (section 13.7).

## 13.2 Intraurban movement and planning

Urban form affects movement patterns in many ways. The propensity to travel is a function of the desire for distant goals and of the ease of movement to them. Hence, the separation of activities creates potential travel needs. Any movement, however, involves overcoming the frictional effect of distance, which in turn involves not only distance but also cost, time and convenience. This frictional effect can be reduced either by decreasing distance or by making movement easier, but it is in any case a function of the density and degree of separation of different land use.

The form of the city is influenced by both planners and their political masters in state and particularly local government. Both groups have emphasised approaches involving low density development and strict zoning, rather than medium or high density multiple use strategies. Segregation of different forms of land use has been a preoccupation of planners. Such a concern stems largely from a reaction against nineteenth century industrial towns with their unfortunate mixtures of houses and environmentally undesirable industry. Furthermore, both industry and commerce have traditionally generated traffic and other impacts (noise, odour) incompatible with residential areas. Strict zoning has been reinforced by community attitudes. In exclusive residential areas, residents resist both non-residential and medium density residential land use. Part of the study area, the Municipality of Ku-ring-gai, was one of the main users of Sydney's earliest form of land use zoning, the restrictive Residential District Proclamation of 1929. Councils (i.e. the elected body), with limited appreciation of the intent and potential of planning and sometimes contrary to planners' recommendations, have also sought the simplest and generally most restrictive zonings rather than the necessarily more complex and less comprehensible mixed use zonings.

Some planners have advocated multiple use, medium to high density planning strategies. Their numbers have grown with the rapid increases in energy costs in the 1970s. Sensitive planning, they claim, allows industry and commerce to be located in, or near to, residential areas without loss of amenity. The length of journeys to work and other forms of movement are potentially greatly reduced.

One difficulty faced by urban planners is that numerous factors are operating at different scales. Many transport planning decisions need to be made at a regional or metropolitan scale and the prerogative to make the decisions is guarded by the authorities operating the facilities. Furthermore, large scale movements relate to broad structural features which, again, require planning at the metropolitan scale. At the same time, however, major transport routes and employment generating land use are often seen as necessarily detracting from local environmental amenity. Local pressure groups and municipal councils understandably and correctly concern themselves with such effects, whether real or imagined. They so often fail to take into account broader issues. The health of the city as a whole depends on accessibility. By resisting the development of transport facilities they may deny people both within and beyond their boundaries adequate access to urban facilities. By resisting the establishment of local employment, they magnify commuting flows and the attendant problems.

## 13.3   Planning and the study region

The County of Cumberland Plan (CCC 1948) was the first attempt since colonial days to comprehensively plan the Sydney region. One of its major concerns was with improving the so called 'living-employment' balance. Growth in the CBD was to be limited, employment dispersed to suburban centres and some satellite towns developed. Each district should have 'dispersed industry providing for local employment', but 'in districts such as Manly-Warringah, Ku-ring-gai, and the northern shore of Port Jackson, natural topography and transport difficulties have retarded industrial development' (CCC 1948:77, 91). Whilst a principle was espoused, practical difficulties were recognised. Within the study region, Chatswood, Manly and Crows Nest were seen as future growth centres. Others, such as Spit Junction, North Sydney, Lindfield and Gordon were to be subsidiary centres. Planning maps accompanying the report show land for industry at Dee Why, Brookvale, East Willoughby, Lane Cove West and Artarmon similar in extent to these areas in 1981. Further sizeable industrial areas are shown to the north of the then existing North Sydney commercial centre and on the waterfront to the south west. These areas were both greatly reduced in later plans. The major regional transport proposal was for 'the Warringah Expressway, a regional road providing access to Manly and the Warringah district, at the same time drawing off heavy transit traffic now passing through Mosman' (CCC 1948:163).

Twenty years later, the Sydney Region Outline Plan tackled similar problems in similar ways. It concluded that the 'living-employment' balance for the study region had not improved since 1948, particularly not in Manly-Warringah and for non-factory employment, despite considerable office development in North Sydney since the late 1950s (NSW. SPA 1967). The balance still needed improvement. 'A basic principle . . . is to encourage the development of a limited number of large new commercial centres offering substantial employment opportunities, more particularly office employment' (NSW. SPA 1967:22). 'It is desirable to divert office employment to centres on the North Shore railway line . . ., but with greater growth at Chatswood because of its strategic location in relation to Warringah Shire' (NSW. SPA 1968:35). Office employment and shopping development at a regional scale were seen as mutually reinforcing. There was no mention of further industrial development in the study region. Commuting flows clearly caused concern: 'one of the biggest movement problems in Sydney is that of journey to work movements across the Harbour' (NSW. SPA 1968:32-5). Both the Harbour Bridge and Roseville Bridge were seen as heavily congested. A proposal for housing 120,000 extra people in North Warringah was floated but, because of the transport and infrastructure problems, was set aside for further study.

Detailed planning was, and is, the prerogative of local government. Municipal schemes have fleshed out the bare bones of the Outline Plan. In areas zoned industrial or commercial little has changed since the Cumberland Plan (Figure 13.2). The only sizeable areas zoned industrial are in the locations designated in the earlier plan. In North Sydney waterfront industrial zoning has been greatly reduced, whilst zoning of much of North Sydney itself has been changed to commercial. Both Mosman and Ku-ring-gai planning maps include a notation that 'there is no land zoned industrial under this scheme', a claim repeated with obvious pride in some Ku-ring-gai Municipal Council publicity material. There are several district commercial centres but Chatswood and the North Sydney to St Leonards area are the only large office/ commercial centres (Alexander ch 3). Hornsby, just north of the study region, offers both commercial and manufacturing jobs.

Finally, the Sydney Area Transportation Study (NSW. SATS 1974b) proposed schemes to overcome transport problems. It began from the dual base of the existing journey to work pattern and the principles of the Outline Plan, but unfortunately no real attempt was made to bring together transport and land use planning in a coherent approach to Sydney's interaction and accessibility problems. The plan's major (or resurrected) proposal for the study region was for a rail link between Newport and St Leonards. An extension to North Sydney would provide a link passing through the employment-rich area along the Pacific Highway. The existing Warringah Expressway would be extended to Narrabeen with a branch to Fairlight. A second branch would connect to Epping Highway at Lane Cove. Hornsby would be linked to North Ryde and the Gladesville Bridge by another freeway, thus taking

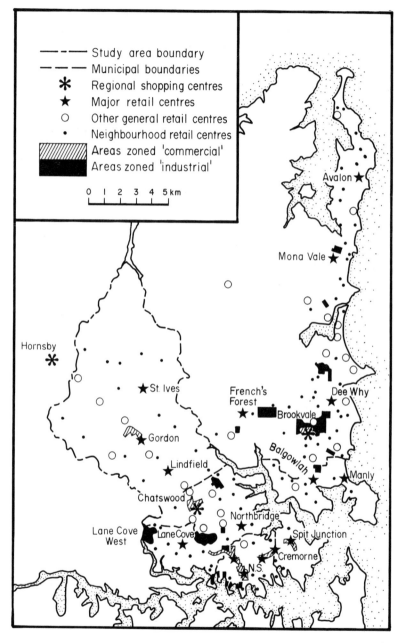

**Figure 13.2  Shopping centres and commercial and industrial land in the North Shore and Northern Beaches region**

pressure off roads in the study region and the Harbour Bridge. Very few of these proposals have been or look like being carried out. Limited upgrading has taken place on the existing North Shore railway; the Warringah Expressway has been extended slightly and might reach Epping Highway in the next few years; and an express bus now links Chatswood and Parramatta. In 1981, the state government announced an inquiry into the future use of land resumed for later stages of the Warringah Expressway. Options mentioned included disposal, use for a freeway and use for some form of public transport.

All of these plans have recognised the possibility of some employment decentralisation to suburban nodes. Despite this, there remains an underlying assumption that overall commuting patterns will remain much as they are. Attention had been focused more on making journeys smoother than on decreasing the need for them or changing the major transport mode employed. In some ways it may be more sensible in the long run to retain a highly concentrated employment pattern but to encourage a major shift away from private cars.

## 13.4    Present transport links

The study region has been chosen to illustrate a number of points. It is not typical of Sydney's suburban districts, nor does it necessarily have the worst transport problems. On the other hand, its movement patterns are greatly influenced by the physical landscape and by the effects of exclusionary zoning and low density development. Furthermore, the region has a particularly strong commuting relationship with the CBD.

Strong physical barriers surround the study region except in the north west. Rugged valleys and reserves severely limit the number of road connections between the region and employment centres to the west and between subregions within it (Figure 13.1). Port Jackson is a formidable barrier to the south, although it also acts as a transport medium. Movement is thus concentrated onto a small number of congested major arteries (Figure 13.1). The limited number of points at which the Harbour and other physical barriers can be crossed also adds greatly to the length of many trips.

Buses are the major form of public transport, in terms of their areal coverage if not in terms of passenger numbers. They feed to railway stations and ferry wharves and link the Northern Beaches district and the southern sections of the North Shore directly to the CBD. They also provide important links between Frenchs Forest and Chatswood and between the North Shore area and the Ryde district. The single rail link runs along the main ridge from Hornsby to North Sydney and then to the CBD. A second link from Hornsby skirts the north western boundary of the study region to link with the Ryde district. Harbour ferries and hydrofoils are the only other non-road transport available.


## 13.5   Living-employment balance

We have seen that planners have paid considerable attention to the balance between residents and jobs. Job ratios give one crude measure of the extent to which such a balance has been achieved. The total job ratio is the number of jobs in an area for each 100 resident workers (Figure 13.3, Table 13.1).

It is, indeed, a crude measure. This crudeness stems in part from the use of LGAs as the areal data units. No LGA is homogenous. Furthermore, any movements across the boundary between two LGAs may involve very short distances. For many purposes the units are far too coarse. They also vary greatly in size. The job ratio relates only to net movements; total movements are often grossly understated. A second measure that partially overcomes the last objection, but not the others, is the percentage of the local workforce employed in their 'home' LGA (Figure 13.4).

Job ratios for Sydney LGAs range from 1,028 for the City of Sydney to 28 for Woollahra. Major employment centres, other than central Sydney, are South Sydney (422), Auburn (179), and Botany (168). All other job ratios are below 125. Some outer suburban LGAs employ nearly half their resident workforce, isolation being a probable factor in their relatively high degree of self-sufficiency. Some inner residential suburbs have lower job ratios and lower percentages employed locally, but their accessibility problems are less severe.

In 1971, Ku-ring-gai had a job ratio of only 36, giving a net outflow of 23,248 workers (Table 13.1). In fact, only 20 per cent of the workforce was employed in the LGA and nearly 30,000 commuted elsewhere. North Sydney and Willoughby both had a net inflow of workers, but the former, despite the job ratio of 108, employed 26 per cent of its resident workforce, whilst 36 per cent worked in the CBD (Table 13.2). Many people bypass local jobs for others which are more suitable, more attractive, or which just happen to be available at the right time (Manning 1978).

Total job ratios also hide important differences between occupational and industrial groupings. By far the largest net flows in 1971 were from Ku-ring-gai and Warringah, but the composition of these flows differed markedly. In the former case, white collar workers, especially those of managerial or professional status, were most important. Workers commuting from Warringah included many more in clerical and manufacturing occupations. North Sydney had significant inflows of managerial personnel and employees in the finance and public administration

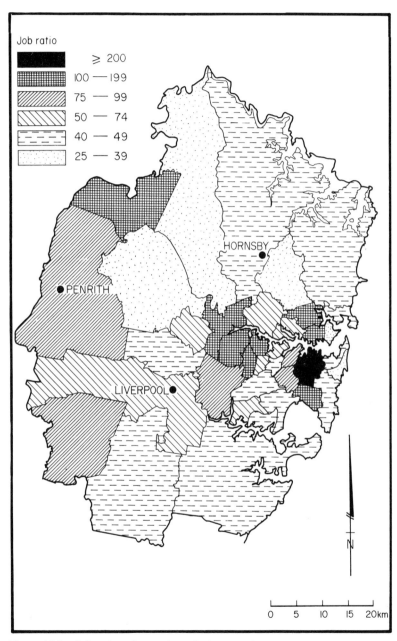

**Figure 13.3   Job ratios: the number of jobs in each LGA for every 100 resident workers, 1971**

**Table 13.1  Job ratios and commuting flows, 1971**

| Local government area | | Occupational Groups | | | | | Industrial Groups | | | | Total |
|---|---|---|---|---|---|---|---|---|---|---|---|
| | | Professional | Management | Clerical | Sales | Craftsmen | Manufacturing | Wholesale & retail trade | Transport & Communications | Finance Public Administration | |
| Ku-ring-gai | job ratio[a] | 30 | 16 | 27 | 51 | 69 | 16 | 43 | 27 | 19 | 36 |
| | number[b] | -6957 | -6794 | -5887 | -1681 | -1036 | -4638 | -4496 | -1272 | -7637 | -23248 |
| Lane Cove | job ratio | 42 | 45 | 48 | 64 | 125 | 119 | 60 | 51 | 34 | 63 |
| | number | -1645 | -940 | -1733 | -414 | +565 | +470 | -1129 | -374 | -1799 | -4777 |
| Manly | job ratio | 41 | 35 | 32 | 52 | 46 | 22 | 50 | 22 | 33 | 43 |
| | number | -1475 | -1273 | -2798 | -885 | -1854 | -2232 | -1859 | -902 | -1536 | -9437 |
| Mosman | job ratio | 26 | 23 | 16 | 46 | 54 | 12 | 41 | 21 | 28 | 34 |
| | number | -2228 | -1477 | -3395 | -769 | -706 | -1541 | -1672 | -732 | -3010 | -9142 |
| North Sydney | job ratio | 110 | 140 | 104 | 112 | 116 | 94 | 111 | 80 | 143 | 108 |
| | number | +577 | +1101 | +350 | +278 | +773 | -280 | +600 | -463 | +3171 | +2435 |
| Warringah | job ratio | 40 | 40 | 35 | 52 | 63 | 69 | 54 | 23 | 22 | 47 |
| | number | -4962 | -4587 | -8766 | -3388 | -6385 | -4136 | -6770 | -3418 | -9132 | -33721 |
| Willoughby | job ratio | 95 | 99 | 91 | 142 | 168 | 158 | 154 | 73 | 59 | 115 |
| | number | -209 | -14 | -525 | +896 | +3629 | +2739 | +2800 | -397 | -1984 | +3606 |

Notes: [a] the job ratio is defined as (number of jobs/number of resident workers) × 100
[b] number indicates net volume of out-commuting (−) or in-commuting (+)
Source: Calculated from data in NSW. PEC (1976b) Tables 3-6

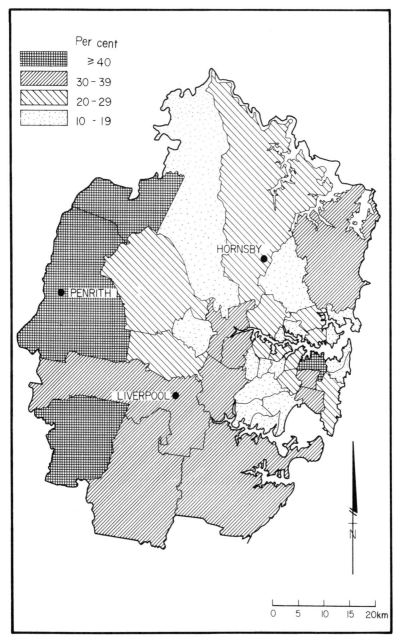

**Figure 13.4    Percentage of the resident workforce employed within the same LGA, 1971**

**Table 13.2   Journey to work movements, 1971**

| Workplace | | Ku-ring-gai | Lane Cove | Manly | Mosman | North Sydney | Warringah | Willoughby | CBD | Inner Southern | Inner Western | Hornsby | Other |
|---|---|---|---|---|---|---|---|---|---|---|---|---|---|
| *Residence* | | | | | | | | | | | | | |
| Ku-ring-gai | number | 6536 | 515 | 66 | 96 | 2543 | 529 | 2783 | 10607 | 4375 | 2828 | 1051 | 1230 |
| | per cent[a] | 19.7 | 1.6 | 0.2 | 0.3 | 7.7 | 1.6 | 8.4 | 31.9 | 13.2 | 8.5 | 3.2 | 3.7 |
| Lane Cove | number | 253 | 1859 | 23 | 84 | 1379 | 144 | 1737 | 3209 | 1792 | 916 | 89 | 355 |
| | per cent | 2.1 | 15.7 | 0.2 | 0.7 | 11.7 | 1.2 | 14.7 | 27.1 | 15.1 | 7.7 | 0.8 | 3.0 |
| Manly | number | 86 | 130 | 3253 | 410 | 1172 | 2586 | 635 | 4212 | 1704 | 381 | 43 | 208 |
| | per cent | 0.6 | 0.9 | 21.9 | 2.8 | 7.9 | 17.4 | 4.3 | 28.4 | 11.5 | 2.6 | 0.3 | 1.4 |
| Mosman | number | 88 | 203 | 110 | 2006 | 1808 | 305 | 782 | 4679 | 1781 | 438 | 54 | 150 |
| | per cent | 0.7 | 1.6 | 0.9 | 16.8 | 14.5 | 2.4 | 6.3 | 37.4 | 14.3 | 3.5 | 0.4 | 1.2 |
| North Sydney | number | 348 | 581 | 105 | 535 | 6963 | 391 | 2462 | 9272 | 4039 | 1057 | 125 | 582 |
| | per cent | 1.3 | 2.2 | 0.4 | 2.0 | 26.3 | 1.5 | 9.3 | 35.1 | 15.3 | 4.0 | 0.4 | 2.2 |
| Warringah | number | 812 | 622 | 3183 | 802 | 3689 | 23955 | 3450 | 11016 | 5812 | 2101 | 306 | 1139 |
| | per cent | 1.4 | 1.1 | 5.6 | 1.4 | 5.5 | 42.1 | 6.1 | 19.4 | 10.2 | 3.7 | 0.5 | 2.0 |
| Willoughby | number | 619 | 764 | 66 | 173 | 2507 | 372 | 6473 | 5496 | 3007 | 1153 | 153 | 533 |
| | per cent | 2.9 | 3.6 | 0.3 | 0.8 | 11.8 | 1.7 | 30.4 | 25.8 | 14.1 | 5.4 | 0.7 | 2.5 |

*Note:* [a] Percentages are of the total workforce for which a place of employment could be determined; workplaces were 'unknown' for between 8 and 11 per cent of employed residents of each LGA.
*Source:* Calculated from data in NSW. PEC (1976b) Table 1

grouping. Important industrial areas at Lane Cove West, East Willoughby and Artarmon are reflected in the job ratios for manufacturing for Lane Cove and Willoughby LGAs. The latter also had a large inflow in wholesale and retail trade due to the importance of Chatswood in this field. However, it is still largely a regional service centre, lacking the major concentrations of financial and administrative employment of North Sydney or the CBD.

## 13.6 Journeys to work

It is evident that there are large scale outward movements to work from the region as a whole and from Ku-ring-gai and Warringah in particular (Table 13.2). However, problems arise from the use of LGAs, and some local movements across LGA boundaries to the large employment zones in Willoughby and North Sydney are included.

The proportion of residents employed in their 'home' LGA varied considerably but was generally low. Isolation may explain the higher figure for Warringah, as self-reliance might be expected to stem from separation from other centres and from the LGA's large size. More residents worked in the CBD than in their own LGA in all cases except Warringah and Willoughby. In 1971, the CBD employed a total of 207,547, largely white in collar positions in wholesale and retail trade, finance, and public administration (NSW. PEC 1976b: Table 9). Despite the absence of direct evidence, it can be safely assumed that a large part of the cross-Harbour commuting flow consisted of professional, managerial, and clerical employees. The inner southern suburbs (Sydney outside the CBD, Leichhardt, Marrickville, South Sydney, Botany, Randwick, Waverley and Woollahra) attracted a further 10 to 16 per cent of the workforce of each study region LGA. The majority of these commuters worked in manufacturing industry but often at the higher professional and managerial levels. In total, 71,000 people from the study region crossed the Harbour on their journey to work.

There were also important flows within the study region, notably to North Sydney and Willoughby LGAs. A third major employment centre, Brookvale, drew mainly from within its LGA, so that movements to it are not shown in Table 13.2. Many professional and managerial workers commuted to North Sydney as an alternative to the longer journey to the CBD.

Traffic counts are a second source of information in intraurban movement (Table 13.3). These have the advantage of providing more recent data than that available from other sources. Whilst not all travel recorded was journey to work in nature, such journeys constitute the bulk of traffic recorded.

First and foremost, the large flow across the Harbour Bridge has

increased steadily. Main routes from Manly-Warringah also had significant increases, as did routes from the North Shore region to areas
further west. This second group of increases probably reflects an
increase in the number of North Shore residents working in industrial
areas in the western half of Sydney. One clear trend in recent years has
been the decentralisation of office jobs at all levels to such areas
(Alexander ch 3).

**Table 13.3    Average daily traffic flows**

| Code[a] | Location | 1965 | '000 of vehicles 1971 | 1977 |
|---|---|---|---|---|
| 1 | Comenarra Parkway, Thornleigh | – | – | 11 |
| 2 | Pennant Hills Road, Pearce's Corner | 20 | 24 | 27 |
| 3 | Pacific Highway, Pearce's Corner | 25 | 41 | 29 |
| 4 | De Burgh's Bridge | 17 | 28 | 37 |
| 5 | Fuller's Bridge | 11 | 19 | 17 |
| 6 | Epping Highway, Lane Cove River | 23 | 38 | 44 |
| 7 | Fig Tree Bridge | 28 | 38 | 37 |
| 8 | Pacific Highway, Chatswood | 29 | 36 | 37 |
| 9 | Pacific Highway, St Leonards | 45 | 35 | 36 |
| 10 | Roseville Bridge | 23 | 44 | 50 |
| 11 | Warringah Expressway, Mount Street | – | 74 | 88 |
| 12 | Military Road, Neutral Bay | 29 | 38 | 49 |
| 13 | Sydney Harbour Bridge | 107 | 135 | 151 |
| 14 | Spit Bridge | 28 | 51 | 54 |
| 15 | Pittwater Road, Collaroy | 21 | 28 | 34 |
| 16 | Mona Vale Road, Middle Harbour Creek | 12 | 18 | 26 |
| 17 | Forest Way, Frenchs Forest | 9 | 17 | 30 |
| 18 | Warringah Road, Beacon Hill | 16 | 23 | 32 |

*Note:* [a] Survey locations are marked on Figure 13.1
*Source:* NSW. DMR (1965, 1971, 1977)

**Table 13.4    Modes of travel used in the journey to work, 1971**

| | car | % travelling by train/ferry | bus | walk |
|---|---|---|---|---|
| *Employment area* | | | | |
| City of Sydney | 30 | 47 | 19 | 4 |
| North Sydney/Willoughby | 62 | 14 | 11 | 12 |
| *Residential Area* | | | | |
| Ku-ring-gai | 66 | 29 | 2 | 2 |
| Manly-Warringah | 71 | 11 | 13 | 4 |
| Inner North | 51 | 22 | 15 | 12 |

*Source:* Manning (1978) Tables 10.1 and 10.2

It is difficult to obtain data on modes of travel. Each of the residential areas listed in Table 13.4 had a clear majority of commuters using private cars. Ku-ring-gai, however, had a higher level of rail patronage than any other suburban area of Sydney. This was partly because of the relatively good service provided but, more significantly, because residents' jobs were so heavily concentrated in the CBD and North Sydney. Overall, 47 per cent of all commuters to the CBD travelled by train and nearly 70 per cent arrived by some form of public transport, a very high figure for Australian and American cities. Manly-Warringah residents, by necessity, relied very largely on road transport. If congestion on the Harbour Bridge is to be relieved and the use of cars in the CBD maintained at a low level or even reduced, planners will need to consider the transport problems of the Northern Beaches.

## 13.7 Conclusions and future developments

Large areas of Sydney's North Shore are almost entirely dormitory suburbs, a feature that reflects a combination of planning practice and the influence of elected representatives who have generally supported the preferences of residents. Major employment zones are concentrated within the funnel of transport routes in the south of the region which feeds across the Harbour to further employment in the CBD and the central industrial area. The relative lack of employment elsewhere in the region is being reduced gradually with the general pattern of dispersal of employment in Sydney, but opportunities are constrained by the nature of the physical landscape, the very peripheral location of the extremities of the region and by community pressures against expansion of commercial zones.

Potential for commercial expansion is strong at several points along the North Shore line: Hornsby, Pymble-Gordon, Chatswood and St Leonards to North Sydney. Also in Warringah, demand for industrial and commercial land is surprisingly strong for such an off-centre region. Frenchs Forest has considerable potential for expansion but there are problems with the attitudes of existing non-residential users, the merits of protecting the Arndale shopping centre and the development standards set for the industrial land.

Large scale movements, especially from the study region to the CBD, will nevertheless continue. What can be done to further facilitate such flows and to increase accessibility? Two vocal groups in the community offer radically different solutions.

One group, backed by the state opposition (Liberal Party) and the NRMA, advocates building an extensive freeway system to reduce congestion on the roads. A key part of their approach has been a second Harbour crossing by bridge or tunnel. In addition, they have advocated the extension of the highway system with particular emphasis on the Warringah Expressway. While it is clear that motor vehicles will continue to play an important part in urban transport and that it is necessary to continue to improve roads, it is by no means evident that massive investment in new freeways is justified. Problems associated with freeways include the adverse effects of motor traffic on the inner city environment and the realisation that new freeways almost inevitably attract congestion to them.

A second group has advocated public transport improvements as the first priority. The present state government has generally taken this view, although by late 1981 it was actively exploring the possibility of constructing a second Harbour crossing. A railway serving Manly-Warringah has been advocated at least since the County of Cumberland Plan. Such a link would cater for the major commuting flows from that area to Chatswood (if one changed trains), North Sydney and the CBD and greatly reduce the need for a major freeway to the area. It has been estimated that 50,000 people per day would use such a rail facility by the year 2000 (NSW. SATS 1974b Vol 3:III-2). This need not be a full heavy rail system: a light rail tramway might well prove more flexible and cheaper. Other light rail links, such as from the study region to Ryde, might also be advantageous. And, as the SATS report (1974b) suggests, ferry and hydrofoil services on the Harbour, along with express and other bus services, could be extended and improved.

Accessibility and ease of movement are of the utmost importance for the continuing health of Sydney as a city. Either of two major approaches is possible: reduce distances by intermixing land uses more and distributing facilities more evenly or improve transport facilities to facilitate travel. Planning will undoubtedly involve elements of both. It must also involve social planning and considerations of equity. Groups within our cities are unequal in many ways but inequality in access to urban facilities is one of the most obvious and most important. It is also, perhaps, the form of inequality that can most readily be reduced (or increased) through the planning process.

In these terms, the study area does not have a major access problem at the moment. Such problems are greater in other areas of Sydney and the differential is likely to increase. Outer suburban areas are now highly dependent on the private car and, if it becomes more costly to run, many residents of outer working class suburbs may well become increasingly disadvantaged in terms of access to work, shops and recreational facilities. A high priority of transport and other planners should be providing for the future needs of such areas. Much of the study region has relatively good public transport. Those who do not have access to it or who do not wish to use it generally belong to households who have one or two or more cars. They are also the very people who will be able to afford to continue using their cars in the future. Journeys to work and to other urban facilities are, and will be, easier than in some other parts of suburban Sydney. Nevertheless, there is undoubtedly considerable room for improvement. Dependence on the car should be decreased further, particularly in Manly-Warringah. It may be possible to reduce the length of journey to work flows. If not, it is at least possible to use the most efficient and most environmentally acceptable forms of transport, adapting them to suit individual flows as much as possible.

The options for the North Shore and Northern Beaches region involve both major regional transport infrastructure improvements and realisation of the potential for increased employment opportunities within the region. These solutions will not be fully realised without the abandonment of obsolete planning policies and change in attitudes of both sections of the community and their elected representatives.

Flexibility and integration need to be the two key words for all future urban planning. No one can accurately predict future circumstances. Cities need to be able to cope with any problems that arise and to take advantage of any opportunities that come their way. They cannot afford to be bound into tightly structured, restrictive plans that do not allow this to happen. Cities also need to be recognised for what they are — highly complex objects, depending for their continued vitality on an extremely dynamic series of interactions and exchanges within them. Accessibility, movement and communication are all essential aspects of the dynamic state we call urbanism.

# 14 Campbelltown
## A case study of planned urban expansion
H.W. FAULKNER

## 14.1 Introduction

The proliferation of sprawling sparsely populated suburbs, particularly on Sydney's western and south western fringes, has been one of the most perplexing problems confronting urban planners in their efforts to guide postwar metropolitan expansion towards acceptable standards of equity, efficiency, convenience and environmental amenity. Generated largely by the car's impact on urban development patterns, this phenomenon has resulted in excessive demands on public authorities responsible for extending essential services to new areas, and local governments on the periphery have been hard pressed to cope with growing demands arising from the influx of new residents. People moving into these areas have to adjust to increased isolation from facilities and jobs, owing to delays in dispersion of urban activities from the metropolitan core.

This chapter traces the link between the postwar development of Campbelltown, on Sydney's south western fringe, and successive metropolitan planning strategies. In doing so, it provides insights into the way planning approaches have evolved and into the obstacles encountered. Campbelltown is an appropriate example because the most recently developed approach to managing Sydney's metropolitan expansion (the Macarthur Growth Centre) has had a profound effect on this area's recent development. Being the most innovative and comprehensive planning scheme yet developed in the Sydney area, the Macarthur program has undoubtedly succeeded in counteracting many of the problems normally experienced in fringe areas. It has performed an essential role in coordinating activities of various government and private agencies and it has enabled funds and technical resources to be channelled directly into infrastructural development. Even so, the

This chapter is based on research conducted before the author joined the Bureau of Transport Economics. The views expressed do not necessarily reflect the opinions or philosophy of this organisation.

Campbelltown case reveals that programs based on the growth centre principle are vulnerable to uncertainties arising from a volatile economic and political environment. As a consequence, the Macarthur project's capacity to enhance accessibility to facilities and job opportunities has been severely restricted. This critical deficiency, rather than the positive achievements, is the focus of the following analysis.

The impact of Campbelltown's incorporation into the metropolitan region is described so that the principal forces influencing the fringe population's access to work and facilities can be isolated. Different approaches to the management of Sydney's growth are then described and evaluated in terms of their repercussions in the Campbelltown area. In the final section a specific aspect of the Macarthur Growth Centre strategy, the industrial development program, is considered to further highlight some of the problems confronting this scheme.

## 14.2    The incorporation process

Before its incorporation in the metropolitan area, the Campbelltown LGA comprised a series of six villages that had grown around railway stations along the main southern line (Figure 14.1). Until World War II, the principal function of the area was to provide dairy products, fruit and poultry to the Sydney market (Bayley 1965). The villages serviced the rural population and primary industries of the area and had experienced a modest growth rate in the interwar period. By 1947 their total population was 7,000. Then, between 1947 and 1961, the area's population increased by 167 per cent to 18,701.

Accelerated growth during the 1950s signalled the transformation of villages in the area from rural service centres to detached commuter suburbs. The influence exerted by the railway system during the incipient stage of suburb formation in the 1950s had a lasting effect on the area's spatial structure. Railway stations became the focal points of the expanding communities' spatial organisation, as commuters settling in the area depended on trains for the journey to work. Retail and commercial establishments required to serve the growing population consolidated in clusters around the stations. In the 1960s increasing car ownership diminished the importance of proximity to railway stations as a priority in residential location. Despite this, increments to the retail-commercial system continued to concentrate at the original railway based centres. Indeed, the structure established in the railway era has to some extent become more entrenched as increased mobility has made agglomeration advantages more significant and enabled greater economies of scale to be achieved through the establishment of larger but fewer service units.

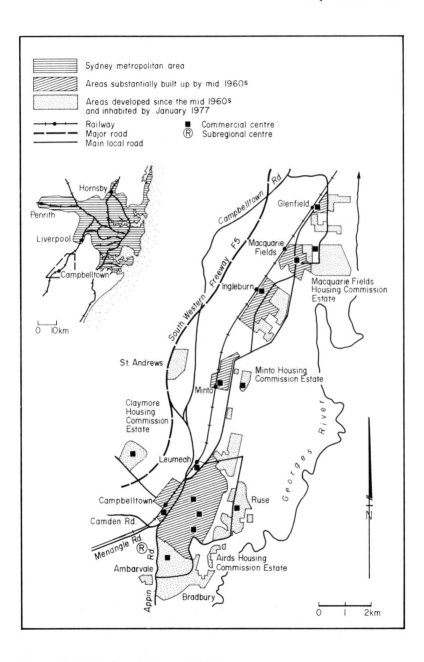

**Figure 14.1   The Campbelltown district**

These inertial forces have not only maintained the predominance of the original service centres within the Campbelltown area, they have also operated on a metropolitan scale to resist the dispersion of higher order services (for example, comparison shops, tertiary education, specialist medical services) and job opportunities to newer fringe areas such as Campbelltown. Inertial tendencies are reinforced by lag effects which inhibit the extension of services and facilities to new areas immediately demands for them are expressed. Such delays are inevitable simply because it takes time for the area's population to reach the threshold required to justify the establishment of central functions. Also, lead times are required for planning and construction processes. These delays are often prolonged on parts of the fringe where development is fragmented and where large areas therefore remain partially developed for extended periods. The effect is to increase the distance separating residents from facilities and jobs.

Special efforts have been made in Campbelltown to avoid or alleviate problems associated with urban growth. For the purpose of interpreting the influence of metropolitan planning on Campbelltown's development, it is convenient to divide Sydney's planning history into two parts: the Cumberland County Council (CCC) era (1945-1963); and the Sydney Region Outline Plan and the Macarthur Growth Centre project (1964 to date). Planning schemes in both these periods explicitly acknowledged the accessibility problems posed by rapid population growth in peripheral areas, which were becoming increasingly isolated from urban activities as the metropolis expanded. However, most attention has been devoted to counteracting the forces resisting the diffusion of job opportunities and higher order services at the metropolitan scale. In the earlier period developments in Campbelltown were only indirectly influenced by the metropolitan planning scheme and plans to coordinate this area's development with that of the whole metropolis were not implemented. In the later period the impact of metropolitan expansion on the Campbelltown sector of the fringe was stronger, and this demanded more direct planning action.

## 14.3   The Cumberland County Council era

The first steps towards the development of a metropolitan planning scheme in Sydney were taken when the CCC was established in 1945. To some extent its formation anticipated intensifying problems of urban growth, but it also reflected a growing planning consciousness aroused by the challenge of postwar reconstruction (Winston 1957:31). The rapid uncoordinated spread of urban development on the periphery was a major problem confronting the CCC. With the return of troops and the relaxation of wartime building restrictions, the pace of residential developments was intensifying, while the freedom and flexibility of movement permitted by the automobile's growing popularity enabled this development to become increasingly dispersed in peripheral suburbs. Urban development on the fringe was occurring at such a rapid rate that demand for basic services and facilities had exceeded the capacity of local government and public authorities to extend them.

The CCC submitted a masterplan for Sydney's development in 1948; it was assented to in June 1951. The plan was intended to provide a framework for local government planning decisions which would reduce the growth problems referred to above and produce a more efficient and socially beneficial pattern of urban development. The main aspects of the plan were described by Winston (1957:39):

a) the *coordination* of land uses on a metropolitan scale to foster a spatial arrangement which maximises convenience and separates incompatible activities;
b) the *consolidation* of development to enable the backlog in the provision of services to be rectified; and
c) the *conservation* of natural and historical assets.

Two features of the scheme were specifically associated with the coordination objective. First, sixteen suburban and six rural district centres were designated as alternative business centres to the CBD. Thus, the suburban population would have better access to higher level services and facilities and also to office employment. The Campbelltown business district was one of the rural district centres. However, as with most other centres, nothing was done to promote its development along the lines proposed by the planning scheme. The second aspect of land use coordination involved the segregation of industrial areas and their dispersal to the suburbs so that jobs would be closer to the newer residential areas. This was to be achieved by restricting industrial development to a limited number of suburban areas and simultaneously freezing developments in the inner urban areas. The CCC thus reinforced a combination of conditions which made deconcentration of industry inevitable (Logan 1964, 1966) and far reaching (Cardew and Rich ch 6).

Postwar suburbanisation of industry, particularly in the western and south western sectors, enhanced the growth potential of dormitory satellite areas beyond the periphery. It became feasible for more urban workers to live in Campbelltown and still be within reasonable commuting distance from work. As part of the more general trend towards industrial deconcentration within the metropolitan region, two major manufacturing plants were established in the Campbelltown area in the late 1950s. These were an electrical engineering firm and a garment manufacturer; each initially employed about one hundred persons. Also at this time intensification of mining activities in the Bulli-Burragorang coalfields contributed to the growth of job opportunities within commuting range. Between 1954 and 1966, population growth accelerated in Campbelltown and changes in the composition of the resident workforce reflected the increased accessibility to industrial and mining jobs (Table 14.1).

The main feature of the masterplan associated with the consolidation and conservation objectives was the demarcation of a greenbelt around the metropolis (Figure 1.1). This strategy was based on the assumption that Sydney's population would reach 2.3 million by 1980 and then stabilise. As vacant land contained within the greenbelt neared exhaustion, surplus population was supposed to be accommodated in satellite towns, including Campbelltown, Penrith, Richmond and Windsor. The intention was to encourage these towns to develop a 'well balanced' set of facilities and job opportunities to serve the population they would receive. Nothing positive was done in this respect, even though it was evident by the late 1950s that Sydney's growth potential had been grossly underestimated. Sydney's population exceeded the 1980 projection in the early 1960s.

Diminution of vacant space within the limits of the greenbelt towards the end of the 1950s resulted in pressure from government and private developers for its release for urban purposes. In 1958 the CCC resisted pressure from the NSW Housing Commission to release land at Minto (within the Campbelltown area) for a satellite town to accommodate 50,000 people (NSW Housing Commission 1957). In 1959 a study was undertaken to assess the feasibility of establishing Campbelltown as a planned satellite but the decision was to defer it (Fraser 1959). The original intention of the masterplan, which saw satellites outside the greenbelt as a long range possibility only, was reaffirmed. In making these decisions, the CCC believed that there was sufficient vacant land

Table 14.1   Changing composition of Campbelltown's workforce, 1954-1966

| Employment sector | 1954[a] (%) | 1966[b] (%) |
|---|---|---|
| Primary | 8.8 | 2.4 |
| Manufacturing | 21.6 | 32.2 |
| Mining | 0.2 | 2.2 |
| Other | 69.4 | 63.2 |
| Total | 100.0 | 100.0 |

Notes: [a]Total number employed in 1954 was 9,690.
   [b]Total number employed in 1966 was 22,801.
Sources: Commonwealth Bureau of Census and Statistics (1954) Census of the Commonwealth of Australia, Analysis of Population in Local Government Areas, Vol 1, Pt 1, Table 7
   Commonwealth Bureau of Census and Statistics (1966) Census of Population and Housing, Vol 4, Pt 1, Table 7

within the area confined by the greenbelt to accommodate Sydney's expansion in the immediate future. However, pressure for the release of large areas of the greenbelt was sustained and the Minister for Local Government eventually capitulated. In 1959 11,900 hectares of the greenbelt were released and this was followed by further encroachments in the 1960s (Harrison 1966).

Although Campbelltown's growth accelerated during the CCC period, it would have been greater had the scheme been executed according to its stated principles. No specific action was taken to promote expansion of satellites such as Campbelltown. Indeed, development proposals involving Campbelltown were shelved. Release of greenbelt areas finally reduced Campbelltown's growth potential by diverting development to other areas. Subsequently, however, Campbelltown became a key component in a plan for Sydney's metropolitan expansion in which the planned satellite concept was resurrected and elaborated within the framework of a more comprehensive urban planning system. Far from being a disadvantage, therefore, postponement of Campbelltown's development ultimately benefited the area by delaying its growth until more effective planning measures had been introduced.

### 14.4 The Sydney Region Outline Plan and the Macarthur Growth Centre project

The CCC was dissolved in 1963 and replaced by the SPA in 1964. Its first action with respect to Campbelltown was to increase the target population to 50,000. In view of the rapid growth the area was already experiencing in the absence of explicit measures to promote that growth, this was simply a formal recognition of the inevitable. A new plan for Sydney's metropolitan expansion was already being prepared.

This new plan, the Sydney Region Outline Plan, promulgated in 1968 envisaged the expansion of Sydney taking place in a linear fashion along communication corridors (NSW. SPA 1968). Community serving activities generating traffic were to be located at nodes along the main transport axes; within each corridor new cities were to be developed as separate spatial and functional entities. Growth was to be directed along three major corridors: a northern corridor towards Newcastle and encompassing Gosford and Wyong; a western corridor towards Katoomba and including Blacktown, Mt Druitt and Penrith; and a south western extension incorporating Campbelltown, Camden and Appin. A fourth corridor, from Blacktown north west to Colo, was considered a possibility at a later stage. The intention was for Sydney to become an integrated metropolitan complex consisting of corridors incorporating Wollongong, Newcastle and the Blue Mountains. Since all these corridors are aligned with major railway routes, the plan perpetuated the railway's influence on the spatial pattern of Sydney's growth.

In theory, at least, the defunct greenbelt-satellite strategy of the CCC scheme recognised that it was not feasible for Sydney to continue to develop as a single unit and at the same time ensure efficiency, economy and convenience for the urban community. Similarly, the new plan saw the need to promote the development of integrated communities at suburban locations. To the extent that the aim of developing relatively self-sufficient communities within corridors resembles the aim of developing planned satellites, the new plan can be regarded as an extension of the superseded CCC plan. However, the approach to achieving this end differed substantially from that adopted previously.

In 1970 a development committee was established to advise the SPA on the planning and coordination of development and public works programs in the Campbelltown-Camden-Appin area. This committee consisted of representatives of the SPA and local government of the area. In July 1973 a structure plan was released proposing that Campbelltown, Camden and Appin be developed as an integrated complex of cities within the south western corridor (NSW. SPA 1973). Some 4,000 hectares of land within the project area had been acquired by the SPA for a town centre, industrial areas, housing estates, open space and educational facilities (Harrison 1978:146).

The Campbelltown-Camden-Appin project was conceived at a time when there was a rising tide of political and professional opinion in favour of the development of new cities as a means of alleviating problems of metropolitan growth (Neilson 1976:472–4). The political rationale underlying the new cities approach was expressed by E. G. Whitlam when he was Leader of the federal Labor opposition in 1970:

> ... differences in the standard of living which Australians enjoy arise increasingly from their access to government services such as hospitals, schools, recreation facilities, sewerage and public transport. Under present arrangements, these things are provided with a growing geographical discrimination against those who live on the expanding perimeters of cities and regional centres (Whitlam 1977:117).

This appreciation of the social ramifications of rapid urban growth was reflected in the ALP's 1972 election platform in which explicit urban and regional development proposals aimed at alleviating problems associated with urban growth were presented to the Australian electorate. These proposals became government policy when the ALP assumed office after the subsequent election. Professional support for the new cities approach was articulated by the AIUS (1972) and Neutze (1974) although others (e.g. Payne and Mill 1973) disagreed. In essence, though, the new cities idea was largely a restatement and refinement of arguments upon which the planned satellite concept had been based.

In September 1975 the Macarthur Development Board (MDB) was set up to continue the planning role of the previous development committee and to facilitate key developments in the Campbelltown-Camden-Appin area. Its formation was encouraged by the promise of federal funding owing to the incorporation of the Macarthur project into the growth centres program of the 1972-1975 Labor government. Unlike other centres in the program, this project was an extension of a metropolitan area and so its growth was more assured. Further, with its power to develop as well as acquire land, the MDB was more likely to achieve its development objectives than agencies relying entirely on the traditional restrictive methods of statutory planning (Harrison 1974:218).

However, major projects, such as the Macarthur scheme, face many difficulties. As they usually have a long gestation period, their planning depends on long term projections which are often unreliable. By 1976, Campbelltown's population growth was more than 30,000 short of the target identified in 1973 (Table 14.2). This shortfall, coupled with the conclusions of the National Population Inquiry, resulted in major revisions of the area's population projections (Table 14.3).

**Table 14.2   Original population targets for Campbelltown-Camden-Appin New Cities project, 1971-2000**

| Location | Target population | | | | |
| | 1971 | 1976 | 1981 | 1991 | 2001 |
|---|---|---|---|---|---|
| Campbelltown | 33,875 | 83,000 | 186,000 | 225,000 | 230,000 |
| Camden | 7,931 | 15,000 | 31,500 | 95,000 | 100,000 |
| Appin | 1,642 | 2,000 | 2,500 | 70,000 | 170,000 |
| *Total* | 43,448 | 100,000 | 220,000 | 390,000 | 500,000 |

*Source:* NSW. SPA (1973:52)

**Table 14.3   Revised population targets for the Macarthur Growth Centre, 1980-2005**

| Location | Target population | | | | |
| | 1980 | 1985 | 1990 | 1995 | 2000 | 2005 |
|---|---|---|---|---|---|---|
| Campbelltown | 93,000 | 150,000 | 188,000 | 210,000 | 224,000 | 230,000 |
| Camden | 16,000 | 27,000 | 52,000 | 78,000 | 97,000 | 100,000 |
| Appin | 2,000 | 4,000 | 12,000 | 26,000 | 54,000 | 100,000 |
| *Total* | 111,000 | 181,000 | 252,000 | 314,000 | 375,000 | 430,000 |

*Source:* MDB (1977:3)

Another major difficulty stems from the need for high levels of funding over an extended period. This requirement cannot be guaranteed when the project spans the period of office of several governments which have different values and funding priorities. Almost from the outset the MDB's programs have been inhibited by financial uncertainties arising from the change in government which occurred within months of its formation. The Liberal-National Country Party coalition, which succeeded the Labor government in 1975, drastically curbed public expenditure because of its fixation on reducing budgetary deficits and because of its ideological opposition to public sector involvement in areas perceived as being the province of private enterprise. Thus federal urban and regional development programs have been virtually dismantled. After receiving $19.5 million from federal sources in 1975/76, the MDB's funds were cut to $5 million in 1976/77 and $1.5 million in 1977/78. No specific allocation was made to the MDB in subsequent budgets.

Nevertheless, the MDB undertook two significant projects, one aimed at promoting industrial development and the other at the development of a subregional centre at Campbelltown. The importance of these projects is reflected in the fact that, together, they accounted for nearly two thirds of the MDB's expenditure in 1977/78, with the former accounting for 48.7 per cent and the latter for 17 per cent (MDB 1978). Progress of the subregional centre clearly illustrates the impact of changing government policy.

The original plan of the Macarthur area envisaged a subregional centre at Campbelltown consisting of: an office complex providing employment for 23,000 workers; an education complex consisting of a university, a college of advanced education and a technical college; a major public hospital; a retailing and wholesaling centre employing 6,250 workers; and entertainment and personal services employing 3,000 workers (NSW. SPA 1973:88). Progress has been made towards fulfilling some of these goals. The first stage of the hospital (120 beds) was completed in October 1977 but the commencement of stage two (to include crucial paediatric and maternity facilities) has been indefinitely postponed. An 'annexe' to the technical college has been completed at Macquarie Fields and presently provides courses mainly in business and secretarial studies to 500 students. The main technical college centre is adjacent to the regional retail centre (Macarthur Square) and was scheduled to receive its first students in mid 1980.

The first stage of the regional retail centre (Macarthur Square) was opened in September 1979. Costing about $50 million, it was a joint venture involving Lend Lease Development Pty. Ltd., the State Super-annuation Board and the NSW Government. Comprising a major department store, a large discount store and 100 specialty shops, it has been claimed that Macarthur Square will provide employment for 1,000 people. However, the extent to which this increase is offset by reduced employment in the older Campbelltown shopping centre remains to be seen. A study commissioned by the MDB in 1977 estimated that 35 per cent of local residents travel to commercial centres outside Campbelltown LGA. Whether Macarthur Square can be successful without seriously affecting trade (and, therefore, employment) in the older centre will depend largely on the degree to which this figure can be reduced. The possibility that many of these trips are linked with other trips (especially work trips and visits to relatives — see Faulkner 1981) may mean that consumer drift to other areas will continue and intense competition between the two centres will consequently occur.

While developments related to the hospital, retailing centre and technical education have occurred substantially (though not totally) according to plan, programs involving office development and tertiary education have been shelved indefinitely. With the contraction of expenditure in tertiary education, there is little chance that a university or college of advanced education will be established in the immediate future. Similarly, budgetary constraints have curtailed programs to relocate government offices, although the potential growth of office activities in suburban areas is greater than often realised (Alexander ch 3; Cardew and Rich ch 6).

## 14.5    Residential and industrial development

Campbelltown's population was estimated as 96,000 in June 1981, close to the revised target (Table 14.3). The uncharacteristic accuracy of this projection is partly attributable to the fact that continued growth has been to some extent assured by public residential development projects undertaken by the NSW Housing Commission and the NSW Land Commission. The Housing Commission has had the major impact. In the 1960s and up to 1973/74 it made a modest contribution to Campbelltown's growth with between five and 20 per cent of dwelling construction. Since 1974 this figure has escalated to around 50 per cent as a result of large estates at Macquarie Fields, Airds, Minto and, more recently, at Claymore (Figure 14.1).

The Housing Commission's close involvement in Campbelltown's development has had a substantial impact on the social profile of the population. In 1978/79 nearly 60 per cent of the incoming population were taking up residence in Housing Commission estates; the proportion of the area's total population in these estates was almost 34 per cent (Campbelltown City Council n.d.). Eligibility criteria adopted in the Commission's allocation of housing ensures a high proportion of: large families; single parent families (especially deserted wives); and families whose breadwinner is unskilled and therefore vulnerable to periodic and long term unemployment. Many of these families have special needs and disabilities, and the problems they face are aggravated by their concentration into segregated communities on the metropolitan fringe (Brennan 1973; Bryson and Thompson 1972; McLelland 1968). However, the Housing Commission's experience in earlier suburban projects at Green Valley and Mt Druitt has at least made it more sensitive to these problems; attempts have been made to reduce some of them in the Campbelltown estates through the provision of community development officers and low cost temporary accommodation to encourage the early establishment of shops, schools, health services and community facilities. Furthermore, comprehensive forward planning and the ability to phase in large scale developments has minimised delays in the provision of permanent services and facilities. By contrast many privately developed residential estates in the area (e.g. Ruse and St Andrews) have remained deprived of facilities for extended periods owing to fragmented and spasmodic development patterns.

Efforts to improve public transport within the area have been limited to periodic rerouting and schedule adjustments to existing bus services. Beyond this, the MDB has not been particularly active in improving the access in new residential estates to services and facilities normally supplied at the neighbourhood level. Instead, resources have been concentrated on programs to reduce the length of work journeys by generating job opportunities within the area.

Since their population normally grows in advance of expansion 'n local employment, areas on the metropolitan periphery traditionally produce a daily flow of commuters which intensifies as the incorporation process advances (Logan 1968a). This trend was evident in Sydney's outer south western sector during the 1960s and early 1970s, when the proportion of the resident workforce employed within the sector declined from 76 per cent in 1945 to 66 per cent in 1961 and then to 57 per cent and 40 per cent in 1966 and 1971 respectively (CCC 1948; NSW. SPA 1966, 1968, 1973). In Campbelltown itself nearly 69 per cent of the workforce commuted to jobs outside the area in 1971 (Table 14.4). Only 26.9 per cent of the male workforce was employed locally while the corresponding figure for the female workforce was 42.5 per cent.

Data from the 1971 census reveal that the average length of the journey to work of both male and female workers from Campbelltown is higher than for any other LGA in Sydney (Manning 1978:92). This is not surprising given Campbelltown's remoteness relative to the remainder of the metropolitan area and in view of the high proportion of the working population that commutes. There are many factory and office workers among these commuters, as is indicated by the major workplace concentrations of Campbelltown residents in the industrial areas of the south western (Liverpool-Moorebank-Bankstown) and inner southern suburbs (South Sydney-Botany-Marrickville) and in Sydney's CBD. Forty four per cent of Campbelltown's commuter journeys terminate in these three areas.

The CCC plan, the Sydney Region Outline Plan and the Campbell-town-Camden-Appin New Cities program have all explicitly recognised the necessity to reduce distances separating residences and workplaces by promoting diffusion of employment opportunities to suburban locations. As far as Campbelltown is concerned, no direct action aimed at achieving this goal eventuated until creation of the MDB enabled public resources to be directed into development projects with the potential to attract employment creating activities to the area. Developments associated with the subregional centre complex (including Macarthur Square, the hospital and the technical college) have, and will, increase local job opportunities in the tertiary sector. However, this project is equally important as a facility serving the needs of the region's population and it may not have the same significance in the job creation field as other projects involving office and manufacturing activities. As the previous discussion indicates, proposals which would have increased government office employment in the area have not been put into action and the outlook is not promising. On the other hand, the MDB has actively promoted growth in manufacturing through its industrial land development program, and it is this program which has become the mainstay of the drive to increase local employment opportunities. The high proportion of unskilled workers settling in the area as a result of the Housing Commission's operations suggests that the emphasis on manufacturing is appropriate. Yet a closer examination of what is happening in manufacturing, in Campbelltown and in Australia generally, raises doubts about the effectiveness of this approach in accomplishing its objective (Rich ch 5).

Campbelltown's first substantial industrial development in the late 1950s was not directly attributable to planning initiatives. Subsequent developments during the 1960s were mainly small scale enterprises

**Table 14.4** **Proportion of Campbelltown's resident workforce employed locally, 1971**

|  | Employed within the LGA | Commuting to other areas | Total workers | % locally employed |
|---|---|---|---|---|
| Male | 2,592 | 7,046 | 9,638 | 26.9 |
| Female | 1,856 | 2,377 | 4,133 | 42.5 |
| *Total* | 4,348 | 9,423 | 13,771 | 31.6 |

*Source:* Australian Bureau of Census and Statistics, 1971 Census, unpublished journey to work tabulations

(Table 14.5). Between 1969 and 1974 a minor increase in the number of larger establishments occurred. Since 1974, and particularly after the MDB's program came into operation, there has been a considerable amount of industrial development in the area. Major employers operating in mid 1978 included Millards Caravans (500 employees), Nile Industries (422 employees), Crompton Parkinson (338 employees) and Pirelli Cables (200 employees) (Campbelltown City Council 1978). A measure of the success of the MDB's industrial development activities is perhaps provided by the observation that it managed to secure 80 per cent of the Sydney metropolitan area's industrial land sales between January 1976 and January 1977 (Campbelltown-Ingleburn News, 11 January 1977).

The scale of recent industrial development in the Campbelltown area has encouraged planners and politicians to exaggerate the impact of this development in reducing the level of commuting. Emphasis is placed on the amount of land consumed by industrial development and on the number of people employed by firms establishing in the area rather than on the number of new positions filled by local residents. Analyses by Manning (1978) and Alexander (1979b) raise doubts about the capacity of increased job suburbanisation to reduce journeys to work. These doubts hinge on the observation that the mobility of the workforce often means that such changes in the pattern of job opportunities are likely to generate more circumferential and reverse commuting.

Two examples in the Campbelltown area support these reservations. Upon relocating its plant from Smithfield to Campbelltown, Millards Caravans recruited only 40 per cent of its workforce from the local population. This firm, which at one stage employed 500 people, has since ceased operations at its Campbelltown plant. Similarly, 57 per cent of the 300 positions that will be created when Crompton Parkinson transfers its electrical motor manufacturing plant to Campbelltown will

**Table 14.5   Industrial development in Campbelltown, 1961/62-1974**

| No. | Number of manufacturing establishments | | | | |
|---|---|---|---|---|---|
| employees | 1961/62 | 1963/64 | 1965/66 | 1967/68 | 1974 |
| 1 — 20 | 38 | 45 | 50 | 57 | 58 |
| 21 — 50 | 0 | 0 | 1 | 2 | 6 |
| 51 — 99 | 0 | 0 | 0 | 1 | 2 |
| 100 + | 2 | 2 | 2 | 2 | 2 |
| Total | 40 | 47 | 53 | 62 | 68 |

*Sources:* Australian Bureau of Census and Statistics, *Manufacturing establishments: Summary statistics of operations in local government areas and statistical divisions of NSW,* 1961/62 to 1967/68
1974 figures based on a survey of establishments in the Campbelltown industrial area

be occupied by skilled workers presently employed at the firm's existing Five Dock plant. With these transfers some workers may migrate with their jobs to Campbelltown but many, preferring not to disrupt their families, will remain in their existing homes and commute to Campbelltown. These trends are undoubtedly accentuated by prevailing economic conditions. High levels of unemployment, especially in manufacturing, encourage workers to retain their existing jobs despite the increased burden in the journey to work resulting from plant relocation. However, over time an increasing percentage of the workforce of these companies is likely to be local in origin.

The general pattern of employment in Campbelltown's industrial sector suggests that the Millards and Crompton Parkinson cases are possibly extreme examples. A survey of industrial development conducted by the Campbelltown City Council early in 1978 reveals a proliferation of small scale service industries. Sixty nine firms in the service sector employed 395 persons while 32 manufacturing firms employed 1,680 workers (Campbelltown City Council 1978: Table 2). Thus, even though manufacturing industries account for less than one third of the firms, they employ 80 per cent of the workers. Manufacturing industries also appear to have been marginally more effective in creating local job opportunities. While 64 per cent of the workers employed in service industries reside locally, the corresponding figure for manufacturing employees is 66 per cent. However, the number of resident workers registered as being locally employed in the 1978 survey still represents only 34.4 per cent of the total resident manufacturing workforce recorded in the 1976 census. Among the manufacturing industries, the garment category has a conspicuously high proportion of local residents in the workforce (97.2 per cent). There are two reasons for this. First, the major garment manufacturer in the area (Nile Industries) employs 422 people and this firm, as we have already noted, is one of the earliest to be established in the area. Second, garment manufacturers traditionally have a relatively high proportion of female workers who tend to be less mobile than male workers (Table 14.6).

**Table 14.6   Workforce sex ratios in Campbelltown manufacturing industries**

| Industry | Workforce sex ratio (males per female) |
|---|---|
| Engineering/steel fabrication | 21.0 |
| Building materials/furniture | 2.0 |
| Baby products | 1.5 |
| Garments | 1.1 |
| Others | 7.0 |

*Source:* Campbelltown City Council (1978 Table 3)

The outlook for industrial development and employment in Campbelltown is clouded by uncertain economic conditions that emerged in the 1970s. As these conditions have reduced consumer demand, many of the new factories in Campbelltown are presently operating below capacity. Furthermore, the economic climate has made many industrialists reluctant to commit themselves to expansion and modernisation programs which may require the relocation of plant on the fringe. The Ford Australia assembly plant proposal, which was to be located at Ingleburn, is a case in point. This plant would have initially employed 1,300 workers and later an additional 2,700. On these grounds, it was given extensive media coverage as a major breakthrough in the area's industrial development program. However, commencement of the first phase of the project was indefinitely postponed soon after negotiations with the MDB were completed in mid 1977.

An optimist might claim that the employment potential of industrial development in the area is far from being realised and progress towards this potential has simply been delayed until economic conditions improve. On the other hand, there are grounds for being rather more pessimistic when the present economic malaise is viewed in terms of permanent structural changes (Linge 1979b). Contraction in the manufacturing sector, the tendency to counter relatively high wages by replacing workers with machines, and the stagnation of domestic and external markets all suggest that the industrial development approach may be limited as a means of reducing journeys to work from Campbelltown. Indeed, the irony of the Macarthur experience is that those manufacturers who have taken advantage of the cheap industrial land made available there have done so mainly to reduce their labour component through plant modernisation. Even if substantial industrial development continues at Campbelltown, diminishing job opportunities in Sydney's manufacturing sector will encourage high levels of reverse commuting. Consequently, local residents will not necessarily occupy a large proportion of the new positions.

## 14.6  Conclusion

Over ten years ago Hugh Stretton expressed some hopes and fears on the eventual outcome of what was then seen as an imaginative approach to planned development on the metropolitan fringe:

> . . . Campbelltown may yet see a good city, or a tolerable industrial satellite like Elizabeth, or another lifeless outer-suburban corridor redeemed for some of its people by patches of good local design within it, and by the beautiful countryside around it (Stretton 1970:256).

Most observers have probably oscillated between the optimistic and pessimistic scenarios over the intervening period. Expectations were raised in the first half of the decade when the project received tangible support and encouragement from the federal Labor government. With the withdrawal of this support by the Liberal-Country Party government and the realisation that the Macarthur scheme was perhaps feasible only in the economic growth environment of the 1950s and 1960s rather than the contractionary environment which prevailed in the 1970s, many observers have either begrudgingly or eagerly acknowledged that the reality is closer to Stretton's 'tolerable industrial satellite'.

Some of the reasons for this outcome include the onset of the economic recession in Australia and the lack of substantive support from a government determined to reassert the private enterprise ethic and to extricate the nation from recession through a 'fight inflation first' strategy which hinged on cutting government expenditure. In view of the constraints inherent in this political environment, and when comparisons are made with what has happened elsewhere on Sydney's metropolitan fringe, the Campbelltown experiment still represents an important advance in planned urban expansion. Given these restrictive conditions, however, an important question remains to be answered: are there elements of the Macarthur project which have made it less effective in alleviating problems experienced on the fringe than it might have been? There are two aspects of the MDB's approach which warrant attention in this regard.

First, the Board has a distinctly long term metropolitan planning outlook, which is reflected in the vision of Campbelltown as a relatively self-contained satellite (with Camden and Appin) by the turn of the century. Such a perspective is undeniably essential if the pattern of metropolitan expansion is to be rationalised and if living conditions in growing peripheral areas are to be improved. Even so, the extended planning horizon exposes programs to greater uncertainty, both in terms of the predictions upon which they are based and in terms of the economic and political environment which influences levels of commitment on the part of governments and commercial interests. More importantly, the preoccupation with long term objectives diverts attention and resources away from more immediate problems. Thus, the Board's inactivity regarding the need for improved local and commuter transport services stands out in stark contrast with its investigations into the feasibility of a light rail transit system for the year 2000 (NSW. PEC and MDB 1978). The tacit assumption that existing problems do not warrant attention because they will be rectified by future development implies a degree of faith in predictions and future public and private investment trends which is not consistent with previous experience.

The other deficiency of the MDB's performance concerns the way its physical planning and development functions have been conducted independently of, and perhaps at the expense of, any systematic monitoring of the social impact of development in the area. This bias is manifest in the fact that, while considerable emphasis has been placed on promoting industrial development, no serious attempt has yet been made to evaluate how effective this program has been in reducing commuting from the area. To some extent the neglect of socially oriented planning requirements is inherent in the structure and purpose of the organisation. Indeed, the Board's professional staff, comprised mainly of engineers and architects, lack the inclination and skills to analyse social trends, needs and problems in a rapidly growing population. One social scientist, an anthropologist, is left to this task. Unfortunately, the 'bricks and mortar' mentality will probably become more firmly entrenched as declining financial support from government sources forces the Board to become increasingly dependent upon revenue derived from its development activities.

# References

Abramovitz M (1961) 'The nature and significance of Kuznets cycles', *Economic Development and Cultural Change*, 9, pp 225-48

Aird W V (1961) *The water supply, sewerage and drainage of Sydney*, MWSDB, Sydney

Albertson L (1977) 'Telecommunications as a travel substitute: some psychological, organizational and social aspects', *Journal of Communication*, 27, pp 32-43

Alexander I (1976a) 'Suburbanisation of the private office sector — fact or fiction?', in Linge G J R (ed) *Restructuring employment opportunities in Australia*, Publication HG 11, Department of Human Geography, Australian National University, pp 185-215

Alexander I (1976b) *Office relocation: an impossible dream?*, Paper presented to the 47th ANZAAS Congress (Section 21), Hobart

Alexander I (1978) 'Office decentralisation in Sydney', *Town Planning Review*, 49, pp 402-16

Alexander I (1979a) *Office location and public policy*, Longman, London

Alexander I (1979b) 'Job location and journey to work: three Australian cities, 1961-1971', *Australian Geographical Studies*, 17, pp 155-74

Alexander I (1980a) 'Office dispersal in metropolitan areas I: a review and framework for analyses', *Geoforum*, 11, pp 225-47

Alexander I (1980b) 'Office dispersal in metropolitan areas II: case study results and conclusions', *Geoforum*, 11, pp 249-75

Alexander I (1981) 'Post-war metropolitan planning: goals and realities', in Troy P N (ed) *Equity in the city*, Allen and Unwin, Sydney, pp 145-71

Alexander I and Dawson J (1979) 'Suburbanisation of retail sales and employment in Australian cities', *Australian Geographical Studies*, 17, pp 76-83

Alford J (1979) 'Australian labour, multinationals and the Asian-Pacific region', *Journal of Australian Political Economy*, 6, pp 4-23

Alonso W (1964) *Location and land use*, Harvard University Press, Cambridge, Mass.

Armstrong R (1972) *The office industry: patterns of growth and location*, MIT Press, Cambridge, Mass.

Australia (1970) *Report from the Senate Select Committee on the container method of handling cargoes: Part 2 — minutes evidence (1968)*, Parliamentary Paper No 46A, Commonwealth Government Printing Office, Canberra

Australia. BIE (1978) *Industrialisation in Asia — some implications for Australian industry*, BIE Research Report 1, AGPS, Canberra

Australia. BIE (1979a) 'Employment patterns in Australian industry', *Journal of Industry and Commerce*, 20, pp 6–9

Australia. BIE (1979b) *Australian industrial development — some aspects of structural change*, BIE Research Report 2, AGPS, Canberra

Australia. BIE (1981a) *The structure of Australian industry — past developments and future trends*, BIE Research Report 8, AGPS, Canberra

Australia. BIE (1981b) *Mining developments and Australian industry: input demands during the 1980s*, BIE Research Report 9, AGPS, Canberra

Australia. BIE (1981c) *The long-run impact of technological changes on the structure of Australian industry to 1990-91*, BIE Research Report 7, AGPS, Canberra

Australia. Cities Commission (1975) *Sydney position paper*, Internal report by W. Richardson, Canberra

Australia. Commission of Inquiry into Poverty [the Henderson report] (1975) *Poverty in Australia*, AGPS, Canberra

Australia. Committee of Inquiry into the Australian Financial System [the Campbell report] (1981) *Final report*, AGPS, Canberra

Australia. Committee to Advise on Policies for Manufacturing Industry [the Jackson committee] (1975) *Report*, AGPS, Canberra

Australia. Department of Industry and Commerce (1980a) *The Australian electronics industry: a report by the Electronics Industry Advisory Council*, AGPS, Canberra

Australia. Department of Industry and Commerce (1980b) *The Australian textile and apparel industries: a report by the Textile and Apparel Industry Advisory Council*, AGPS, Canberra

Australia. Department of Industry and Commerce (1980c) *The Australian footwear industry: a report by the Footwear Industry Advisory Council*, AGPS, Canberra

Australia. IAC (1977) *Structural change in Australia*, AGPS, Canberra

Australia. IAC (1980a) *Annual report 1979-80*, AGPS, Canberra

Australia. IAC (1980b) *Passenger motor vehicles — import restrictions and quota allocation*, IAC Report 250, AGPS, Canberra

Australia. IAC (1981) *The regional implications of economic change*, AGPS, Canberra

Australia. Migrant Services and Programs [the Galbally report] (1978) *Report*, Volume 1, AGPS, Canberra

Australia. National Population Inquiry [the Borrie report] (1975) *Population in Australia; a demographic analysis and projection*, AGPS, Canberra

Australia. Report of the Committee of Inquiry into Technological Change in Australia [the Myers report] (1980) *Technological change in Australia*, Volume 1, AGPS, Canberra

Australia. Royal Commission on Australian Government Administration [the Coombs report] (1976) *Report*, AGPS, Canberra

Australia. Senate Standing Committee on National Resources (1978) *The Commonwealth's role in the assessment, planning, development and management of Australia's water resources*, AGPS, Canberra

ACTU (1979) *Submission to the Myers Committee on Technological Change*, Sydney

AIUS (1970) *Manufacturing development in the Sydney region — problems and opportunities*, Canberra

AIUS (1972) *Efficient and humane alternatives to over concentrated growth: first report of the task force on new cities for Australia*, Canberra

AIUS (1973) *Urban development in Melbourne*, Canberra

AIUS (1980) *Urban strategies for Australia: managing the 80's*, Publication 88, Canberra

Australian Population and Immigration Council (1976) *A decade of migrant settlement*, AGPS, Canberra

Australian Stock Exchange Journal (1979) 'The retail industry — an industry in turmoil', October, pp 11-15

Badcock B (1973) 'The residential structure of metropolitan Sydney', *Australian Geographical Studies*, 11, pp 1-27

Balmain Residents (1975) *Case against cargo trucking from Mort Bay*, Balmain

Barnet R J and Muller R E (1974) *Global reach: the power of the multinational corporations*, Simon and Schuster, New York

Baumann D and Dworkin D (1978) *Water Resources for our cities*, Resource Papers for College Geography No 78-2, Association of American Geographers, Washington, D. C.

Bayley W A (1965) *History of Campbelltown, New South Wales*, Halstead Press, Sydney

Beed T W (1964) *The growth of suburban retailing in Sydney*, unpublished Ph.D. thesis, Department of Geography, University of Sydney

Bell F C (1972) 'The acquisition, consumption and elimination of water by the Sydney urban system', *Proceedings of the Ecological Society of Australia*, 7, pp 161-72

Bell G (1981) 'The last of the major shopping centres', *The Bulletin*, October 27, pp 112-4 and 116

Bellin H (1976) 'The challenge for small business', *National Bank Monthly Summary*, June, pp 5-7

Bernasek M (1978) 'Australian manufacturing industry: the challenge of structural change', *Current Affairs Bulletin*, 55(2), pp 4-29

Berry B J L (1967) *Geography of market centers and retail distribution*, Prentice-Hall, Englewood Cliffs, New Jersey

Black J (1977) *Public inconvenience*, Urban Research Unit, Australian National University, Canberra

Blake J (1976) 'Brent Cross shopping centre', *Town and Country Planning*, 44, pp 231-36

Borrie W D (1978) 'Population trends and policy', in Scott P (ed) *Australian cities and public policy*, Georgian House, Melbourne, pp 1-22

Brennan T (1973) *New community: problems and policy*, Angus and Robertson, Sydney

Brotherson W H (1975) 'Port operations in Australia', *Australian Transport*, 17(9), pp 33-5

Bryson T and Thompson F (1972) *An Australian new town: life and leadership in a new housing suburb*, Penguin, Harmondsworth

Burnley I H (1974a) 'International migration and metropolitan growth in Australia', in Burnley I H (ed) *Urbanization in Australia: the postwar experience*, Cambridge University Press, Cambridge, pp 99-117

Burnley I H (1974b) 'Social ecology of immigrant settlement in Australian cities', in Burnley I H (ed) *Urbanization in Australia: the post-war experience*, Cambridge University Press, Cambridge, pp 165–83

Burnley I H (1977) 'Mortality patterns in Sydney', in McGlashan N D (ed) *Studies in Australian mortality*, University of Tasmania Press, Hobart, pp 29–62

Burnley I H (1978) 'The ecology of suicide in an Australian metropolis: the case of Sydney', *Australian Journal of Social Issues*, 13, pp 91–103

Burnley I H (1980) *The Australian urban system: growth, change and differentiation*, Longman Cheshire, Melbourne

Burnley I H and Walker S (1978) 'Immigrant group adjustment at the neighbourhood level in selected districts of Sydney', in *Participation, Report to the Premier*, Ethnic Affairs Division, Premiers Department, NSW Government, pp 465–90

Butlin N G (1964) *Investment in Australian economic development 1861–1900*, Cambridge University Press, Cambridge

Butlin N G (1970) 'Some perspectives on Australian economic development', in Forster C (ed) *Australian economic development in the twentieth century*, Allen and Unwin, London, pp 266–327

Butlin N G (ed) (1976a) *The impact of Port Botany*, Australian National University Press, Canberra

Butlin N G (ed) (1976b) *Sydney's environmental amenity 1970–1975: a study of the system of waste management and pollution control*, Botany Bay Project Report No 1, Australian National University Press, Canberra

Byrt W J (1981) *The Australian company*, Croom Helm, London

Callus R and Quinlan M (1979) 'The new unskilled worker', *Journal of Australian Political Economy*, 6, pp 74–84

Cameron J R and Klaassen B (1977) 'Development of an Australian water policy', *Water Resources Bulletin*, 13, pp 387–400

Campbelltown City Council (n.d.) *Estimates of Housing Commission dwellings and population, 1970–82*, Campbelltown

Campbelltown City Council (1978) *Survey of Campbelltown industrial area*, Campbelltown·

Cardew R V (1976) *Residential development in the south coast urban region of New South Wales*, unpublished MA hons. thesis, Department of Geography, University of Sydney

Cardew R V (1979) *The real cost of housing*, Publication 81, AIUS, Canberra

Cardew R V (1980) 'The future of flats and home units in Sydney', in Archer R (ed) *Planning for urban consolidation*, Planning Research Centre, University of Sydney, pp 76–85

Cardew R V (1981a) *Government regulation of industrial property development*, Publication 92, AIUS, Canberra

Cardew R V (1981b) 'Liberalising land use classes', *Proceedings of the Sixth Conference of Local Government Planners Association of NSW, 1980*, Sydney

Carter H (1981) *The study of urban geography*, (third edition), Arnold, London

Chait S (1978) 'Models and the urban planning crisis: a comment', *Town Planning Review*, 49, pp 228–31

Chamberlin E H (1956) *The theory of monopolistic competition*, (seventh edition), Harvard University Press, Cambridge, Mass.

Chapman C (1981) 'Cutting big government down to size', *Australian Business*, 7 May, pp 37–40

Choi C Y and Burnley I H (1974) 'Population components in the growth of cities', in Burnley I H (ed) *Urbanization in Australia: the post-war experience*, Cambridge University Press, Cambridge, pp 51-61

Chong F (1981) 'Millionaire Ho gambles on a white elephant', *Business Review*, 18-24 July, pp 31-2

City of Sydney (1971) *City of Sydney strategic plan*, Urban Systems Corporation, Sydney

City of Sydney (1980) *1980 City of Sydney plan*, Council of the City of Sydney, Sydney

Cleaver A (1979) 'Beating the sewerage backlog', *Sydney Water Board Journal*, 29(1), pp 13-28

Cochrane P J (1980) *Industrialization and dependence: Australia's road to economic development*, University of Queensland Press, St Lucia

Cohen R (1977) 'Multinational corporations, international finance, and the Sunbelt', in Perry D C and Watkins A J (eds) *The rise of the Sunbelt cities*, Sage, Beverly Hills, California, pp 211-26

Cohen R (1979) 'The changing transactions economy and its spatial implications', *Ekistics*, 46, pp 7-15

Commonwealth Banking Corporation (1979) *Submission to the Inquiry into Technological Change*, Sydney

Connell R W (1977) *Ruling class, ruling culture*, Cambridge University Press, Cambridge

Cox K R, Reynolds D R and Rokkan S (1974) *Locational approaches to power and conflict*, Wiley, New York

Crane E (1967) 'Market segmentation: an evaluation', *Conference Proceedings, American Marketing Association*, Chicago, No 26, pp 69-71

Crough G J (1981) *Superannuation funds in Australia: their investment, control and social significance*, Working Paper 8, Transnational Research Project, University of Sydney

CCC (1948) *The planning scheme for the County of Cumberland*, Sydney

CCC (1959) *Growth of population in Australia and the County of Cumberland*, Sydney

Daly M T (1980) *Capital and migration: forgotten factors in regional development*, paper given at International Geographical Union Congress, Tokyo

Daly M T (1982) *Sydney Boom Sydney Bust*, Allen and Unwin, Sydney

Daly M T and Webber M J (1973) 'The growth of the firm within the city', *Urban Studies*, 10, pp 303-17

Daniels P W (1975) *Office location. An urban and regional study*, Bell, London

Dare T (1981) 'Services limp behind as urban sprawl marches west', *SMH*, 30 September

Davis B W (1980) 'Professional values and accountability in government: the case of Australian public investment', in Weller P and Jaensch D (eds) *Responsible government in Australia*, Drummond Publishing, Melbourne, pp 161-67

Davis S I (1976) *The Euro-Bank*, Macmillan, London

Dawson J A (1979) *The marketing environment*, Croom Helm, London

Dawson-Grove T (1979) 'Pressure on to rationalise tyre industry', *AFR*, 10 April

De Leuw Cather (1976) *Parramatta region public transport study*, for the Joint Commonwealth-State Steering Committee, Canberra

DJ's Properties Ltd (1972) *Prospectus*, Sydney

Dridan J R (1964) 'The urban uses of water', in *Water resources use and management*, Proceedings of a symposium held at Canberra by the Australian Academy of Science, 9-13 September 1963, Melbourne University Press, Melbourne, pp 44-53

Easterlin R A (1961) 'Influences in European overseas emigration before World War I', *Economic Development and Cultural Change*, 9, pp 331-51

Edgerton D, James G and Jordan F (1979) 'Port container movements in Sydney', *Australian Transport Research Forum: Forum Papers — Sydney 1978*, pp 63-84

Encel S and Walpole S (1980) 'The effects of technological change in Australia', *Papers of the Australian and New Zealand Regional Science Association*, fifth meeting, Tanunda, pp 1-13

Fagan R H (1981a) 'Spatial organisation in the brewing industry: a study of corporations in the Australian manufacturing recession', in Donnelly P (ed) *Geography in the 80s*, Sydney Teachers College, Sydney

Fagan R H (1981b) 'Geographically uneven development: restructuring of the Australian aluminium industry', *Australian Geographical Studies*, 19, pp 141-60

Fagan R H, McKay J and Linge G J R (1981) 'Structural change: the international and national context', in Linge G J R and McKay J (eds) *Structural change in Australia: some spatial and organisational responses*, Publication HG 15, Department of Human Geography, Australian National University, Canberra, pp 1-49

Faulkner H W (1981) 'Journey pattern adjustments on Sydney's metropolitan fringe: an exploratory study', *Australian Geographer*, 15, pp 17-25

Fiegel N (1980) *Growth of planned retail centres in suburban Sydney*, unpublished hons. thesis, School of Town Planning, University of New South Wales

Frank R E (1967) 'Market segmentation research: findings and implications', in Bass F M, King C W and Pessemier E A (eds) *Application of the sciences in marketing management*, Wiley, New York

Fraser R D L (1959) 'Proposal to examine the problems of establishing Campbelltown as a large satellite town', *Cumberland County Council, Chief County Planner's Report*, M2015, 5 August, Sydney

Freeman C (1974) *The economics of industrial innovation*, Penguin, Harmondsworth

Fröbel F, Heinrichs J and Kreye O (1980) *The new international division of labour: structural unemployment in industrialised countries and industrialisation in developing countries*, Cambridge University Press, Cambridge

Gallagher D R (1976) 'Pricing for water demand management: possibilities and limitations', in *Pricing and demand management policies in the provision of water and sewerage*, AGPS, Canberra, pp 20-30

Gallagher D R (1977) 'Some implications of water rates', *Economics*, 10(2), pp 41-4

Gallagher D R and Robinson R W (1977) *Influence of metering, pricing policies and incentives on water use efficiency*, Australian Water Resources Council Technical Paper No 19, AGPS, Canberra

Gibbons R P (1976) 'Finance and planning: the Water Board and the 1959 green belt releases', *Australian Journal of Public Administration*, 35, pp 147-59

Gibson J (1979) *Biological maps of Sydney*, Reed, Sydney

Gilmour P (1974) 'Development of physical distribution models', in Gilmour P (ed) *Physical distribution management in Australia*, Cheshire, Melbourne, pp 319-24

Goddard J B (1975) *Office location in urban and regional development*, Oxford University Press, Oxford

Golledge R G (1979) *Consultant's report on retail centre policy*, Town and Country Planning Board, Melbourne

Gottman J (1970) 'Urban centrality and the interweaving of quaternary activities', *Ekistics*, 29, pp 322-31

Grace Bros. (1981) *Annual report*, Sydney

Gruen V (1978) 'The sad story of shopping centres', *Town and Country Planning*, 46, pp 350-3

Gudgin G (1978) *Industrial location processes and regional employment growth*, Saxon House, Farnborough

Guirdham N (1972) *Marketing: the management of distribution channels*, Pergamon Press, Oxford

Hall A R (1968) *The export of capital from Britain 1870-1914*, Methuen, London

Hamilton F E I and Linge G J R (1981) 'International industrial systems', in Hamilton F E I and Linge G J R (eds) *Spatial analysis, industry and the industrial environment volume 2, international industrial systems*, Wiley, Chichester

Hanke S H (1972) 'Pricing urban water', in Mushkin S J (ed) *Public prices for public products*, The Urban Institute, Washington, D.C., pp 283-306

Harrison P F (1966) 'City planning in Australia: what went wrong?', in Australian Institute of Political Science *Australian cities: chaos or planned growth?*, Angus and Robertson, Sydney, pp 60-87

Harrison P F (1972) 'Planning the metropolis — A case study', in Parker R S and Troy P N (eds) *The politics of urban growth*, Australian National University Press, Canberra, pp 61-99

Harrison P F (1974) 'Planning the metropolitan areas', in Burnley I H (ed) *Urbanization in Australia: the post-war experience*, Cambridge University Press, Cambridge, pp 203-20

Harrison P F (1978) 'City planning', in Scott P (ed) *Australian cities and public policy*, Georgian House, Melbourne, pp 141-73

Hastings J S (1978) *The long term effects of the pedestrianisation of the Lane Cove shopping centre*, unpublished B.Sc. hons. thesis, School of Geography, University of New South Wales

Healey P (1977) 'The sociology of urban transportation planning: a sociopolitical perspective', in Hensher D A (ed) *Urban transport economics*, Cambridge University Press, Cambridge

Heeps D P (1977a) *Efficiency in industrial, municipal and domestic water use*, Australian Water Resources Council Technical Paper No. 20, AGPS, Canberra

Heeps D P (1977b) 'The use of water by urban communities', *Victoria's Resources*, 19(4), pp 19-23

Hickie D (1981) 'Who owns Australia's manufacturing industry?', *National Times*, 28 June, pp 23-34

Hood N and Young S (1979) *The economics of multinational enterprise*, Longman, London

Hymer S (1975) 'The multinational corporation and the law of uneven development', in Radice H (ed) *International firms and modern imperialism*, Penguin, Harmondsworth, pp 37-62

Jay C (1981) 'Population smorgasbord: is Australia facing a people boom?' *AFR*, 11 June

Jenkins C and Sherman B D (1979) *The collapse of work*, Methuen, London

Johnson J H (ed) (1974) *Suburban growth: geographical processes at the edge of the western city*, Wiley, London

Johnston R J and Rimmer P J (1969) *Retailing in Melbourne*, Publication HG 3, Department of Human Geography, Australian National University, Canberra

Jones J, Shipway M and Simpson J (1979) *Impact of Macquarie regional shopping centre*, Urban Studies No 5, Macquarie University

Jones Lang Wootton (1979) *Property review*, February, Sydney

Kain J F (1975) *Essays in urban spatial structure*, Ballinger, Cambridge, Mass.

Kasper W (1978) 'Australia's economic and industrial structures: past patterns and prospective trends', in Kasper W and Parry T G (eds) *Growth, trade and structural change in an open Australian economy*, University of New South Wales, Sydney, pp 90-124

Keeble D E (1968) 'Industrial decentralization and the metropolis: the North-West London case', *Transactions of the Institute of British Geographers*, 44, pp 1-54

Kendig H (1979) *New life for old suburbs: post-war land use and housing in the Austrlian inner city*, Allen and Unwin, Sydney

Kilmartin L and Thorns D C (1978) *Cities unlimited. The sociology of urban development in Australia and New Zealand*, Allen and Unwin, Sydney

King R (1977) 'Social and community issues in port development', *Australian Transport Research Forum: Forum Papers — Melbourne* (no pagination)

Lamberton D McL (1977) 'Structure and growth of communication services', in Tucker K A (ed) *The economics of the Australian service sector*, Croom Helm, London, pp 143-66

Langdale J V (1975) 'Nodal regional structures of New South Wales', *Australian Geographical Studies*, 13, pp 123-36

Langdale J V (1979a) 'Telex and data transmission and the Australian economic system', *Proceedings of the Tenth New Zealand Geography Conference*, Auckland, pp 97-104

Langdale J V (1979b) 'The role of telecommunications in the information economy', *Background papers for a seminar on social research and telecommunications planning*, Planning Directorate, Telecom Australia, Melbourne, pp 30-50

Lever W F (1974) 'Manufacturing linkages and the search for suppliers and markets', in Hamilton F E I (ed) *Spatial perspectives on industrial location and decison making*, Wiley, London, pp 309-33

Linge G J R (1967) 'Governments and the location of secondary industry in Australia', *Economic Geography*, 43, pp 43-63

Linge G J R (1971) 'Government and spatial behaviour' in Linge G J R and Rimmer P J (eds) *Government influence and the location of economic activity*, Publication HG 5, Department of Human Geography, Australian National University, Canberra, pp 25-52

Linge G J R (1977) 'Manufacturing', in Jeans D N (ed) *Australia: a geography*,

Sydney University Press, Sydney, pp 466-90

Linge G J R (1978) 'The Australian environment and industrial location analysis', in Hamilton F E I (ed) *Industrial change: international experience and public policy*, Longman, London, pp 144-54

Linge G J R (1979a) 'Australian manufacturing and the role and responsibilities of geographers', *Australian Geographical Studies*, 17, pp 193-203

Linge G J R (1979b) 'Australian manufacturing in recession: a review of the spatial implications', *Environment and Planning A*, 11, pp 1405-30

Linge G J R (1979c) *Industrial awakening: a geography of Australian manufacturing, 1788-1890*, Australian National University Press, Canberra

Linge G J R and McKay J (eds) (1981) *Structural change in Australia: some spatial and organisational responses*, Publication HG 15, Department of Human Geography, Australian National University, Canberra

Living City (1980) 'Holding down that peak demand', 28, p 17

Lloyd P E and Dicken P (1977) *Location in space: a theoretical approach to economic geography*, (second edition), Harper and Row, New York

Logan M I (1963) 'Industrial location trends in Sydney region', *Australian Planning Institute Journal*, 2, pp 155-60

Logan M I (1964) 'Manufacturing decentralisation in the Sydney metropolitan area', *Economic Geography*, 40, pp 151-62

Logan M I (1966) 'Locational behaviour of manufacturing firms in urban areas', *Annals of the Association of American Geographers*, 56, pp 451-66

Logan M I (1968a) 'Work-residence relationships in the city', *Australian Geographical Studies*, 6, pp 151-66

Logan M I (1968b) 'Capital city development in Australia', in Dury G H and Logan M I (eds) *Studies in Australian geography*, Heinemann Educational Australia, Melbourne, pp 245-301

Logan M I, Whitelaw J S and McKay J (1981) *Urbanization: the Australian experience*, Shillington House, Melbourne

McAfee R J (1980) 'Historical climatology for Sydney 1788-1850', *Sydney Gazette*, 1(3), p 4

MDB (1977) *Macarthur growth centre: population projections 1976-2015*, Campbelltown

MDB (1978) *Administrative report*, No 16, Campbelltown

McDonald C N (1978) *Rationalistion of the pharmacy industry: a case study*, unpublished B.Sc. hons. thesis, School of Geography, University of New South Wales

Mackett R L (1977) 'Models and the urban planning crisis', *Town and Country Planning Review*, 48, pp 287-98

McKinsey and Co (1978) *Reshaping the Water Board's strategy to suit future requirements*, Sydney

McLelland M (1968) 'Needs and services in an outer suburb', *Australian Journal of Social Issues*, 3, pp 44-62

McMahon T A and Weeks C R (1973) 'Climate and water use in Australian cities', *Australian Geographical Studies*, 11, pp 99-108

Manning I G (1978) *The journey to work*, Allen and Unwin, Sydney

Meier R (1962) *A communications theory of urban growth*, MIT Press, Cambridge, Mass.

MWSDB (n.d.a) *The Shoalhaven scheme*, Sydney

MWSDB (n.d.b) *Water: the key to development*, Sydney

MWSDB (1968) *The Shoalhaven scheme*, Sydney

MWSDB (1977) *Metropolitan Water Sewerage and Drainage Board: Eighty-ninth Annual Report for the Year Ended 30th June 1977*, Sydney

MWSDB (1978) *Shoalhaven water supply and power generation scheme: stage I: technical details*, MWSDB and Electricity Commission of NSW, Sydney

MWSDB (1979) *Deepwater submarine outfalls for Sydney*, Sydney

MWSSDB (1979a) *Metropolitan Water Supply, Sewerage, and Drainage Board: Annual Report 1979*, Perth

MWSSDB (1979b) *Metropolitan Water Board: Development Plan 1979-1984*, Perth

Mills B (1981a) 'The godfathers of Australian business', *AFR*, 14 April

Mills B (1981b) 'Institutions show how to handle the big money', *AFR*, 16 April

Muller R E (1979) *National economic growth and stabilization policy in the age of multinational corporations: the challenge of our post-market economy*, Occasional Paper 3, Transnational Research Project, University of Sydney

Munro C H (1974) *Australian water resources and their development*, Angus and Robertson, Sydney

Muth R F (1969) *Cities and housing*, Chicago University Press, Chicago

Neilson L (1972) *Business activities in three Melbourne suburbs*, Urban Research Unit, Australian National University, Canberra

Neilson L (1976) 'The growth centres programme', in McMaster J C and Webb G R (eds) *Australian urban economics: a reader*, Australian and New Zealand Book Co, Sydney, pp 471-86

Neutze G M (1974) 'The case for new cities in Australia', *Urban Studies*, 11, pp 259-75

Neutze G M (1977) *Urban development in Australia*, Allen and Unwin, Sydney

Neutze G M (1978) *Australian urban policy*, Allen and Unwin, Sydney

NSW (1967) *Report of the Royal Commission of Inquiry into rating, valuation and local government finance*, [the Else-Mitchell report] Government Printer, Sydney

NSW (1976) *Report of the Botany Bay port and environment inquiry* [the Simblist report] Parliamentary Papers 1976 (Second Session) No. 103, Government Printer, Sydney

NSW (1979) *Environmental Planning and Assessment Act*, No. 203, NSW Government, Sydney

NSW (1980a) *Commission of Inquiry into the Kyeemagh-Chullora road* [the Kirby report] *Vol. I: Containers*, NSW Government, Sydney

NSW (1980b) *Report of the Commission of Enquiry into the New South Wales road freight industry* [the McDonnell report], NSW Government, Sydney

NSW (1981) *Commission of Inquiry into the Kyeemagh-Chullora road* [the Kirby report] *Vol. II: criteria for evaluation, Vol. III: criteria for evaluation, Vol. IV: the options*, NSW Government, Sydney

NSW. DMR (1945) *Main road development plan for Sydney and the County of Cumberland*, Sydney

NSW. DMR (1965) *Traffic volumes and supplementary data 1965: County of Cumberland Volume 1*, Sydney

NSW. DMR (1971) *Traffic volumes and supplementary data 1971: County of Cumberland Volume 1*, Sydney

NSW. DMR (1977) *Traffic volumes and supplementary data 1977: County of Cumberland Volume 1*, Sydney

NSW. DMR and PEC (1979) *Report on the Kyeemagh-Chullora route study*, Sydney

NSW. Housing Commission (1957) *Annual Report*, Sydney

NSW. PEC (1976a) *Population projections for New South Wales 1975-2000*, Sydney

NSW. PEC (1976b) *Work places and work trips 1971*, Sydney

NSW. PEC (1978) *Parramatta town centre*, internal report, Sydney

NSW. PEC (1979) *Population projections for New South Wales 1976-2001*, Sydney

NSW. PEC (1980a) *Sydney's inner area: a study of six inner municipalities*, Publication 79/21, Sydney

NSW. PEC (1980b) *Review: Sydney Region Outline Plan*, Publication 80/5, Sydney

NSW. PEC and MDB (1978) *Macarthur growth centre public transportation study*, Volume 1, Pak-Poy and Associates, Crows Nest

NSW. SPA (1966) *Journey to work survey: metropolitan Sydney*, Sydney

NSW. SPA (1967) *Growth and change, prelude to a plan*, Sydney

NSW. SPA (1968) *Sydney Region: Outline Plan 1970-2000A.D. A strategy for development*, Sydney

NSW. SPA (1973) *The new cities of Campbelltown, Camden and Appin: structure plan*, Sydney

NSW. SPCC (1977) *The quality of Sydney's natural waterways in relation to its growth*, Sydney

NSW. SATS (1974a) *SATS; Volume 1 — base year (1971) data report*, Sydney

NSW. SATS (1974b) *Sydney area transportation study*, Sydney

Nilles J *et al.* (1976) *The telecommunications transportation trade-off*, Wiley, New York

Nora S and Minc A (1980) *The computerization of society*, MIT Press, Cambridge, Mass.

Norcliffe G B (1977) *Inferential statistics for geographers*, Hutchinson, London

Northam R M (1979) *Urban geography* (second edition), Wiley, New York

Nugent E (1977) *Wholesaling and urban structure*, unpublished B.A. hons. thesis, School of Earth Sciences, Macquarie University

OECD (1981) *Microelectronics, productivity and employment*, Committee on Information, Computers and Communications Policy, Paris

Paterson J (1978) 'Urban management: the Australian context', in Ryan P F (ed) *Urban management processes*, Australian National Commission for UNESCO, AGPS, Canberra pp 7-14

Payne M and Mill G (1973) 'The case for new cities in Australia', *Royal Australian Planning Institute Journal*, 11, pp 5-7

Perrons D C (1981) 'The role of Ireland in the new international division of labour: a proposed framework for regional analysis', *Regional Studies*, 15, pp 81-100

Plant Location International Pty Ltd and W D Scott and Co Pty Ltd (1972) *The office space markets, Sydney metropolitan area: 1972-1980*, Volume I, Sydney

Porat M (1978) 'Emergence of an information economy', *Economic Impact*, 24, pp 29-34

Porter M G (1974) 'The interdependence of monetary policy and capital inflows in Australia', *The Economic Record*, 50, pp 1-13

Potter R J (1977) 'Electronic mail', *Science*, 195, pp 1160-4

Power N A (1980) *An investigation of the factors affecting urban water consumption in Northern Australia*, Department of Civil and Systems Engineering, James Cook University of North Queensland, Townsville

Pratten C F (1976) *Labor productivity differentials within international companies*, Occasional Paper 50, Department of Applied Economics, University of Cambridge, Cambridge

Puu T and Wibe S (1980) *The economics of technical progress*, Macmillan, London

Pye R (1977) 'Office location and the cost of maintaining contact', *Environment and Planning A*, 9, pp 149-68

Rees J A (1976a) 'The need for and general method of demand control in the provision of water and sewerage services', in *Pricing and demand management policies in the provision of water and sewerage*, AGPS, Canberra, pp 7-19

Rees J A (1976b) 'Rethinking our approach to water supply provision', *Geography*, 61, pp 232-45

Reid H (1981) *Urban consolidation in Sydney*, Planning Research Centre, University of Sydney

Reserve Bank of Australia (1979) *Submission to the Committee of Inquiry into the Australian Financial System*, Occasional Paper 7, Reserve Bank, Sydney

Rich D C (1981a) 'Structural change in Australian manufacturing: an analysis of employment and productivity', in Linge G J R and McKay J (eds) *Structural change in Australia: some spatial and organisational responses*, Publication HG 15, Department of Human Geography, Australian National University, Canberra, pp 143-87

Rich D C (1981b) 'The geography of productivity in Australian manufacturing', *Proceedings of 17th Conference of the Institute of Australian Geographers*, Mitchell College of Advanced Education, Bathurst, pp 231-43

Richardson H W (1977) *The new urban economics: and alternatives*, Pion, London

Rimmer P J (1969) *Manufacturing in Melbourne*, Publication HG 2, Department of Human Geography, Australian National University, Canberra

Rimmer P J (1978) *Urban goods movement in Sydney*, Bureau of Transport Economics Occasional Paper No 17, AGPS, Canberra

Rimmer P J and Hicks S K (1979) 'Urban goods movement: process, planning approach and policy', in Hensher D A and Stopher P R (eds) *Behavioural travel modelling*, Croom Helm, London, pp 525-52

Rimmer P J and Hooper P (1977) *Launceston urban freight study: a reconnaissance report*, Commonwealth Bureau of Roads, Melbourne

Rimmer P J and Tsipouras A (1977) 'Ports and urban systems: framework and research needs in resolution of port generated conflicts', *Australian Transport Research Forum: Forum Papers*, Melbourne (no pagination)

Robinson P (1980) 'Defence firms fight a little-known war … and may be winning', *AFR*, 1 December

Robinson P (1981a) 'How business shocked Hamer', *AFR*, 3 February

Robinson P (1981b) 'How to plan an economic shambles, Victorian-style', *AFR*, 4 February.

Robinson P (1981c) 'Defence Dept assuming the role of industry protector', *AFR*, 7 December

Rowland D T (1979) *Internal migration in Australia*, ABS, Canberra
Royal Australian Planning Institute Journal (1981) 'Pedestrianisation and a renascence of civil design', 19, pp 46-67
Russell J A (1980) 'Effects of computerisation on casual women workers — South Australian Totalizator Agency Board', in *Technological change in Australia*, Vol 4, Report of the Committee of Inquiry into Technological Change in Australia, AGPS, Canberra, pp 189-235
Rydges (1978) 'Retailing: why investor demand exceeds investment supply in Sydney', April, pp 117-18
Rydges (1979) 'Where the money is in retail sites', April, pp 164-66
Rydges (1981) 'Too many shops but top locations still thrive', April, pp 118-21
Saddington A L (1974) *The efficiency of shopper movement within planned and unplanned shopping centres*, unpublished B.Sc. hons. thesis, School of Geography, University of New South Wales
Salter W E G (1966) *Productivity and technological change*, (second edition), Cambridge University Press, Cambridge
Sandercock L K (1975a) 'Capitalism and the environment: The failure of success', in Wheelwright E L and Buckley K (eds) *Essays in the political economy of Australian capitalism*, Volume 1, pp 153-78
Sandercock L K (1975b) *Cities for Sale*, Melbourne University Press, Melbourne
Sandercock L K (1979) 'Urban policy', in Patience A and Head B (eds) *From Whitlam to Fraser: reform and reaction in Australian politics*, Oxford University Press, Melbourne, pp 140-56
Scargill D I (1979) *The form of cities*, Bell and Hyman, London
Scott A J (1970) 'Location—allocation systems: a review', *Geographical Analysis*, 2, pp 95-119
Scott A J (1980) *The urban land nexus and the state*, Pion, London
Scott W D and Co Pty Ltd (1975) *Empirical investigation of issues arising from urban goods workshop*, (2 vols), unpublished report, Commonwealth Bureau of Roads, Melbourne
Shiels G (1979) *Optimum retail levels — a case study of retailing patterns in Woollahra, Waverley and Randwick*, unpublished Master of Urban Studies thesis, Macquarie University
Simmons J W (1966) *Toronto's Changing Retail Complex*, Research Paper No. 104, Department of Geography, University of Chicago, Chicago
Simons P L (1966) *Sydney's wholesale district*, Research Paper 10, Department of Geography, University of Sydney
Simons P L (1967) *Wholesaling in Sydney*, unpublished Ph.D. thesis, Department of Geography, University of Sydney
Smith A (1980) *Goodbye Gutenberg: the newspaper revolution of the 1980s*, Oxford University Press, Oxford
Smith D M (1977) *Patterns in human geography*, Penguin, Harmondsworth
Snow D (1981) 'Increased immigrant intakes planned', *AFR*, 3 November
Solomon R J (1975) *Industrial land in Sydney*, Publication 51, AIUS, Canberra
Sorensen A D and Cooper M J (1981) 'Australian overseas investment: some locational considerations', in Linge G J R and McKay J (eds) *Structural change in Australia: some spatial and organisational responses*, Publication HG 15, Department of Human Geography, Australian National University, Canberra, pp 119-41
Souter G (1981) *Company of heralds: a century and a half of Australian*

*publishing by John Fairfax Limited and its predecessors 1831-1981,* Melbourne University Press, Melbourne

South Australia. Engineering and Water Supply Department (1980) *A guide to the Engineering and Water Supply Department,* Adelaide

Spann R N (1979) *Government administration in Australia,* Allen and Unwin, Sydney

Spann R N and Curnow R G (eds) (1975) *Public policy and administration in Australia: a reader,* Wiley, Sydney

Spearritt P (1978) *Sydney since the twenties,* Hale and Iremonger, Sydney

Spicer D (1980) *Birkenhead Point: changes in the market area of a new shopping centre,* unpublished, B.Sc. hons. thesis, School of Geography, University of New South Wales

Stilwell F J B (1980) *Economic crisis, cities and regions: an analysis of current urban and regional problems in Australia,* Pergamon Press, Sydney

Stretton H (1970) *Ideas for Australian cities,* privately published, Adelaide

Struyk R J and James F J (1975) *Intrametropolitan industrial location: the pattern of change,* Heath, Lexington, Mass.

Stubbs P (1980) *Technology and Australia's future: industry and international competitiveness,* Australian Industries Development Asociation, Melbourne

Sydney Water Board Journal (1976) 'The Shoalhaven scheme', 26(2), pp 2-10

Sykes T (1978) *The money miners; Australia's mining boom, 1969-70,* Wildcat Press, Sydney

Taylor M J and Thrift N J (1980) 'Large corporations and concentrations of capital in Australia: a geographical analysis', *Economic Geography,* 56, pp 261-80

Taylor M J and Thrift N J (1981a) 'Spatial variations in Australian enterprise: the case of large firms headquartered in Melbourne and Sydney', *Environment and Planning A,* 13, pp 137-46

Taylor M J and Thrift N J (1981b) 'British capital overseas: direct investment and corporate development in Australia', *Regional Studies,* 15, pp 183-212

Taylor M J and Thrift N J (1981c) 'Some geographical implications of foreign investment in the semiperiphery: the case of Australia', *Tijdschrift voor Economische en Sociale Geografie,* 72, pp 194-213

Taylor M J and Thrift N J (1981d) 'The changing spatial concentration of large company ownership and control in Australia 1953-1978', *Australian Geographer,* 15, pp 98-105

Thomas B (1972) *Migration and urban development,* Methuen, London

Thomson J M (1977) *Great cities and their traffic,* Gollancz, London

Townroe P M (1972) 'Some behavioural considerations in the industrial location decision', *Regional Studies,* 6, pp 261-72

Townsley W A (1976) *The government of Tasmania,* University of Queensland Press, St Lucia

Troy P N (ed) (1981) *Equity in the city,* Allen and Unwin, Sydney

Tyler R S (1973) *Report on the price of land,* Institute of Real Estate Development, Sydney

Urban Transport Study Group of NSW (1978) *URTAC review: deficient road corridors—present and future—report to UTS technical advisory committee,* Sydney

Vance J E (1970) *The merchants' world. The geography of wholesaling,* Prentice-Hall, Englewood Cliffs, New Jersey

Vandermark E and Harrison P F (1972) *Development activities in four Sydney suburban areas*, Urban Research Unit, Australian National University, Canberra

Vipond J (1981) 'Changes in unemployment differentials in Sydney, 1947-76', *Australian Geographical Studies*, 19, pp 67-77

Wadley D A (1979) 'Enterprises in trouble: the geography of wholesaling in the Australian agricultural machinery industry, 1967-72', in Hamilton F E I and Linge G J R (eds) *Spatial analysis, industry and the industrial environment. Progress in research and applications. Volume 1. Industrial systems*, Wiley, Chichester, pp 187-211

Walder E J (1969) 'Water supply and sewerage in an expanding metropolis', *Public Administration* (Sydney), 28, pp 171-80

Walsh M (1979) *Poor little rich country: the path to the eighties*, Penguin, Ringwood

Water Resources Newsletter (1979) 'Water conservation in Greater Hobart', 46, p 3

Webber M J and Daly M T (1971) 'Location of manufacturing growth within cities: a predictive model for Sydney, 1954-1966', *Royal Australian Planning Institute Journal*, 9, pp 130-36

Westfield Holdings Ltd (1981) *Annual Report*, Sydney

Wettenhall R L (1976) 'Report on statutory authorities', in Australia. Royal Commission on Australian government administration [the Coombs report] *Report*, Volume 1, appendix, AGPS, Canberra, pp 311-408

Wheelwright E L (1971) 'Development and dependence: the Australian problem', *Australian Quarterly*, 43, pp 22-39

White R L and Watts H D (1977) 'The spatial evolution of an industry: the example of broiler production', *Transactions of the Institute of British Geographers, New Series*, 2, pp 175-91

Whitlam E G (1977) *On Australia's constitution*, Widescope International Publishers, Camberwell, Victoria

Wilde P D (1980) *Industrial structure and change in Tasmania: regional development in a peripheral economy*, Occasional Paper 7, Department of Geography, University of Tasmania, Hobart

Wilde P D (1981a) 'From insulation towards integration: the Australian industrial system in the throes of change', *Pacific Viewpoint*, 22, pp 1-24

Wilde P D (1981b) 'Industrial change, structural adjustment and the periphery: the case of Tasmania', in Linge G J R and McKay J (eds) *Structural change in Australia: some spatial and organisational responses*, Publication HG 15, Department of Human Geography, Australian National University, Canberra, pp 219-36

Wilderness News (1981) 'New role for the H.E.C.', 2(3), p 3

Wilenski P (1977) *Directions for change: interim report of the review of New South Wales government administration*, Government printer, Sydney

Wilenski P (1978) 'New South Wales: Review of New South Wales government administration', in Ryan P F (ed) *Urban management processes*, Australian National Commission for UNESCO, AGPS, Canberra, pp 74-85

Windschuttle K (1979) *Unemployment: a social and political analysis of the economic crisis in Australia*, Penguin, Ringwood

Winkler R C (1979) 'Social factors and water consumption', in *Hydrology and water resources symposium, Perth 1979: Symposium Papers*, Institution of

Engineers Australia, Canberra, pp 269-70

Winston D (1957) *Sydney's great experiment: the progress of Cumberland County plan*, Angus and Robertson, Sydney

Wolfers H (1980) 'The big stores between the wars', in Roe J (ed) *Twentieth century Sydney: studies in urban and social history*, Hale and Iremonger, Sydney, pp 18-33

Wood P A (1974) 'Urban manufacturing: a view from the fringe', in Johnson J H (ed) *Suburban growth: geographical processes at the edge of the western city*, Wiley, London, pp 129-54

Wynyard J (1972) *Subdivision of residential land in New South Wales — its history, operation, problems and effects*, unpublished dissertation, Diploma in Town and Country Planning, University of Sydney

# Index